Mastering Anti-Money Laundering and Counter-Terrorist Financing

Mastering Anti-Money Laundering and Counter-Terrorist Financing

A compliance guide for practitioners

TIM PARKMAN

Harlow, England • London • New York • Boston • San Francisco • Toronto • Sydney • Auckland • Singapore • Hong Kong
Tokyo • Seoul • Taipei • New Delhi • Cape Town • São Paulo • Mexico City • Madrid • Amsterdam • Munich • Paris • Milan

In memory of Ronald Sidaway
1939 – 2010

PEARSON EDUCATION LIMITED

Edinburgh Gate
Harlow CM20 2JE
Tel: +44 (0)1279 623623
Fax: +44 (0)1279 431059
Website: www.pearson.com/uk

First published in Great Britain in 2012

ISBN: 978-0-273-75903-4

British Library Cataloguing-in-Publication Data
A catalogue record for this book is available from the British Library

Library of Congress Cataloging-in-Publication Data
A catalog record for this book is available from the Library of Congress

10 9 8 7 6 5 4 3 2 1
16 15 14 13 12

Typeset in 11.5pt Garamond by 30
Printed and bound in Great Britain by Ashford Colour Press Ltd, Gosport, Hampshire

Contents

Author's acknowledgements

The author wishes to thank Gill Peeling for her hard work in assisting with the preparation of this book, along with numerous industry colleagues and friends, without whose insights it would not have been possible. He would also like to thank Christopher Cudmore, Sundus Pasha and all the other editing staff at Pearson for their invaluable support and guidance.

Publisher's acknowledgements

We are grateful to the following for permission to reproduce copyright material:

Figures on pages 208, 210, 212, 214, 217, 219, 222, 224, 227, 229, 231, 233, 234, 236, and 238 are used with permission from Lessons Learned Ltd, © Lessons Learned Ltd 2012.

Extract on pages 71–72 is used with permission from www.jmlsg.org.uk. Extracts on pages 65, 98, and 105 are used with permission from FATF, Copyright © FATF/OECD. All rights reserved.

Chapters 2 and 3 contain material from *Countering Terrorist Finance: A Training Handbook for Financial Services* by Tim Parkman and Gill Peeling, used with permission from Gower Publishing.

In some instances we have been unable to trace the owners of copyright material, and we would appreciate any information that would enable us to do so.

How to use this book

AML CFT TRAINING VIDEOS AT DISCOUNTED RATES

Throughout *Mastering Anti-Money Laundering and Counter-Terrorist Financing* you will see occasional 'WWW' icons in the margin of the page. This indicates a preview link to the author's website *www.antimoneylaunderingvideos.com* and to a training film which is relevant to the AML CFT issue being discussed at that point in the book.

Subscriptions, whether to a particular film or to the complete library, are available to purchasers of *Mastering Anti-Money Laundering and Counter-Terrorist Financing* at discounted rates. Further details can be obtained by emailing proof of purchase to *info@lessonslearned.co.uk*

FREE SUSPICION RECOGNITION TRAINING MATERIALS

Free electronic copies of the suspicion recognition materials in Chapter 6 are also available to purchasers of the book, again by emailing proof of purchase to *info@lessonslearned.co.uk*.These opportunities, too, are indicated by the 'WWW' icon in the relevant page margin.

'MASTERING ANTI-MONEY LAUNDERING AND COUNTER-TERRORIST FINANCING': THE COURSE

Mastering Anti-Money Laundering and Counter-Terrorist Financing is also available in classroom course form in either a two-day or a five-day format led by qualified and experienced instructors from Lessons Learned Ltd including, on certain courses, the author himself, Tim Parkman.

From February 2013, the book will also be available as an online certificated course. Again, further details of each can be obtained by emailing *info@lessonslearned.co.uk*.

DISCLAIMER

The content of this book is intended solely for educational purposes, to describe and explain key concepts, processes, laws and standards. It should not be relied upon for operational purposes and purchasers should take care to obtain local legal advice on all operational issues affecting their business.

Introduction

Unfortunately, this is a complex book about a simple subject. It's full of laws and regulations, policies and procedures, checklists and diagrams, international standards and a large range of examples and case studies, both real and synthesised. That's how this subject is. Armies of politicians, regulators and Compliance Officers have spent the past 25 years or so erecting the edifice you see described here. They have attended meetings and conventions, persuaded sceptical colleagues about the need for action, drafted and amended long pieces of legislation and sat in parliaments and legislatures around the world late into the early morning, debating the smallest amendments. They have, together, produced hundreds of thousands of pages of policies and procedures descending right to the most granular level of detail and there are, as you read this, almost certainly at least several hundred thousand employees of financial and other institutions laboriously engaged in completing questionnaires, filling out checklists or photocopying 'something for the file'.

Unsurprisingly, a discussion along the lines of *'Is all this really necessary?'* is even today, after so long doing this, never really far from the surface. Frustration can boil over and tempers flare as directors and business heads, relationship managers and leading sales persons, branch managers, supervisors and tellers (who thought they were here to meet and exceed targets and beat the world) are compelled instead to grapple with the minutiae of Know Your Customer (KYC) documentation, transaction reporting and records maintenance.

People get upset, and when they do it's worthwhile asking an old question: what's is all for? Beyond simply 'obeying the law…', why *do* Anti-Money Laundering (AML) and Counter Terrorist Financing (CFT)? It's a worthwhile question and one you'd better have an answer to if you plan on implementing the types of processes described in this book. In an attempt to answer it, I can do no better than to refer to the three sources which highlight, to my mind, what this fight is all about. The first example is a summary of relevant parts of 'The State of the Future, 2010' a survey by the Millennium Project of the World Federation of United Nations Associations.

Example

The survey states that international organized crime continues to grow in the absence of a coherent global strategy to counter it and then lists some of the statistics. The best estimate for the annual value of counterfeiting and intellectual property piracy is about $300 billion to $1 trillion. For the global drug trade, about $386 billion; for the trade in environmental goods, about $63 billion; for human trafficking and prostitution – $141 billion; and for the weapons trade, about $12 billion. It goes on to report the FBI's estimate that online fraud cost U.S. businesses and consumers alone $560 million in 2009, up from $265 million in 2008, and points out that The overall organised crime figures don't include extortion or its part of the $1 trillion in bribes that the World Bank estimates is paid annually, nor its part of the estimated $1.5–6.5 trillion in laundered money that exists. Hence the total income, the survey estimates, could be $2–3 trillion—about twice as big as all the military budgets in the world. Governments, it states, can be understood as a series of decision points, with some people in those points vulnerable to very large bribes. Decisions 'could be bought and sold like heroin, making democracy an illusion.'

Specifically, about 2.5 million people from 127 different countries are being trafficked around the world, out of which approximately 70% are women and girls and up to 50% are minors. There are more slaves now than at any time in human history; estimates are that as many as 27 million people are forced to work without pay and are not free to leave – more than at the height of the African slave trade in the first half of the 19th century.

The survey further cites the International Atomic Energy Agency's report that between 1993 and the end of 2009, the Illicit Trafficking Database recorded 1,784 nuclear trafficking incidents (up from 222 during 2009 – a startling 700% increase), ranging from illicit disposal efforts to 'nuclear material of unknown provenance.' There are approximately 1,700 tons of highly enriched uranium, and 500 tons of separated plutonium that could produce nuclear weapons, all needing continued protection.

Source: http://www.millennium-project.org/millennium/2010SOF.html

The second source is an excerpt from a book that I wrote with Gill Peeling in 2007, dealing with terrorist financing. It deals with the statistics in time and numbers of the September 11th 2001 attacks on the United States. We were interested, in amongst all the legal details and political debate, to strip out the bare facts. It retains the power to shock.

Example

Effect of the 9/11 financing

It is worth reminding ourselves of what this innocuous stream of transactions actually led to. In the days before 11 September 2001, having returned the remaining money – $26 000 in total – to Hawsawi in the UAE the hijackers assembled in their various departure cities, ready to carry out arguably the most psychologically devastating attacks in American history. They were armed only with small knives, box cutters and cans of mace or pepper spray.

Atta and fellow hijacker Omari flew to Boston and spent their last evening shopping, eating pizza and making ATM withdrawals. Their three accomplices stayed in a hotel just outside Boston. Next morning they were among the 81 passengers who boarded American Airlines Flight 11, a Boeing 767 bound from Boston to Los Angeles. The plane took off at 7.59 a.m.; at 8.46, under the control of the hijackers, it ploughed into the North Tower of the World Trade Center in New York, the impact killing all the passengers, nine flight attendants and an unknown number of people in the tower.

Al-Shehhi and his team were also in Boston hotels the night before the attack. They took off from Boston on another Boeing 767, United Airlines Flight 175, an 8 a.m. departure for Los Angeles. There were 56 passengers and seven attendants on the flight, all of whom were killed instantly when the plane hit the South Tower of the World Trade Center at 9.03 a.m. Within 90 minutes both towers collapsed completely, killing more than 2600 people in total.

At 8.20 a.m., American Airlines Flight 77 – a Boeing 757 carrying 58 passengers and four attendants – left from Washington Dulles, again bound for Los Angeles. The five hijackers on board diverted the flight and at 9.37 a.m. flew it into the Pentagon in Washingon at 530 miles per hour. Everyone on the plane was killed. The death toll in the building was 125.

The fourth plane to be targeted was a Boeing 757, United Airlines Flight 93 from Newark to San Francisco. Unlike the other planes, Flight 93 was hijacked by only four terrorists, led by Jarrah and apparently destined for the White House. But in this case the 37 passengers fought back. After what must have been a desperate struggle, the plane came down in a field in Shanksville, Pennsylvania, about 20 minutes' flying time from Washington. Everyone on board was killed outright.

In total, 256 people died on the four planes.

When taken with those who lost their lives in the World Trade Center buildings and the Pentagon, the final death toll was greater than at Pearl Harbor in December 1941.

Source: Tim Parkman and Gill Peeling (2007) *Countering Terrorist Finance: A Training Handbook for Financial Services*, Gower Publishing Ltd.

The third and final source is a newspaper article from Britain's *Daily Telegraph* describing the activities of French law enforcement agencies in seeking an international arrest warrant for Teodorin Obiang Mangue, the high-living son of oil rich Equatorial Guinea's dictator-president, stemming from a case brought in France by Transparency International (TI), the global anti-corruption campaigning NGO, claiming that the Obiangs had plundered and laundered billions in oil wealth that rightfully belonged to the people of Equatorial Guinea. In reading the below, bear in mind that the OECD said of Equatorial Guinea in 2010 that 'The...increase in oil revenue, however, has had very little effect on poverty reduction in the country and on improving the general standard of living of the population. The poverty rate... remains extremely high. The country also suffers from a high infant-mortality rate, persistent epidemics, a poor rate of access to drinking water, low vaccination coverage and a weakly managed public administration, education sector and health sector.'

Source: http://www.oecd.org/dataoecd/12/56/40577917.pdf

Example

The Telegraph article describes how inside Mr. Obiang's Paris apartment overlooking the Arc de Triomphe, police found a disco, cinema, steam baths, a sauna, a hair salon, gold and jewel encrusted taps, a pink marble dining room, a Rodin statue, 10 Fabergé eggs, 300 bottles of Chateau Petrus wine worth €2.1 million, art works worth €18.5 million bought from Yves St. Laurent's private collection, a Piaget Polo watch encrusted with 498 diamonds worth €598,000, a Regency chest of drawers worth €2.8 million, a €72,000 caviar service and champagne holder, hundreds of designer suits and pairs of shoes (most unused), coloured tap water to match the marble basins ('sometimes blue, sometimes pink') and a fleet of eleven turbo-charged cars including Bugattis, Ferraris, Maseratis and Porsches.

Source: http://www.telegraph.co.uk/news/worldnews/africaandindianocean/equatorialguinea/9169755/International-arrest-warrant-sought-for-playboy-son-of-Equatorial-Guinea-president.html

The intriguingly named NGO website, Africandictator.org, then describes how the Obiang government, stung by TI's assault on its reputation, has ordered its public prosecutor to "launch a probe into whether [TI] has slandered the country."

Source: http://www.africandictator.org/?p=8147

No need to enquire about the outcome of that enquiry, I would guess.

Complexity, unfortunately, is an inevitable by-product of what happens when you try to do something like trying to prevent criminals, WMD proliferators and corrupt tyrants, terrorists enjoying unfettered access to the world financial system, whilst at the same time allowing that system to be accessed freely and conveniently by ordinary people. The myriad different types of products and services produce complexity. The different categories of customer and the different business sectors and circumstances that they face produce complexity, as does the bewildering array of different types of information – about a person, a country, a relationship, a transaction – which may be relevant to determining what risk they pose. And the need to maintain a balance in the system, such that ordinary folk aren't discriminated against and have their inconvenience kept to a minimum, produces complexity. Of course it does. But you get where I'm going with this. We don't really have a choice.

I once moderated an event in Kosovo (of all places). Since the laws there were very new, we had instigated a debate about what role the financial services industry should play in the fight against money laundering and terrorist financing. It quickly turned into a discussion about *whether* the financial services industry should have *any* role in combating money laundering and terrorist financing. The debate got quite lively and a number of people (including the diplomatic representative of a western government, who clearly forgot his brief 'in the moment') argued quite forcefully that the financial services industry had no, or at least only a very limited, role to play. They viewed the new legislation as an attempt by governments to sub-contract their own obligations on to commercial enterprises and, in the process, save money and help themselves in the collection of taxes.

I'm glad to report that a significant number of people in the room took a different view. One older gentleman put the case elegantly. He asked some simple questions, thus.

> 'Given that governments and societies put so much effort into dealing with crime itself; given that they invest large sums of public money in police forces to detect and investigate crime, in prosecutors to gather evidence and bring cases before the courts, in the judiciary and court system for trying and convicting criminals, in prison and probation services for punishing criminals and rehabilitating them into society after they have served their sentences; given all of that, should the financial services industry really be allowed to say in effect: "If you commit crime and you are detected and investigated, and a case is prepared against you and brought to court and you are convicted and punished with a prison sentence, have no fear. You're just a customer like anyone else! We will keep your information secret and your money safe and it'll be ready and waiting for you on the day you come out of jail! Thank you for banking with us!"'
>
> *Source*: Anonymous

Of course it cannot. Of course it has a bigger role to play.

Imagine a world in which you could walk into a bank and open an account, place money in it, wire that money to someone else in another country and then close your account without anyone having any idea who you are or what you are up to.

Imagine a world in which nobody was required to know or understand anything about what was happening on a customer's account so that anything – literally anything – which occurred on it was considered normal and unnoteworthy.

Imagine a world in which a person could receive millions of unexplained dollars each month through their account without anybody being obliged to ask where the funds had come from and what they were being used for.

Imagine a world in which records were destroyed as soon as a customer had closed his account and where it was common practice to warn a customer that they were under suspicion by the authorities.

It's not acceptable and it never should have been.

The question remains, though; could the system be made less complex? Could the broad principles outlined in this book be made generally available, to be interpreted by different institutions and different staff, as they saw fit? No, that wouldn't work. Apart from the inevitable commercial pressures that would intervene – to please customers (of course), to increase revenues (of course) – more than anything else people are busy. Less people, doing more work, with less time, seems to be the way things are going. People can't make it up as they go along, they need guidance. So the policies and the procedures must be detailed and precise. So far as they can, they must describe all the foreseeable situations that a person fulfilling a particular role may encounter, and then tell them what to do in each case – and if they are unsure, to ask for guidance. The devil is in the detail, but the detail is, unfortunately, unavoidable.

This intense pressure on people creates another risk; the risk that they will forget why they are doing what they are being required to do: what the end purpose is. People don't think anymore – we're all too busy. We're so busy checking spreadsheets, double checking controls, completing reports, photocopying documents for the file, all within a time limit that gets reduced each year, that we don't have the time or the perspective to stand back and simply *think* about something or ask questions about it. Why is this customer doing it this way and not that way? Why does everybody else's account look like this, but X's account looks like that? What possible reason could this person have for asking me to arrange this transaction?

As much as anything else, through all the policies and procedures, this is about getting people to *think* again.

US $1.5 trillion in laundered money, US$ 1 trillion paid in bribes each year, 27 million held in slavery, 2,971 people killed in a terrorist attack, high infant mortality and 300 bottles of Chateau Perris wine worth €2.1 million.

1

Fundamental Concepts

Where you see the **WWW** *icon in this chapter, this indicates a preview link to the author's website and to a training film which is relevant to the AML CFT issue being discussed.*
*Go to **www.antimoneylaunderingvideos.com***

BACKGROUND AND DEFINITIONS

Definitions

Money laundering is the conversion or transfer of money to disguise its illegal origins; or the use of the financial system to convert or transfer money or other assets so as to disguise their illegal origins. (AML is the acronym used for Anti-Money Laundering.)

Terrorist financing is the use of the financial system to facilitate the funding of terrorist acts, and to disguise both the origins and intended purpose of the funds used. *Note:* The generally used acronym CFT has been used for Countering the Financing of Terrorism.

In historical terms, even though banks and other financial institutions have been used by criminals since the dawn of modern commerce for hiding, transferring money and disguising their source of wealth, the emergence of money laundering and terrorist financing as a bank risk in its own right has been relatively recent.

One can distinguish between *money laundering and terrorist financing risk* on the one hand, and *Know Your Customer (KYC) and regulatory risk* on the other. The first is the risk that a financial institution will actually be used as a conduit for criminally derived money, or for money that turns out to have been destined for a terrorist purpose. The second is the risk that, without having actually handled criminal or terrorist funds, a financial institution will nevertheless be deemed to have been negligent or in some other way sub-standard in its adoption and enforcement of adequate policies and procedures designed to prevent actual usage of its facilities occurring.

This distinction is important because it impacts upon the *reputational* risks faced by financial institutions. Money laundering can be difficult to identify, terrorist financing even more so. Accordingly, the mere presence of criminal or terrorist funds within a financial institution will rarely be sufficient to attract censure or punishment. It must usually be accompanied by an individual or corporate failure in expected standards. The counterpoint is that, conversely, a failure in standards *is* usually sufficient to attract censure or punishment, along with attendant reputational damage, even *without* the actual presence of criminal/terrorist funds within the organisation, although clearly it will be much worse when both elements are present.

Example

Amy Elliott was a vice president and senior relationship manager with the Citibank private bank during the 1990s, based in New York. Raul Salinas, the brother of the former President of Mexico, Carlos Salinas (and hence a Politically Exposed Person (PEP)), was introduced to her by a longstanding client of the private bank, Carlos Hank Rohn. Elliott opened multiple accounts for Salinas and his wife in London and Switzerland, using a variety of measures to ensure maximum confidentiality, such as code name accounts, offshore trust company accounts and a unique funds transfer method which succeeded in moving funds to these accounts from Mexico without creating any documentary evidence identifying Salinas as the owner of the funds.

Based on her knowledge of the region, and on her general perceptions of the Salinas family, Elliott made assumptions about the legitimacy of Salinas' wealth which later proved to be unfounded. With her supervisors looking on, she made no independent checks on the sources of his wealth and waived all references other than the one given by Carlos Hank Rohn. Later on, after Salinas had been arrested on suspicion of murder and after the Swiss authorities had frozen all the accounts and brought charges for laundering the proceeds of illicit narcotics trafficking, the case was the subject of hearings by the US Senate Committee on Investigations and Elliott was questioned on the issue of what enquiries she had made about the origins of the money going through the accounts. An excerpt appears below.

Senator Levin: Now, did you know the source of his funds? Did you ask him the source of his funds? Let us put it that way.

Ms Elliott: Source of funds is where the money is coming from, and I knew two things. I knew that for his personal account the funds were going to be approximately $100,000, and it was going to come from one of the Mexican banks. And he told me it was going to be either Bancomer or Banca Cremi. He did not know which one.

Senator Levin: All right. Now, when he deposited the money later on...

Ms Elliott: Excuse me?

Senator Levin: When he deposited the millions later on, because it says here, 'and thereafter', did you know the source of those millions that he deposited later on?

Ms Elliott: I knew they were coming from Mexican banks.

Senator Levin: But did you know the source of his funds, where he got the funds from?

Ms Elliott: I believed at the time, Senator, that we were talking about monies that were a combination of things ...

Senator Levin: Did you also believe that he had sold a construction company?

Ms Elliott: I did.

Senator Levin: And did you know the name of the construction company?

Ms Elliott: I do not.

Senator Levin: Did you ask him?

Ms Elliott. I did not.

Senator Levin: Did you ask him how much he received from the construction company?

Ms Elliott: I did not, sir.

Senator Levin: Did you ask him about any projects that that alleged construction company had ever undertaken?

Ms Elliott: Carlos Hank told me that they had worked on a road together ....

Source: http://www.gpo.gov/fdsys/pkg/CHRG-106shrg61699/html/CHRG-106shrg61699.htm

Compare this example with the situation involving those US banks that opened accounts for some of the 9/11 hijackers after they had arrived in the United States and were planning their attacks. The National Commission on the Terrorist Attacks upon the United States described their involvement as follows:

Example

'All of the hijackers opened accounts in their own name, using passports and other identification documents. Contrary to numerous published reports, there is no evidence the hijackers ever used false Social Security numbers to open any bank accounts. In some cases, a bank employee completed the Social Security number field on the new account application with a hijacker's date of birth or visa control number, but did so on his or her own to complete the form. No hijacker presented or stated a false number ...

The hijackers' transactions themselves were not extraordinary or remarkable. The hijackers generally followed a pattern of occasional large deposits, which they accessed frequently through relatively small ATM and debit card transactions. They also made cash withdrawals and some occasionally wrote checks. In short, they used their accounts just as did many other bank customers. No one monitoring their transactions alone would have had any basis for concern ... Even in hindsight, there is nothing ... to indicate that any SAR [Suspicious Activity Report] should have been filed ....'

Source: *National Commission on Terrorist Attacks upon the United States: Monograph on Terrorist Financing, Staff Report to the Commission* p.140 (www.9-11commission.gov/staff_statements/911_TerrFin_Monograph.pdf)

The effect of this distinction is that financial institutions need to pay very close attention, *in advance* of any problems, to the issue of how their policies and standards (and just as importantly their adherence to those policies and standards) will stand up to scrutiny *if* it turns out that there is a problem subsequently.

KEY PROCESSES IN MONEY LAUNDERING AND TERRORIST FINANCING

Money laundering and terrorist financing bear many similarities, but there are some key distinctions.

With non-terrorist criminal money laundering, the funds in question always have a criminal origin. The process has been described as having three distinct phases:

- *Placement*: the moment at which criminally obtained money is first 'dematerialised' and put into the financial system (e.g. as a credit entry on a bank account).
- *Layering*: the movement of the money through a large series of transactions with no real economic purpose, in order to make it more difficult to prove the criminal origin of the funds and disguise ownership.
- *Integration*: the eventual use of the money for a genuine economic purpose (e.g. the purchase of a luxury item or a business capable of generating further profits from legitimate business activities).

With money laundering, the basic aim is to hide the criminal *origin* of the funds. The amounts in question are typically large and hence easier to detect. (Note: a training film of the money laundering process can be previewed at http://www.antimoneylaunderingvideos.com/player/tew.htm.) **WWW**

With terrorist financing, the key difference is that the funds passing through the financial system *need not* have a criminal origin, even though quite often they do. They can stem from a variety of different sources, many of them legitimate at the point of acquisition.

A particular feature of terrorist financing (and not just so-called 'Islamist' terrorist financing, but extending to other groups as well over the past few decades) is the use of non-profit, charitable, religious or cultural organisations as 'cover' for the passage of funds.

With terrorist financing, the basic aim is to hide the criminal *purpose* of funds. By the time funds have been designated and made available for a specific terrorist attack, the amounts in question are typically quite small and hence harder to detect.

The key differences between money laundering and terrorist financing processes are represented diagrammatically in Figure 1.1.

Perhaps the most important difference between the two is between the people who undertake each activity. Money laundering is done by criminals – particularly those involved in organised crime. Their goal is solely to enrich themselves, essentially the more the better. They are trying to wash as much money as possible through the system. Terrorists are different animals. One either deeply and genuinely committed to a religious, ideological or

Figure 1.1 **The key differences between the two processes**

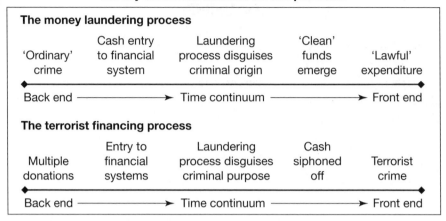

The money laundering process

'Ordinary' crime	Cash entry to financial system	Laundering process disguises criminal origin	'Clean' funds emerge	'Lawful' expenditure
Back end →		Time continuum →		Front end

The terrorist financing process

Multiple donations	Entry to financial systems	Laundering process disguises criminal purpose	Cash siphoned off	Terrorist crime
Back end →		Time continuum →		Front end

political cause, or brainwashed into believing they want to use the financial system only insofar as it assists in the funding of their campaign of violence. (Note: a training film of the terrorist financing process can be previewed at http://www.antimoneylaunderingvideos.com/player/ftm.htm.)

WWW

MONEY LAUNDERING

Money launderers use various elements of the financial and commercial system for their activities.

Transportation and consolidation

This is basically the conversion of criminal cash into larger denomination notes. Large amounts of small currency (coins or notes) derived from crime are difficult to manage and very difficult to transport from one physical location to another. A smaller amount of large denomination notes is much easier to handle and can be more easily concealed if, for example, the money launderers want to smuggle it across borders to be laundered in other countries.

Customers who appear regularly to be exchanging large amounts of small currency units for much larger denominations and who do not appear to have any logical reason for doing this might well be cause for suspicion.

Placement

Placement involves the various methods used by money launderers to dematerialise their criminal money within the financial system.

One method involves the use of 'smurfs'. The money launderer gives a sum of cash to an individual known as a 'smurf'. The 'smurf' deposits the cash in small amounts into a number of different bank accounts, probably held at several different banks. The deposit amounts are small enough that they do not attract attention or suspicion. Once the money is deposited, the placement stage is complete. (Note: a training film of this can be previewed at http://www.antimoneylaunderingvideos.com/player/smurfing.htm.) **WWW**

A second method involves the use of 'front companies'. The launderer selects company and business bank accounts belonging to apparently respectable, high net worth individuals. The money launderer gives a much larger sum of cash to these people. The cash is then paid into their accounts and, with the support of forged documentation, is explained as a legitimate receipt from the sale of a property or the sale of an interest in a business for example. Once the cash is deposited and the purpose of the transaction successfully explained, the placement stage is complete.

Any business that is cash intensive is useful, since it already handles large amounts of legitimate cash, and the criminal cash can be mingled with this and banked as if it were the legitimate proceeds of the business. Examples of cash intensive businesses include supermarkets, restaurants and jewellery shops. (Note: a training film dealing with a front company account can be previewed at http://www.antimoneylaunderingvideos.com/player/red_flags_aml.htm.) **WWW**

Yet another method involves the purchase of different types of insurance and investment policies for cash, through independent financial advisers or brokers who have persuaded themselves that the cash is of legal provenance. At a selected moment, the policy is surrendered and a redemption cheque or funds transfer is received from the issuer.

Ultimately, amounts so 'placed' in apparently legitimate accounts held by other people may then be transferred to a single account which acts as a conduit for the money as it is moved on elsewhere, as part of the layering process described below.

Layering

This is essentially the technique used by money launderers to process their money in such a way as to disguise its connection with crime. There are a number of possible examples:

- investment in financial products which have good liquidity and which can be bought and sold easily (e.g. unlisted stocks and shares)
- purchase and sale of real estate – apartments, houses, flats, commercial premises
- transfer of the money to a business, ostensibly as a 'loan' with documents such as loan agreements and receipts to support the illusion that the loan is real

- transfer of the money overseas or to other accounts under the guise of money destined for a specific purpose (e.g. education overseas of a family member)
- using fictitious business transactions to move money around (e.g. giving money to suppliers against invoices raised for goods that were never issued; or raising invoices to customers in respect of sales that never took place)
- transferring money to companies overseas in payment for non-existent shipments of imported goods
- use of shell companies and shell banks, i.e. entities that have no real function, no real place of business and no real business operations, but which exist in name only as a conduit for the receipt and distribution of money
- use of the international financial markets to buy and sell securities and move money across international borders.

Use of criminally owned or sympathetic investment firms and banks

Investment business and banking gives money launderers an opportunity to move large amounts of money into the international financial markets. The high turnover of such markets (customers might legitimately buy and sell many times in any one day) is useful in helping the money launderers to move their money around as much as possible.

Investment firms will legitimately transact very large volumes of purchase and sale deals in any one day. A criminally owned investment firm can, of course, use its business systems and resources to launder large amounts of criminal money through large-scale transactions.

Use of shell companies and shell banks within the overall laundering process

Shell companies have no purpose other than to act as a conduit for money. Money launderers will use shell companies as a vehicle for their money movements; as somewhere where money can be received and co-mingled with other funds, before it is transferred on to another destination.

Any activity which appears to have no real economic purpose should be an immediate cause for suspicion. Any activity which does not match your understanding of a customer's likely needs and which does not seem plausible for that particular customer should also give you cause to be suspicious.

Integration of laundered assets into the legitimate economy and repatriation to the home territory

Once the proceeds of criminal activity have been transported, consolidated, placed and layered they will, by the end of the process, have all the appearance of legitimately earned wealth, which can then be integrated into the legal economy. This could be done, say, through an investment in a business that produces a legally earned dividend or in a work of art or other item of intrinsic value which can either be enjoyed for what it is or sold. Investment income or sale proceeds may now be repatriated back into the country where the crimes were committed, so that they are available there to the ultimate criminal beneficial owner.

At a certain point in a person's life, he or she may decide to give up the criminal life, seek respectability and even political office, whereupon the powers of the state can then be used to legalise or pardon past acts and confer legitimacy on the criminal and those with whom he or she has consorted.

TERRORIST FINANCING

It is possible to discern two strands of terrorist financing, which occur at different ends of the chain shown in Figure 1.1. Type 1 terrorist financing refers to the financing of a terrorist movement over time, whilst Type 2 refers to the funding of specific attacks.

Terrorist groups such as Al-Qaeda, Jemaal Islamiyah, the Liberation Tigers of Tamil Eelam (the LTTE or 'Tamil Tigers') and the Provisional IRA have all used the financial and commercial system in similar ways to fund their activities.

Type 1 terrorist financing

The methods used to obtain, collect and/or disguise funds for terrorist movements or causes have included:

- donations from charities sympathetic to the terrorists' cause (or possibly even set up by the terrorist group itself), or from charities whose administration systems have been infiltrated and 'hijacked' by terrorists who then divert legally obtained charitable donations to their own terrorist cause
- criminal activities including drug trafficking, people trafficking, gun running, counterfeiting operations, fraud, identity theft, etc.
- voluntary payments from ethnic diaspora (both legal expatriates and illegal immigrants)
- funds extorted from ethnic diaspora under threat of exposure to the immigration authorities or harm to their families
- legitimate business activities carried out by front companies, or 'donor' businesses sympathetic to the terrorists' cause.

Type 2 terrorist financing

The methods used to fund specific terrorist attacks have included:

- ATM and credit card withdrawals on personal accounts – used to retrieve money from accounts in one country from a point of retrieval in another country
- use of the Hawala banking system, which is largely unregulated and as such allows for anonymous movements of money between jurisdictions
- physical importation of funds in cash or traveller's cheques either by the terrorists themselves on arrival in a country of operation or via couriers
- use of company structures and commercial banking operations to transfer money across borders
- wiring of funds between accomplices in different parts of the world, either using their own accounts or those of sympathisers.

In a sophisticated financing operation, cash and proceeds from cheques, cash cards, gold, shares, policies, houses, cars, works of art and any number of items representing 'value' are collected into the accounts of charities, high street traders, other legitimate businesses, 'front' companies, 'clean' individuals, mosques, churches, import–export houses, art galleries etc. ready for onward transmission as invoice payments, investments, contributions, loan repayments, expense reimbursements, intra-entity transfers, salaries and dividend payments, all available for use or further onward movement as and when required. The full range of payment methods can be deployed from formal wire transfers, money transmission (e.g. Western Union), unofficial money transfer ('hawala' or 'hundi') schemes right through to the withdrawal of cash and its physical transportation via cars, boats, planes, rickshaws, pack animals or people.

Well organised groups will exploit synergies in the process. For example, throughout the 1980s the LTTE in Sri Lanka (which used to raise an estimated $50 million per annum from various sources) operated a fleet of tankers. The ships not only made profits on legitimate lading contracts, but were also used for smuggling the weapons once they had been purchased and for carrying illegal immigrants to foreign countries as another method of earning money to finance the campaign. Often, business activity and terrorism feed off each other in a mutually dependent relationship. Despite its periodic public slayings of 'drug dealers', the Taliban funded itself from Afghanistan's poppy trade for many years. The Provisional IRA took over and ran profit-making taxi-cab businesses, and bombed Belfast buses and bus stations, ostensibly as part of its campaign of violence, but also to remove the commercial competition.

FURTHER DIFFERENCES BETWEEN TERRORIST FINANCING AND CLASSICAL MONEY LAUNDERING

As can be seen from the above, in its deployment of disguising activities to create the appearance of transactional legitimacy, Terrorist Financing (TF) has much in common with its elder sibling, Money Laundering (ML), but there are additional differences:

- *The volume of funds involved.* For serious money launderers handling the proceeds of serious crime, the amounts involved are very large indeed. Current estimates are that there are approximately $1 trillion in criminal assets hiding within the global economy at any given time. That is far more than is likely to be allocated towards the financing of terrorism worldwide. And whilst many terrorist groups are organised enough to collect very substantial sums running into tens of millions each year, not every attack is spawned from those funds. As the UK's 7/7 bombers showed, a lethal attack on a transport system can be planned and funded well within the confines of an average monthly salary. This poses severe operational difficulties for those organisations (currently primarily banks and other 'gatekeepers' involved in financial services) charged with trying to disrupt the flow of terrorist funds through the financial system. In combating ML, systems are constructed to detect 'suspicious' transactions, where 'suspicious' tends to mean 'unusual', and 'unusual' tends (though not always) to mean 'unusually large'. But as far as the funding of individual attacks is concerned, this approach simply doesn't work. How do you detect an 'unusual' retail purchase or a 'suspicious' mobile phone bill?
- *The status of terrorism (and hence terrorist financing) as a political issue.* Subject to continuing arguments about legal details such as categorisation and mutual enforceability, to a large extent the world now recognises what a criminal is, what criminal money laundering is, and agrees that criminals and money launderers deserve to be caught, punished and stripped of their ill-gotten gains. This is not yet true of terrorism, for the basic reason that there is still no full international agreement on what a 'terrorist' actually is and on what constitutes 'terrorism'. Whilst very few will promote or defend the concept of deliberately causing civilian deaths as a legitimate means of pursuing a cause, the old axiom that 'one man's terrorist is another man's freedom fighter' still applies. Consequently terrorist financing as an issue has a political 'edge' to it that money laundering does not. It makes it a much more sensitive and complicated issue for organisations and governments to deal with, especially in light of the invidious ways in which, in free societies, terrorist groups operate within what we may call innocent society.

- *The extension of terrorist financing into innocent society.* Non-terrorist criminals and terrorists tend to treat innocent society very differently. If you are not actually a criminal, if you do not live a 'criminal lifestyle' (basically spending lots of cash whose origins you can't explain) and if you do not consort with criminals or seek their company, then other than through mistaken identity, you are unlikely to be thought of as a criminal by society at large. Moreover, other than in your designated role as victim, criminals themselves will most likely leave you alone. They are unlikely to try to recruit you to their cause, ask you to drive their getaway car, or request the use of your bank account to collect their cash before wiring it to an offshore haven. Not for nothing is it called 'the underworld' – a phrase aptly denoting the parallel yet separate existence of the criminal community.

The same isn't true of terrorist financing. As has been described, serious terrorist groups committed to long-term operations will finance their activities using any means they can, and the national, ethnic or religious groups from which they are drawn – be they minority communities within specific countries or diaspora spread around the world – will often pay a heavy price for 'the cause'. Many who detest the terrorists' methods will still be viewed with suspicion and fear by wider society. Those who try to disassociate themselves and their families from any connection with terrorism often face pressure to support, to assist or to 'get involved' in some way, shape or form, with punishment or 'discipline', often invisible to the rest of society, being meted out to those who refuse to conform. And even when they seek to give charity for the support of their own community, whether at home or overseas, they risk the conversion of that most humane of acts into murderous purposes.

SUSPICION RECOGNITION

A critical requirement of financial institutions and others charged with responsibilities for the detection and prevention of ML and TF is that they report instances when they suspect that their facilities and services may have been used by their customers and clients for criminal purposes. But when should you be suspicious? We deal with this key question later in more detail, but for now let's track the process of how suspicion might develop in a fairly typical, potential money laundering scenario using the example of the Pecunia Banking Corporation. In this fictitous example we will consider at each stage, and *purely on the information presented*, whether or not we are either 'neutral', 'uncomfortable' or 'suspicious' about this client.

Pecunia Banking Corporation

Example

Stage 1

You are newly employed by AlnaBank Global, and are reviewing existing relationships. The client you are looking at this morning is Pecunia Banking Corporation (PBC) which has a correspondent banking relationship with Alna. PBC is a registered Russian bank with, the file states, a number of important corporate clients and its stated purpose in wanting to set up a correspondent relationship is to be able to service its clients' needs in Europe.

PBC's reason for wanting a correspondent relationship seems perfectly reasonable. There are no particular issues here. The bank is a Russian bank, and everyone knows that Russian banks have been exploited in the past by those wishing to move illicit wealth from the country, but there is nothing on these facts which stands out in that regard.

Stage 2

PBC was incorporated in 2009 and has a registered head office at 23 Sevatskaya Street, Moscow, which a map reveals is in a suburb. A certified copy of PBC's Certificate of Incorporation has been examined and is authentic. PBC's appointed representative is Mr Ginatulin, the Managing Director to whom AlnaBank staff speak to on a weekly basis. A copy of his identification is on the file.

A number of questions are now starting to emerge as we find out more about PBC. The bank is clearly not well established, as it has only existed since 2009. The bank's registered office is not in central Moscow, but rather in a distant suburb. What and where is Sevatskaya Street? Is it possible that the bank might be a 'shell bank', i.e. a bank that does not have a genuine physical presence in the country where it is incorporated?

Stage 3

Mr Ginatulin is on PBC's Board of Directors. Mr Shimanenko is the only other named Director, and his identification details are also on the file. There are 10 shareholders, each owning between 5 per cent and 15 per cent of PBC. All the shareholders are corporate entities (e.g. Infolink, Poldavic Professional Services). All except one are subsidiaries of a company called 'International Distributions'.

PBC's ownership is, effectively, shrouded in mystery because we do not know who exactly controls it. There are two named directors, but they are not shareholders. The shareholders are all corporate entities, and these are almost all owned in turn by another corporate entity called 'International Distributions'. Who owns these businesses? Who are the individual people behind these company names? The extent to which this bank appears to want to hide its ownership is potentially very suspicious indeed.

Stage 4

Your bank has clearly asked Mr Ginatulin about PBC's client base and the nature of its business. Mr Ginatulin has stated that it acts for a number of well-known Russian companies, some of whom are involved in the film industry. There are photocopies of letters of instruction from some of these companies. Mr Ginatulin has also referred staff to PBC's website, where there are printouts about the bank's products and services. There are multiple references to the management team, but no other bank managers or employees are identified or named anywhere on the website.

AlnaBank is really none the wiser about what PBC and its clients really do. The client letters are photocopies not originals so they could be forgeries and 'being involved in the film industry' isn't really a sufficient description of the type of business. Shell banks might attempt to give themselves a legitimate presence by setting up websites and putting out information to give the impression of normal banking business. In this particular instance there is some information about products and services but *still* no information about the bank's history or its ownership.

Stage 5

Transaction records show very large volumes of funds being put through the account over the two years during which it has been open – nearly $1 billion. Many of the transactions are stated to be on account of well-known Russian companies, with monies being received and then forwarded on to other banks in the US, but about half – some $400 million – is stated to be on account of 'International Film Distributions' for purchasing film rights. These payments have been made to Hollywood Bank in the Bahamas, which appears to be a genuine bank.

There is a disturbing lack of any independent verification of any of the information provided. One billion dollars is a very large sum for throughput within two years, so you had better be sure that the business is genuine. It is also particularly noteworthy that funds have been sent to the US and the Bahamas, whereas the business purpose stated on the file was to service clients' European needs. No information is given on the value of the film rights purchased. If the purchase related to the *Lord of the Rings* franchise, then maybe the payment would be justified. But the purchase of valueless offshore assets from associates in order to suppress profits is a well-known tax evasion strategy, and by now it is indeed starting to look as if that may be what is going on here.

In short, this is a relationship about which there is a chronic shortage of information. Whilst technical requirements such as identification and certification documents litter the file, along with 'famous name' clients, we do not really know whether the bank has a physical existence, who ultimately controls it, whether its clients are genuine, what business they are engaged in, and how and why they are making their payments. Definitely suspicious!

2

The International AML and CFT Framework

Key components of the international institutional and legal framework

A developing framework to combat tax evasion

A developing framework to combat proliferation financing

The financial action task force (FATF)

FATF regional style bodies and associate members

Other relevant international bodies

Key requirements for financial institutions

Key components of a national AML/CFT framework

KEY COMPONENTS OF THE INTERNATIONAL INSTITUTIONAL AND LEGAL FRAMEWORK

The best and easiest way to view the international framework for combating money laundering and terrorist financing, is as a scale of activity, ranging from the international, to the regional, to the national, to the institutional and finally to the individual level. The framework is shown in Figure 2.1, with slight variations for each jurisdiction.

UN conventions and resolutions

UN Single Convention on Narcotic Drugs 1961; UN Convention on Psychotropic Substances 1971; UN Convention against Illicit Traffic in Narcotic Drugs and Psychotropic Substances 1988 (the Vienna Convention)

Collectively, these conventions have provided the international legal framework for the 'war on drugs', i.e. the global control and scheduling of various categories of drugs deemed harmful or abusive, including opium, heroin, cocaine, cannabis, ecstasy and LSD to name but a few.

The 1988 Convention agreed in Vienna went further. Its Article 5 (Confiscation) required states to cooperate in various ways in seizing and confiscating the proceeds of trafficking in illegal narcotics. Its particular focus was on mutual legal cooperation in such areas as extradition, search and seizure, service of documents, the transfer of legal proceedings between jurisdictions and preventing bank secrecy laws being used to prevent the mutual transfer of information relevant to a case.

Crucially, Article 3 (Offences and Sanctions) also required states to criminalise the laundering of the proceeds of illegal narcotics trafficking through the financial system, thus paving the way for the setting up of the international anti-money launding (AML) system.

UN Convention for the Suppression of the Financing of Terrorism 1999

The UN has had an anti-terrorist financing regime in place for some time on state actors (the so-called 'rogue states', such as Libya and Iran). It was only in the second half of the 1990s that the financing of terrorism by non-state actors came to the fore.

Following a series of resolutions condemning terrorist action during the 1990s, the UN adopted this convention at the General Assembly held in NewYork in December 1999. The resultant treaty came into force in April 2002. Article 2 of the Convention requires countries to criminalise the act of providing or collecting funds with the intention or knowledge that those funds will be used to carry out a terrorist attack.The Convention asserts that 'financing is at the heart of terrorist activity' and lays out the foundations for

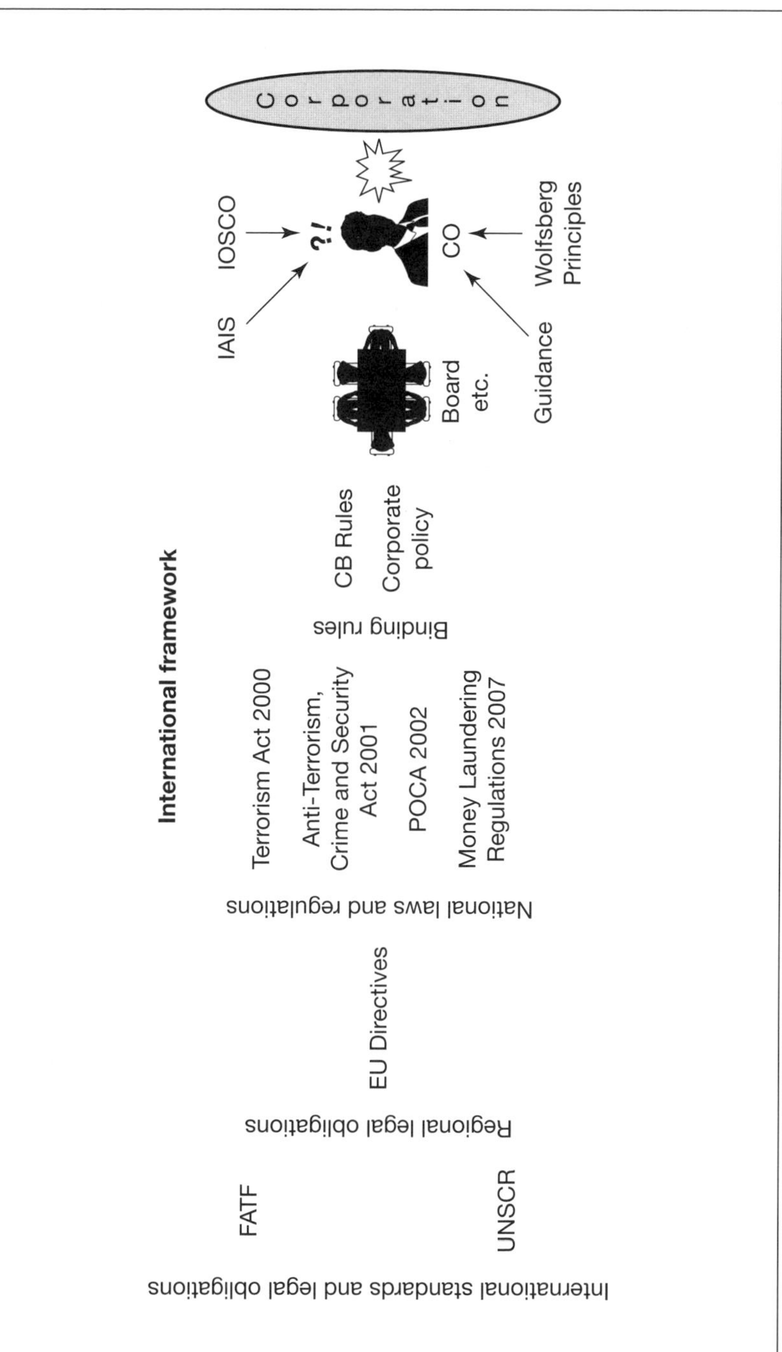

Figure 2.1 **The international AML CFT legal framework (as seen from a UK legislative perspective)**

closer cooperation between law enforcement agencies, financial authorities and individual countries.

Countries that have ratified the treaty (known as State Parties) are required to put into place mechanisms to identify, detect and freeze or seize assets used or earmarked for terrorist activities, and financial institutions are called upon to be vigilant with regard to unusual transactions and to report to the authorities anything that they suspect may have links with terrorism or terrorist activities. They are also obliged to prosecute or extradite offenders, and to cooperate with other countries' investigations. A State Party cannot, for example, turn down a request for mutual legal assistance on the grounds of its own banking secrecy laws.

UN Security Council Resolution 1373 2001

Following the attacks on the World Trade Center in September 2001, the United Nations Security Council passed UNSCR 1373 for the Suppression of the Financing of Terrorism. This is one of the lynchpins of international action against terrorist financing, and includes a range of steps and strategies to combat the financing of terrorism generally.

Resolution 1373 builds on the UN blacklisting regime which started with the creation of the Al-Qaeda and Taliban lists with UN Security Council Resolution 1267, following the 1998 Al-Qaeda attacks on the US embassies in Kenya and Tanzania. Resolution 1267 called upon all states to freeze funds and other property that may be used directly or indirectly to benefit the Taliban. Created in the aftermath of 9/11, Resolution 1373 goes a few steps further and encourages states to create their own blacklists.

Resolution 1373 reconfirms that all states should prevent or suppress terrorist financing, criminalise fundraising or the provision of economic resources for terrorism, and freeze the financial assets of terrorist groups. Terrorist acts should be established as serious criminal offences and anyone involved in their financing, planning or perpetration should be denied any kind of support and brought to justice. Particular emphasis is placed on the exchange of information between countries, not only with regard to terrorist actions and movements but also in light of the close links between terrorist acts and other types of organised crime and money laundering.

Critically, UNSCR 1373 continued the extension of the existing notification and sanctions regime, already applicable to 'rogue states', to individuals and organisations suspected of connections with terrorism. This led to the establishment of an international blacklist of suspected terrorists. Resolution 1373 also established the Counter-Terrorism Committee (CTC) as a monitoring body to try to ensure the Resolution is effectively implemented and to provide assistance for countries that need help in this regard.

UNSCR 1624 2005

The UN's 50-year anniversary in September 2005 saw the adoption of UNSCR 1624, which among other things stresses that countries should criminalise *incitement* to commit terrorist acts and calls upon states to strengthen international border security. This development was a direct response to the open preaching of overtly violent and/or aggressive messages by, in particular, a small minority of Muslim clerics.

European Union Directives and Council Common Positions

European Convention on Laundering, Search, Seizure and Confiscation of the Proceeds from Crime 1990 (The Strasbourg Convention)

This was signed in Strasbourg in 1990 and entered into force in September 1993. The Convention aimed to counter laundering of the proceeds of *all* types of crime (not just drug trafficking) and to improve international cooperation (Chapter III of the Convention), both between Council of Europe member states and with other countries around the world. With specific reference to money laundering the Convention included provisions for the establishment of a range of laundering offences (Chapter II Article 6). It also included provisions for the confiscation of the proceeds of crime and for ordering the disclosure of bank, financial and commerical records to facilitate the tracing and identification of such proceeds (Chapter II, Articles 2 and 4).

European Convention on the Laundering, Search, Seizure and Confiscation of the Proceeds from Crime, and on the Financing of Terrorism 2005 (Convention #198)

Updating and expanding on the 1993 Convention agreed in Strasbourg, this more recent Convention was adopted by the Committee of Ministers in May 2005 and is firmly grounded in the 1999 UN International Convention for the Suppression of the Financing of Terrorism (discussed above). Crucially, in Chapter II Article 2(2) the Convention focuses not only on the laundering and confiscation of criminal proceeds, but also on the interdiction of 'clean' money generated through legitimate sources but destined for criminal purposes – a key activity for financiers of terrorism, as has been noted. The text addresses the fact that quick access to financial information or information on assets held by criminal organisations, including terrorist groups, is key to the successful implementation of preventive and suppressive measures against them.

EU Money Laundering Directives

There have been three EU Directives dealing with Money Laundering. The First Directive, in 1991 (now repealed by the Third Directive) was the 'basic package' and required member states to implement laws centred around the Financial Action Task Force 40 – FATF 40 (see later in this chapter). It applied, however, only to a restricted range of financial institutions and only to the proceeds of drug related crimes. Accordingly, the Second Directive of 2001 extended both the range of crimes to be covered under national legislation and regulation, and also the categories of institutions to be affected, extending the latter to include not just banks but also 'gatekeepers' such as lawyers, notaries, trust or company service providers, accountants, auditors, tax advisers, real estate agents, casinos, auctioneers and other dealers in high-value goods.

The Financial Action Task Force's previous review of its 40 Recommendations in 2003, together with the addition of nine Special Recommendations and other associated international activity in relation to terrorist financing resulted in the creation of a Third EU Directive of October 2005 (which came into force in the member states on 15 December 2007).

The Third Directive explicitly addresses terrorist financing as well as money laundering. It also contains more detailed 'customer due diligence' provisions than previous Directives. In particular these:

- are defined as comprising not just customer identification and verification of identity, but also establishment of the purpose and intended nature of the business relationship and ongoing monitoring
- apply to new and existing customers
- require identification of beneficial owners and the verification of the beneficial owner's identity
- introduce exemptions from full customer due diligence ('simplified due diligence') for certain low risk situations, and
- require 'enhanced due diligence' measures for situations that present a higher money laundering or terrorist financing risk, at least for non-face-to-face business, 'politically exposed persons' and international correspondent banking relationships.

Furthermore:

- The Directive provides for comitology measures – legally binding implementing measures the Commission can adopt to clarify certain provisions of the Directive. Among others, the Commission may adopt criteria for simplified and enhanced due diligence, definitions of, for example, beneficial owner and politically exposed persons, and identify third countries that do not meet the provisions of the Directive.
- It recognises in EC law the concept of a risk-based approach to anti-money laundering.
- It applies a licensing/registration system for 'currency exchange offices', trust and company service providers that involves a fit and proper test for those who direct or beneficially own such businesses.

- It requires financial firms to apply customer due diligence and record-keeping standards to overseas branches and majority-owned subsidiaries (unless not permitted by local law).
- It introduces more explicit obligations on institutions to have systems for AML risk management and compliance.
- It includes miscellaneous provisions on, for example, the suspicious activity reporting regime and the relationship with financial intelligence units.

Council Common Position (2001/931/CFSP)

December 2001 also saw the implementation of a Council Common Position in drawing up a list (since regularly updated) of individuals, groups and entities involved in terrorism whose assets were to be frozen. The list at that time included ETA (Basque Fatherland and Liberty), the IRA (Irish Republican Army), GRAPO (the First of October Anti-Fascist Resistance Group), the terrorist wing of HAMAS, Palestinian Islamic Jihad and other revolutionary activist groups, as well as the names of individuals belonging to such groups. A more recent, updated version of this list (2011/931/CFSP published 31 January 2011) lists, in addition to a number of designated individuals, the following groups and entities:

1. 'Abu Nidal Organisation' – 'ANO' (aka 'Fatah Revolutionary Council', aka 'Arab Revolutionary Brigades', aka 'Black September', aka 'Revolutionary Organisation of Socialist Muslims')
2. 'Al-Aqsa Martyrs' Brigade'
3. 'Al-Aqsa e.V.'
4. 'Al-Takfir' and 'Al-Hijra'
5. 'AumShinrikyo' (aka 'AUM', aka 'Aum Supreme Truth', aka 'Aleph')
6. 'BabbarKhalsa'
7. 'Communist Party of the Philippines', including 'New People's Army' – 'NPA', Philippines
8. 'Gama'a al-Islamiyya' (aka 'Al-Gama'a al-Islamiyya') ('Islamic Group' – 'IG')
9. 'İslami Büyük Doğu Akıncılar Cephesi' – 'IBDA-C' ('Great Islamic Eastern Warriors Front')
10. 'Hamas', including 'Hamas-Izz al-Din al-Qassem'
11. 'Hizbul Mujahideen' – 'HM'
12. 'Hofstadgroep'
13. 'Holy Land Foundation for Relief and Development'
14. 'International Sikh Youth Federation' – 'ISYF'
15. 'Khalistan Zindabad Force' – 'KZF'
16. 'Kurdistan Workers' Party' – 'PKK', (aka 'KADEK', aka 'KONGRA-GEL')
17. 'Liberation Tigers of Tamil Eelam' – 'LTTE'
18. 'Ejército de Liberación Nacional' ('National Liberation Army')
19. 'Palestinian Islamic Jihad' – 'PIJ'

20. 'Popular Front for the Liberation of Palestine' – 'PFLP'
21. 'Popular Front for the Liberation of Palestine – General Command' (aka 'PFLP – General Command')
22. 'Fuerzas armadas revolucionarias de Colombia' – 'FARC' ('Revolutionary Armed Forces of Colombia')
23. 'Devrimci Halk Kurtuluş Partisi-Cephesi' – 'DHKP/C' (aka 'Devrimci Sol' ('Revolutionary Left'), aka 'Dev Sol') ('Revolutionary People's Liberation Army/Front/Party')
24. 'Sendero Luminoso' – 'SL' ('Shining Path')
25. 'Teyrbazen Azadiya Kurdistan' – 'TAK' (aka 'Kurdistan Freedom Falcons', aka 'Kurdistan Freedom Hawks')
26. 'Autodefensas Unidas de Colombia' – 'AUC' ('United Self-Defense Forces/Group of Colombia').

Source: © European Union, http://eur-lex.europa.eu/

Al-Qaeda, Osama bin Laden and his associates were already designated in a separate Council Common Position of February 2001. Effectively this was the implementing mechanism within the EU for UN Security Council Resolution 1373, extending sanctions and account freezing to groups and individuals suspected of terrorism.

Patriot Act 2001

Although the Patriot Act is US legislation and clearly country-specific it needs to be included here as a section in its own right, since it was such a seminal response to the 9/11 terror attacks. Passed in the aftermath of the attacks, this wide-ranging piece of legislation promulgated stiff provisions affecting all financial firms with business touching the US directly or indirectly. In short, the Act is significant because its ramifications extend well beyond US territory and beyond US institutions. It also sets in place a number of counter-terrorist financing measures that have since become adopted as part of the international standard for best practice in combating terrorist financing.

Title III (International Money Laundering Abatement and Financial Anti-Terrorism Act of 2001) prohibits 'covered financial institutions' (basically US banks and US branches of non-US banks) from opening correspondent accounts with foreign shell banks (i.e. banks which did not have a physical presence in the jurisdiction where they were incorporated and which were not part of a larger group), and from doing business with other banks which *did* have relationships with foreign shell banks. It imposed enhanced due diligence requirements in respect of correspondent and private banking relationships with foreign banks (requirements again applying to both US banks and the US branches of foreign banks) and asserted 'long arm' jurisdiction over the assets of foreign money launderers, in so far as their accounts, assets or transactions touched the US.

A DEVELOPING FRAMEWORK TO COMBAT TAX EVASION

Tax evasion usually involves the concealment of *legally* obtained funds in order to avoid paying the taxes due. Tax evasion poses a serious threat to government revenues worldwide, and particularly since the start of the current global economic crisis in 2008 there have been significant developments in the international cooperative effort to combat tax evasion.

The Organization for Economic Co-operation and Development (OECD) has long been engaged in facilitating cooperation across jurisdictions in the fight against tax evasion. The OECD's Global Forum on Transparency and Exchange of Information for Tax Purposes is a multilateral framework which seeks to implement and monitor the implementation of standards of transparency and exchange of information for tax purposes. The OECD standards provide for the international exchange on request of foreseeably relevant information for the administration or enforcement of the domestic tax laws of a requesting party.

With its Foreign Account Tax Compliance Act (FATCA), enacted in 2010, the US is at the vanguard in introducing harsher national measures designed to reinforce internationally agreed standards by legislating to *enforce* the disclosure of US taxable income held outside the US, to place obligations on both taxpayers and the foreign financial institutions holding their assets and to penalise those taxpayers and institutions that do not cooperate or make accurate information about their US-based income available.

Under FATCA, US persons and entities holding financial assets outside the US will be expected to report those assets to the US Internal Revenue Service (IRS). Foreign financial institutions – or FFIs – will also be required to report to the IRS on financial accounts held with them by US persons and entities, or by foreign entities in which US persons have a significant (10 per cent or more) ownership interest. FFIs will need to enter into an agreement with the IRS to comply with FATCA, or otherwise do no further business with US clients or US securities. If an FFI has not entered into such an agreement but nonetheless continues to do business with US entities and securities then it becomes subject to a fairly punitive withholding tax on all its US-based income. In other words, any FFI wishing to continue to do US business really has very little option *but* to comply with FATCA. Compliance with FATCA also requires FFIs to carry out specific due diligence in order to identify its US clients; and to withhold and/or deduct a withholding tax on the US-based income of any US clients who themselves have not complied with their obligations under FATCA. With the due diligence requirements of this law there are obvious parallels with the anti-money laundering and counter-terrorist financing procedures and systems already used by affected financial institutions.

The introduction of FATCA has implications in that financial institutions will need to review and update their existing provisions for account opening, account monitoring, record keeping and reporting in order to ensure compliance and avoid becoming subject to a withholding tax. Other countries and jurisdictions are likely to follow with equivalent legislation of their own and so, from the implementation perspective, it is as well for FFIs to prepare *now* on the assumption that, sooner or later, they will need their operations to be compatible with comparable rules in other countries, and not just FATCA.

A DEVELOPING FRAMEWORK TO COMBAT PROLIFERATION FINANCING

Increasing international concerns regarding the apparent intentions of certain states (notably Iran) to develop a nuclear weapons capacity has led to the development of some international accords and country-specific legislation designed to combat the financing of the proliferation of weapons of mass destruction (WMD).

Measures to combat proliferation financing have much in common with anti-money laundering and counter-terrorist financing. Hence the Financial Action Task Force (FATF), established initially to combat money laundering and subseqeuently terrorist financing, announced in October 2007 that it was extending its remit to combat proliferation financing, and has since issued guidance on this (see the section on FATF, below). The UN responded with Resolutions in December 2006, March 2007, March 2008 and June 2010, aimed at restricting trade with Iran that might enable or facilitate the proliferation of WMD.

EU Council Regulations 423/2007, 617/2007 and 1110/2008 restrict certain trade with Iran and specifically target proliferation financing by requiring credit and financial institutions who conduct business with Iranian financial institutions to:

- exercise continuous vigilance over account activity
- require that all information fields relating to the identification of originators and beneficiaries in payment instructions should be completed and, if the information is not supplied, to refuse the transaction
- maintain all records of transactions for a period of five years and make them available to national authorities on request
- report transactions involving an Iranian entity and, specifically, to report any suspicions that funds may be related to proliferation financing.

The US has also taken specific legislative steps to combat proliferation financing, with the passing into law in July 2010 of the Comprehensive Iran Sanctions, Accountability and Divestment Act (CISADA). This Act requires sanctions for companies that actively invest or intend to invest in

Iran's energy sector. Activities that can trigger sanctions include:

- making an investment that directly and significantly contributes to the enhancement of Iran's ability to develop its petroleum resources, of:
  - $20 million or more, or
  - $5 million per investment, totalling $20 million or more in a 12-month period
- selling, leasing, or providing goods or services that could directly and significantly facilitate the maintenance or expansion of Iran's domestic production of refined petroleum products, with:
  - a fair market value of $1 million or more, or
  - an aggregate fair market value of $5 million or more in a 12-month period
- selling or providing Iran with refined petroleum products, with:
  - a fair market value of $1 million or more; or
  - an aggregate fair market value of $5 million or more in a 12-month period
- providing goods or services that could directly and significantly contribute to the enhancement of Iran's ability to import refined petroleum products, including;
  - insurance or reinsurance services
  - financing or brokering services, or
  - ships and shipping services, with a fair market value of $1 million or more, or an aggregate fair market value of $5 million or more in a 12-month period.

The intention of CISADA is to address the potential connection between such investment and Iran's capability to develop its nuclear programme.

THE FINANCIAL ACTION TASK FORCE (FATF)

The FATF (also known as GAFI – Groupe d'Action Financière, see www.fatf-gafi.org) is an inter-governmental body whose membership at the end of 2011 comprised 34 member countries and two regional organisations. It was set up by the then G-7 Summit held in Paris in 1989 in response to the growing threat posed by international money laundering and was given the task of examining money laundering techniques and trends, setting out measures to combat them and then reviewing the action taken at both the national and international level. As terrorist financing has risen up the international agenda, the FATF's role has naturally extended to encompass CFT as well and its remit was recently extended to include the proliferation of weapons of mass destruction (WMDs). It works in close cooperation with various other international bodies, including the IMF, the World Bank and the United Nations.

The FATF effectively has a manifold role at the heart of the overall AML and CFT regime, described below:

- To monitor the progress of countries in introducing AML and CFT measures, using self-assessments and more detailed mutual evaluations. 'Non-cooperative' governments have found themselves under heavy moral, political and economic pressure to toe the line through the reviews. For example, Austria eventually agreed to prohibit anonymous savings accounts as a result of pressure from the FATF, and the countries of Eastern Europe and the former Soviet Union (including Russia) have embarked upon urgent national legislative programmes in a very short space of time as a result of their inclusion on the 'Non-Cooperative Countries and Territories' List, dealt with in more detail in Chapter 7.
- To review trends, techniques and innovations in money laundering (which has led to annual and specialised money laundering typologies reports), and to keep member states abreast of the findings.
- To build a global AML and CFT network by extending the reach of FATF principles. This has resulted in new member countries joining the group; it has also led to the formation of regional FATF-style groups.
- To define and promulgate international standards on the combating of Money Laundering and Terrorist Financing and WMD Proliferation. At the heart of FATF's activities are their recommendations on measures for the combating of Money Laundering and the Financing of Terrorism and Proliferation. Now known as 'The FATF Recommendations' they were completely revised and refreshed in February 2012. The extension beyond money laundering and terrorist financing into the field of proliferation has been a reaction to one of the major issues of our time. A number of states, notably Iran, appear to be taking steps to build a WMD capability and accordingly we may expect sequential action and guidance from FATF on the issue of WMD proliferation financing. FATF have already in fact responded with a 'Typologies Report on Proliferation Financing', published in June 2008 and focusing specifically on the trends and methods used in financing the development of WMD programmes.

The FATF Recommendations are available from the FATF website at www.fatf-gafi.org. However, for convenience they are summarised here.

The Forty Recommendations (February 2012)

The Forty Recommendations were first published in 1990, revised in 1996, and comprehensively updated in both 2003 and 2012. They were designed to provide a comprehensive plan of action for countries that needed to fight money laundering, terrorist financing and weapons proliferation, encompassing the following key areas:

- AML/CFT Policies and Coordination
- Money Laundering and Confiscation
- Terrorist Financing and Financing of Proliferation
- Preventive Measures
- Transparency and Beneficial Ownership of Legal Persons and Arrangements
- Powers and Responsibilities of Competent Authorities and Other Institutional Measures, and
- International Cooperation.

Countries have diverse legal and financial systems and therefore all cannot take identical measures. The FATF 40 therefore lay out broad principles for countries to implement according to their particular circumstances and constitutional frameworks. They are not a binding international convention, but many countries around the world have made a political commitment to fight money laundering by adopting and implementing the FATF 40 and those who do not face censure and reprisals if they refuse to do so.

What follows is only a brief summary of the recommendations and some of the interpretative notes to provide an overview of the headline requirements. It should not be taken as a substitute for detailed reference to the source document.

A: AML/CFT policies and coordination

Recommendation 1 requires countries to adopt a risk-based approach to combating money laundering and terrorist financing to ensure that resources are as efficiently applied as possible. R1 also requires financial institutions and Designated Non-Financial Businesses and Professions (DNFBPs) to 'identify, assess and take effective action to mitigate their money laundering and terrorist financing risks'.

Recommendation 2 requires national coordination between policy-makers, the FIU, law enforcement authorities, supervisors and others, to ensure that the implementation of policies and activities to combat money laundering, terrorist financing and WMD proliferation is effectively coordinated domestically.

B: Money laundering and Confiscation

Recommendation 3 requires countries to criminalise money laundering as a specific offence and to apply the crime to 'the widest range of predicate offences'. A predicate offence, in this regard, is a serious offence which, legally, can give rise to money laundering where criminal proceeds have resulted from it. Most notably, the 2012 recommendations require that countries include tax evasion as a predicate offence, which was never the case previously.

Recommendation 4 requires countries to empower their competent authorities (such as police and prosecutors) to identify, trace, freeze, seize and confiscate criminal assets. It also permits countries to confiscate such assets ahead of any criminal conviction which is likely to be sought.

C: Terrorist Financing and Financing of Proliferation

Recommendation 5 requires countries to criminalise both the financing of terrorist acts and the financing of individual terrorists and terrorist organisations, as well as designating terrorist financing offences as predicate offences for money laundering purposes.

Recommendation 6 requires countries to implement 'targeted financial sanctions régimes' to prevent and suppress terrorism and terrorist financing pursuant to the various UN Security Council Resolutions, for the purpose of freezing terrorist funds and denying their availability to designated persons and entities.

Recommendation 7 requires that countries also implement targeted financial sanctions régimes aimed at preventing, suppressing and disrupting WMD proliferation pursuant, again, to UN Security Council Resolutions.

Recommendation 8 requires countries to pass laws which prevent the exploitation of NPOs for terrorist financing purposes.

D: Preventive Measures

Recommendation 9 requires that bank (and other financial institution) secrecy laws should be subordinate to the implementation of the FATF recommendations (so that, for example, institutions reporting in good faith cannot be the subject of successful legal actions for damages by customers and clients claiming damages for breach of confidentiality).

Recommendation 10 relates to customer due diligence (CDD). Financial institutions must undertake CDD when:

- establishing business relations
- carrying out occasional transactions above US$/€15,000 or certain wire transfers
- there is a suspicion of money laundering or terrorist financing, or
- there are doubts about the truth or adequacy of previously-obtained identification information.

Under Recommendation 10 institutions must:

- identify and verify the customer's identity using 'reliable, independent source documents, data or information'
- identify the beneficial owner of the account (i.e. the natural person or persons who own or control it, or for whose benefit it exists, and behind whom there are no further interests), and understand the ownership and control structure of corporations and other entities to this effect
- understand the purpose and intended nature of the business relationship; and
- conduct ongoing due diligence and transaction scrutiny throughout the course of the relationship to ensure consistency between account activity and stated purpose.

The CDD measures should be determined according to a risk-based approach (examples of which are dealt with in more detail in Chapter 4 of this book) and although customer identification and verification is not required to precede the opening of business relations, this is subject to the risks being effectively managed. An inability to conduct CDD for any reason should effectively prohibit a financial institution from providing the requested services and generate a need to consider the making of a suspicious transaction report.

Recommendation 10 is the subject of an extensive interpretative note containing expanded requirements on CDD for legal persons and arrangements. In particular, it contains a step-by-step process for the establishment of the identity of beneficial owners. Under this process, institutions should first identify the natural person or persons exercising control of the corporation or trust through ownership; failing that, they should attempt to establish those exercising control by means other than ownership (presumably, for example, through secret agreements, commercial arrangements etc.); failing that, they should establish a relevant natural person who holds a senior management position.

Recommendation 11 requires financial institutions to maintain transaction and CDD records for a minimum period of five years from the date of the transaction (in relation to transaction records) or following the termination of the business relationship (in relation to CDD records). These records must also be made available to competent authorities within the jurisdiction.

Additional Measures for Specific Customers and Activities

Recommendation 12 deals with politically-exposed persons (PEPs) and their family members or close associates and requires institutions to take additional steps to the CDD measures outlined in R10; in particular to put in place systems to determine whether the proposed relationship involves a

PEP, to obtain senior management approval for such relationships, to take 'reasonable measures' to establish the source of wealth and the source of funds and to conduct 'enhanced ongoing monitoring' of the relationship.

Recommendation 13 contains a series of requirements in relation to cross-border correspondent banking, under which, in addition to the CDD measures described in R10, financial institutions must obtain information on and understand their respondents' business, reputation, quality of supervision and quality of AML/CFT controls (particularly where CDD on customers have access to 'payable through accounts'), as well as obtaining senior management approval for the establishment of new correspondent relationships and understanding the respective responsibilities of the respondent and co-respondent.

Recommendation 13 also prohibits the provision of correspondent services to shell banks.

Recommendation 14 requires countries to establish licensing and registration systems for customers who provide money value transfer services (MVTS) with appropriate penalties for unlicensed operators.

Recommendation 15 requires countries and financial institutions to risk assess new products and delivery mechanisms and technologies for money laundering and terrorist financing purposes and to take steps to mitigate those risks.

Recommendation 16 relates to wire transfers and is the subject of extensive guidance in the interpretative notes. The headline requirement is that countries must require financial institutions to include both originator and beneficiary information in wire transfers, and that that information should remain with the transfer throughout the payment chain.

There are also requirements for financial institutions to be able to detect wire transfers which lack the necessary information and also to freeze the processing of wire transfers apparently involving designated persons and entities.

Recommendation 17 allows countries to permit financial institutions to rely on third parties to perform CDD steps (other than ongoing due diligence) in certain circumstances. However, the relying institution must retain ultimate responsibility (in legal terms) for the adequacy or otherwise of the CDD measures.

Recommendation 18 requires that countries should compel their financial institutions to implement AML and CFT programmes which, in the case of institutions with overseas branches and subsidiaries, should be to a consistent standard throughout, based on the home country's requirements.

Recommendation 19 requires that financial institutions should apply enhanced CDD measures to relationships involving countries which have been designated by FATF as higher risk.

Recommendation 20 requires that financial institutions be under an obligation to report suspicions of money laundering or terrorist financing promptly to the country's Financial Intelligence Unit (FIU).

Recommendation 21 requires that national laws should protect financial institutions and their staff who have reported suspicions of money laundering or terrorist financing in good faith, from civil or criminal liability for breach of confidentiality. Recommendation 21 also mandates that countries prohibit by law the practice of 'tipping-off' (informing a customer that a report has been filed with the FIU).

Recommendations 22 and 23 contain a range of requirements in relation to designated non-financial businesses and professions (DNFBPs). Basically the CDD and record-keeping requirements set out earlier apply to DNFBPs in designated situations, as do the recommendations relating to internal controls/foreign branches and subsidiaries, higher-risk countries, the reporting of suspicious transactions and tipping-off.

Specifically, the interpretative notes to Recommendation 23 make it clear that lawyers (and accountants providing legal advice) are not required to file suspicious transaction reports in circumstances where the information forming the basis of their suspicion was acquired in a situation which was subject to professional secrecy or legal professional privilege. Furthermore, lawyers are not deemed to have 'tipped-off' a client if they seek to dissuade them from engaging in certain types of activity that might constitute money laundering.

Recommendations 24 and 25 require countries to ensure that information on beneficial ownership and control in relation to legal persons (e.g. corporations) and legal arrangements (e.g. trusts) is available and can be accessed by competent authorities, and that they should also consider measures to make information on beneficial ownership and control available to financial institutions and DNFBPs.

These greatly-expanded requirements in relation to beneficial ownership are the subject of an extensive interpretative note which makes it clear that, at the heart of the matter, companies are going to have to be able to draw a distinction between legal ownership on the one hand, and beneficial ownership on the other, and to appoint 'one or more natural persons resident in the country' to provide information on beneficial ownership to the authorities.

Recommendations 26, 27 and 28 require countries to maintain adequate regulatory and supervisory frameworks for financial institutions and DNFBPs, and set out the minimum standards applicable.

Recommendation 29 requires countries to establish a FIU for the analysis of suspicious transaction reports and the obtaining of further relevant information in relation to money laundering and terrorist financing.

Recommendation 30 outlines the required responsibilities of law enforcement and investigating authorities and emphasises the importance of 'proactive parallel financial investigation' and inter-agency cooperation.

Recommendation 31 details the required powers of law enforcement and investigating authorities, such as their ability to access all necessary documents for use in investigations and their powers to use investigative techniques such as undercover operations, communications interception and controlled delivery (i.e. participating in the handling and delivery of illegal goods and substances for the purpose of obtaining evidence for prosecution).

Recommendation 32 deals with cash couriers, and the requirement that countries should put in place mechanisms to control the cross-border transportation of cash and negotiable instruments through declaration and/or disclosure systems.

Recommendations 33 and 34 impose obligations on countries to maintain statistics pertaining to the effectiveness and efficiency of their AML/CFT systems and to provide feedback to financial institutions and DNFBPs which will assist them in complying with their obligations, in particular their reporting of suspicious transactions.

Recommendation 35 requires countries to maintain a range of 'effective, proportionate and dissuasive' sanctions against persons and entities which fail to comply with their AML/CFT obligations. These sanctions should also be applicable to directors and senior management of financial institutions and DNFBPs.

Recommendations 36 to 40 then finally cover a range of requirements in relation to international cooperation, including becoming parties to relevant international conventions, mutual legal assistance, cross-border asset freezing and confiscation, extradition and generally providing 'the widest range of international cooperation in relation to money laundering, associated predicate offences and terrorist financing'.

Key differences between the 2012 Recommendations and their predecessors

Apart from bringing the former 'nine special recommendations' relating to terrorist financing within the body of the main AML recommendations, thereby creating a more unified and inclusive set of standards, the new 2012 FATF recommendations are different in the following key areas:

- **Tax crimes are now predicate offences.** Those who have followed the subject over the years will be aware that the absence of tax evasion and other serious tax crimes within the definition of 'predicate offences' which could give rise to money laundering – and therefore trigger the application of the necessary laws and standards – was an issue of hot debate. That debate has now been resolved and tax evasion (and other serious tax crimes) now sit alongside fraud, kidnapping and people- and narcotics-trafficking as offences which can give rise to money laundering.
- **Politically Exposed Persons (PEPs).** Whilst many financial institutions had included domestic PEPs within their PEP risk management processes for a number of years, the old standards did not actually require this, applying, as they did, only to foreign PEPs. This has now been remedied and the requirements for enhanced due diligence and the other standards in relation to PEPs effectively now apply to both foreign and domestic PEPs alike.
- **Wire transfers.** The previous standards (which in themselves significantly increased the information requirements relating to wire transfers) required only that originator information should remain with the wire transfer throughout its journey through the financial system. The new standard requires that both originator and beneficiary and related information should travel with the transfer.
- **Beneficial ownership.** Responding, no doubt, to the growing realisation of the extent to which front companies, front trusts and other types of corporate and legal structures and arrangements can be used for laundering large amounts of criminal money, as well as disguising funds destined for terrorism and proliferation, the new standards have expanded significantly the requirements in relation to the establishment of beneficial ownership.

  Specifically, R10 dealing with CDD now includes a step-by-step process to be followed when identifying beneficial ownership, as described earlier on. In addition, there are now major new requirements for countries to create systems (including a company registry, if they do not already have one) in which information on beneficial ownership is both recorded and available.

  Required measures include the nomination of a specific person or persons who will be responsible for available information regarding beneficial ownership and for providing further assistance to the authorities. Similar requirements apply to trusts and other legal arrangements. There are also requirements for countries to tackle 'obstacles to transparency' such as the misuse of bearer shares and nominee shareholding arrangements.

Practitioners will know that the issue of beneficial ownership in the day-to-day implementation of the standards poses one of the biggest practical challenges of all, so the increased focus on beneficial ownership is certainly hitting the 'sweet spot' in terms of where the real risks lie. Once countries start implementing the new standards, it will be interesting to see how they are met within the companies responsible for implementing them. For example, do many directors and officers of sizeable private companies even understand what the term 'beneficial ownership' means? (After all, it has taken bankers a while to understand it.) If the officer within a company responsible for maintaining and providing information on its beneficial ownership suspects that the information they have been given on beneficial ownership is suspect, will they be under a duty to disclose this? Will they commit a criminal offence if they fail to do so, or if the information which they have certified turns out to be false? How can countries prevent the information they collect on 'beneficial ownership' becoming just another layer of information which actually disguises *true* ownership and control? These are all questions which will have to be answered as the new standards become adopted in each country.

FATF REGIONAL STYLE BODIES AND ASSOCIATE MEMBERS

Several regional organisations and other bodies have been established to carry forward the principles and practices set out by FATF on a more localised/regional basis. They enjoy observer or associate membership status at the FATF and are:

- The Asia/Pacific Group on Money Laundering (APG)
- The Caribbean Financial Action Task Force (CFATF)
- The Eastern and Southern Africa Anti-Money Laundering Group (ESAAMLG)
- The Grupo de Accion Financiera Sud America (GAFISUD)
- The Eurasian Group (EAG)
- The Middle East and North Africa Financial Action Task Force (MENAFATF)
- The Council of Europe Committee of Experts on the Evaluation of Anti-Money Laundering Measures and the Financing of Terrorism (MONEYVAL)
- The Inter Governmental Action Group against Money Laundering in West Africa (GIABA).

All the groups analyse the latest money laundering and terrorist financing trends which have been detected in their region and all look to the FATF as the global leadership organisation in these fields.

OTHER RELEVANT INTERNATIONAL BODIES

International Monetary Fund (IMF)

The IMF has long been involved in international efforts to combat money laundering at a national level, and after the events of 9/11 it intensified and extended the remit of these activities to include combating the financing of terrorism. As a collaborative institution with a near-universal membership of countries (it has 187 members), the IMF is perhaps a natural forum for countries to share information and develop common approaches and appropriate policies to deal with such issues.

The IMF has also brought to bear its capabilities in the assessment of member states' financial sectors, and the provision of technical assistance to help countries strengthen their financial sectors. The Financial Sector Assessment Programme (FSAP), established in 1999, is a joint effort with the World Bank and is designed to provide member countries with a comprehensive evaluation of their financial systems as a whole, rather than those of individual financial institutions. The FSAP aims to alert the national authorities to weaknesses in their systems, and to help them design countermeasures to reduce those weaknesses.The IMF and World Bank are also involved in policy development in the counter-terrorist financing arena and author publications on various issues of concern and interest, including reference guides, handbooks and working papers on topics such as the operation of Financial Intelligence Units, legislative drafting and the impact of terrorism on financial markets

The IMF has taken a number of specific steps to assist countries in strengthening their anti-money laundering counter terrorist financing provisions. In March 2004, the IMF Executive Board agreed to make AML and CTF assessments and technical assistance a regular part of IMF work, and to expand this work to cover the full scope of the FATF recommendations. In 2009, the IMF launched a donor-supported trust fund to finance technical assistance in AML/CFT.

Basel Committee on Banking Supervision (BCBS)

The Basel Committee was established at the end of 1974, and comprises central bank (or banking supervision authority) representatives from 27 countries including the US, Japan and a number of EU states. The Committee formulates broad supervisory standards and guidelines and recommends statements of best practice in the expectation that individual authorities will take steps to implement them through detailed arrangements – statutory or otherwise – suited to their own national systems. Its main guidance documents cover areas such as transparency in payments messages, account opening and customer identification, customer due diligence and international cooperation.

The Egmont Group

The Egmont Group was set up in 1995 to facilitate international cooperation and in its ongoing work aims to support the growing number of Financial Intelligence Units (FIUs) set up by various countries since 11 September 2001. Its purpose is broadly to provide a forum through which FIUs can improve their national AML programmes. Any FIU which considers itself to comply with the criteria of the Egmont Group, of being a central, national agency responsible for receiving (and where permitted, requesting) disclosures of financial information, and analysing and disseminating such information to the competent authorities as appropriate, is eligible to apply to become an Egmont member FIU.

The Wolfsberg Group

The Wolfsberg Group is an association of 11 global banks, which aims to develop financial services industry standards for know-your-customer, AML and CFT policies. The group first came together in 2000 (at the Château Wolfsberg in north-eastern Switzerland – hence the name) to draft anti-money laundering guidelines for private banking in the wake of some very negative money laundering scandals which had affected the industry. *The Wolfsberg Anti-Money Laundering Principles for Private Banking* was subsequently published in October 2000 (and revised in May 2002). Since then the group has published papers on a wide range of areas including 'Terrorist Financing' (January 2002), 'Correspondent Banking' (November 2002), 'Monitoring, Screening and Searching' (September 2003, revised 2009) and the 'Risk Based Approach' (June 2006). The group also publishes FAQs on a range of specific issues including beneficial ownership, Politically Exposed Persons (PEPs) and intermediaries.

IAIS and IOSCO

Beyond the banking sector, international bodies such as the International Association of Insurance Supervisors (IAIS) for the insurance industry, and the International Organization of Securities Commissions (IOSCO) have issued guidance to members on best practice in the combating of money laundering and terrorist financing.

KEY REQUIREMENTS FOR FINANCIAL INSTITUTIONS

There is by now a fairly well-defined suite of activities which, taken together, denote current international best practice in anti-money laundering and counter terrorist financing, and these revolve around the core areas below. More detailed information on best practice approaches is provided in Chapter 3.

Name screening

Before entering into a business relationship, prospective customers' names must be checked against published lists of persons and organisations suspected of being connected with terrorism. Financial services must not be provided to those on the lists.

Risk assessment

Before entering into a business relationship, prospective customers must be assessed as to the degree of money laundering and terrorist financing risk which they pose, and must thereafter be the subject of appropriate risk-based procedures and controls. Risk factors to be considered include:

- location of customer and/or transaction
- type of customer (individual, corporate, trust, etc.)
- nature of customer's business
- age/period of existence of customer
- countries where customer typically conducts its business
- counterparties of customer
- product profile and sales distribution channels.

A detailed explanation of a risk-based approach to money laundering and terrorist financing is provided in Chapter 4.

CDD and EDD

Customer Due Diligence (CDD) and Enhanced Due Diligence (EDD) must be undertaken where necessary, on a risk-sensitive basis, including:

- *Identification*. Evidence and verification of the customer's identity must be obtained prior to the provision of services.
- *Business purpose*. Details of the business purpose of the relationship must be obtained.

- *Beneficial ownership*. Where this is unclear, beneficial ownership must be ascertained, the test being one of significant interest and control.
- *Ongoing monitoring* of accounts on a risk-sensitive basis and scrutiny of transactions to ascertain whether they are consistent with the stated purpose of the account.
- *Prohibition on opening accounts for shell banks*. Banks without a physical presence in the jurisdiction where they are incorporated, and which are otherwise not part of a larger group constituted in a well regulated country, are designated as 'shell banks' and may not be banked. It follows from this that where it is not obvious that a bank is not a shell bank, financial institutions must make reasonable efforts to establish whether or not it is a shell bank and thereafter to act accordingly.
- *Simplified due diligence* is allowed under certain circumstances, for example where customers are counterparties from well-regulated jurisdictions, or where a customer has been introduced by such an entity.

More information on CDD and EDD implementation is provided in Chapter 4.

Suspicion reporting

On a risk-sensitive basis, 'suspicious' transactions must be reported to the authorities and cooperation extended to the authorities in the investigation of such reports. Specifically, financial institutions must not make customers or third parties aware that such reports have been filed.

More information on different typologies, the features that characterise them and how to recognise these in financial business is provided in Chapter 6.

Record-keeping

Customer and transaction records must be retained and kept available for inspection for five years from the date of the end of the relationship (in the case of customer records) and five years from the date of the transaction (in the case of transaction records).

Staff training

Training must take place on a regular basis, in which relevant staff are trained in:

- how to recognise a potentially suspicious transaction
- what to do if they become suspicious

- their own legal obligations and those of the financial institution where they are employed
- the procedures and controls in place for dealing with AML/CFT issues within the financial institution.

More information about staff training and examples of tried and tested training techniques is provided in Chapters 3, 6 and 8.

Cooperation with relevant authorities

Cooperation must be extended, within the parameters defined by law, to law enforcement agencies in the investigation of suspected money laundering and terrorist financing. In suspected terrorism cases, in particular, it is especially important that financial institutions are able to produce records quickly in response to requests.

Responsiveness to international findings

Financial institutions must take account of information made available from reliable sources which is relevant to their assessment of money laundering and terrorist financing risk. For example, if a country appears on the list of Non-Cooperative Countries and Territories issued by FATF then financial institutions should reassess and amend their risk control procedures accordingly.

KEY COMPONENTS OF A NATIONAL AML/CFT FRAMEWORK

As part of the mutual evaluation regime, on an ongoing basis FATF conducts detailed assessments of the extent to which the AML/CFT regimes of different countries do or do not meet the international standards which it has set out in the FATF 40.

The basic requirements, however, for the institutional framework in each country are as follows, and each country must have the following.

Core legislation

The country must have primary statutes which criminalise the process of money laundering and terrorist financing, permit the seizure and confiscation of criminal and terrorist assets, impose criminal penalties (fines and imprisonment) for breaches of the law and which, in all other respects, comply with the requirements laid out in the FATF 40 and the various international conventions and regional treaties to which the country is a party.

Regulations or statutory instruments and interpretative notes or guidance

The country must have regulations or statutory instruments which address in detail the legal requirements contained in the core legislation, and which set out the various steps which regulated parties (i.e. financial institutions and the other 'gatekeepers' who are charged with AML and CFT duties) must take in order to fulfil their obligations. The regulations must cover such issues as:

- risk assessment
- customer identification and due diligence
- account and relationship monitoring
- suspicion reporting
- records maintenance
- internal controls
- staff training.

Along with other key areas identified in the FATF 40, it is not enough that regulations simply be issued; they should also be the subject of interpretative guidance which assists regulated firms in understanding and applying them.

Regulatory bodies

The country must have a regulator or regulators that have powers to inspect firms' compliance with laws and regulations and to compel improvement. Regulators must have powers to censure and impose fines and other punishments in order to give 'teeth' to their inspections. It follows from this that the staff of these regulatory bodies must be knowledgeable about the AML and CFT matters which are the subject matters of their inspections.

Financial Intelligence Units

Countries must have centralised units to receive and analyse reports of suspicions of money laundering and terrorist financing under the legislation and regulation, to build knowledge and expertise of money laundering trends and methods within their country, and to make this intelligence available to the state enforcement bodies (see below) for the purpose of taking effective action.

Law enforcement agencies

Countries need to empower police forces or other investigative agencies to investigate money laundering and its underlying crimes, and terrorist financing and the plots being funded by it. Again, officers within these agencies need to be sufficiently skilled and knowledgeable in this regard, in order to be able to fulfil their tasks successfully. The area is typically so complex that designated agencies may be required to conduct specialised tasks such as asset tracing, asset seizure or terrorist surveillance.

Ultimately, the purpose of law enforcement is to catch criminals, seize their assets and bring cases to court, so they need to work closely with the next component of the national AML/CFT regime, below.

Prosecutory authorities

Countries need to have prosecutory authorities that can work with the police to prepare and bring to court cases of money laundering and terrorist financing. Again, specialist knowledge and expertise is required for the lawyers and case specialists involved in reviewing and preparing the cases for court, and presenting/advocating them in court.

Judicial and penal system

Countries must have judges, courts and prisons capable of administering justice according to the law. This means the system must have the capacity and resources to try cases and appeals which are brought before the courts and to do so within a reasonable time, and to have effective state institutions for punishment, once convictions have been obtained.

Integrity

Finally, and perhaps most importantly, it is worth mentioning here that the 'golden thread' running through all of the above is the requirement that a country's AML/CFT regime and apparatus should have integrity at both the institutional and the individual level, and that decision-making should be free from bribery and corruption. Equally, the state should provide the necessary resources to protect, as far as humanly possible, individuals from threats, coercion and violence at the hands of the criminal community whose power they are trying to attack.

3

The Role, Structure and Positioning of the AML/CFT Compliance Function

Structure and culture

AML/CFT best practice

Best practice in higher-risk products and services

IT systems

Training and communication

A 'pro-business' approach

Management of internal suspicion reporting

Where you see the **WWW** *icon in this chapter, this indicates a preview link to the author's website and to a training film which is relevant to the AML CFT issue being discussed.*
Go to ***www.antimoneylaunderingvideos.com***

STRUCTURE AND CULTURE

Core activities for the AML/CFT role

These can be summarised as follows:

- securing senior management support
- receiving and analysing internal disclosures of suspicious activity from staff
- making external disclosures of suspicious activity to the authorities
- producing, monitoring and updating policies and procedures
- using international findings and UN and other watchlists
- staff training and awareness
- reporting on AML and CFTto senior management
- responding to information requests from competent authorities
- general oversight of the bank's overall AML/CFT effort.

Key policies and procedures

These should include the following as a minimum:

- name screening (client acceptance)
- risk assessment (client acceptance)
- identification (client acceptance)
- due diligence and enhanced due diligence
- account monitoring
- sanctions and prohibited transactions
- suspicion recognition and reporting
- records maintenance
- training, awareness and communication
- incorporation of international findings
- staff screening.

Position of the AML/CFT role within the organisation's structure

The exact place of the AML/CFT compliance role within the overall structure of the organisation is not prescribed internationally, and so will depend upon any national requirements and on the preferences of the organisation and its senior management.

In the largest international banks, the position of Head of AML and CFT is a senior position which is well remunerated and offers enough direct access to senior management to be able to function effectively. Typically the AML/CFT function will fit within one of two models:

1. *As part of a wider financial crime function*. In this model, AML and CFT sit within a specialist unit which also deals with fraud prevention and other types of financial crime such as insider trading, market manipulation, tax evasion and, more recently, proliferation financing.
2. *As part of a wider legal and compliance function*. In this model the AML/CFT function sits within a wider unit which, apart from AML and CFT, also deals with issues such as:
   - compliance with other banking rules and laws
   - compliance with the organisation's code of conduct dealing with issues such as conflicts of interest and other ethical matters relating to integrity and anti-corruption.

It is of course also possible for the unit to sit completely independently, as a statement of the importance attached to it. If that is the case, then the reporting line of the head of the unit should be at least to Executive Director level and preferably to the Chief Executive Officer, in order to avoid the risk of the unit being bypassed in important decision-making processes.

AML/CFT units are rarely part of the audit function. This is because they must themselves be subject to scrutiny and oversight in relation to the effectiveness of the way in which they perform their duties. This would not be possible if they were part of the audit function, whose job it is to provide management with assurance that different functions in the organisation are doing their jobs efficiently, including the AML/CFT function.

The so called 'three-line defence model' for AML and CFT sees the organisation setting up three tiers of protection against the various risks posed. These are:

- *First line of defence – at line management level*. Relationship managers, branch managers and supervisors and their front line staff comprise the outer armour of the organisation's defences. They are relied upon to be aware of the risks and to apply policies and procedures as they have been laid down, for example in relation to issues such as identification, account monitoring, name screening and suspicion reporting.
- *Second line of defence – AML/CFT unit*. The AML/CFT unit itself forms the second line of defence. The unit exercises general oversight of all AML and CFT activities within the organisation including:
  – designing policies
  – conducting training
  – engendering senior management support
  – monitoring and reviewing the application of policies within the business units.

If the unit contains audit skills, then there is no reason why it should not conduct audit-type activities to satisfy itself that policies are being applied successfully. Nevertheless, such activities will not constitute formal audit assurance in governance terms. Such assurance can only be provided by the audit department.

- *Third line of defence – audit department.* The organisation's audit department provides the third line of defence, conducting full audits not only of business units (which should also include AML and CFT checks and sampling) but also of the AML/CFT function itself, to provide assurance to the Board and Audit and Risk Committees that it is doing its job properly.

Organisation of the AML/CFT role

In terms of who does what within the AMT/CFT function, in a small organisation one or two people may handle everything from business queries to training, to writing policy, to arranging IT support for name screening, etc. As an organisation gets larger and more complex, however, this clearly becomes inappropriate and a division of responsibilities becomes necessary.

The precise nature of the division, if not prescribed by local law, is a matter for the Head of the AML/CFT function to decide. For example, a Head in a reasonably large organisation might split the responsibilities of the function as follows or, where resources are tight, allocate clusters of them to individuals:

- regulatory and FIU liason and reporting
- receipt and analysis of internal Suspicious Transaction Reports (STRs)
- sanctions, blacklists, name screening and client acceptance
- policy, training and international compliance
- day-to-day operational advice to business units.

The very largest organisations will need to operate matrix structures in which different roles are performed across multiple products in different business streams across multiple jurisdictions (if the organisation is expanding internationally). These structures may, for example, see different heads of AML/CFT distributed through the organisation on a business or geographic basis, with double reporting lines to both the general managers of those businesses and into a main, centralised AML/CFT function sited in head office.

In such cases, the more complex the structure needs to become, the more important it is that there is great clarity as to who is responsible for what – in particular the statutory responsibilities laid down under national law and, of course, clarity within the organisation as to whom suspicious transactions should be reported.

Importance of a strong compliance culture

Whereas all core activities in the AML/CFT role are important there is one activity in particular which is paramount, and that is securing senior management support. Compliance starts from the top and without the commitment of senior management the role of the AML/CFT Compliance Officer becomes that much more difficult, and some might even say impossible.

Why is this? The answer is that the senior managers in organisations occupy positions of such power that effectively they determine the culture of the organisations which they lead. Whether it is because subordinates want to impress them, or because they are fearful for their jobs, or because they act purely from habit may differ from case to case. But the general indication is that people's propensity to follow orders at work and 'go with the flow' is extremely high.

What is the evidence for this? Much research has been done in this area but two psychological studies conducted in America in the 1960s are particularly worthy of mention. The first, undertaken by Stanley Milgram, placed subjects in a situation where they thought they were taking part in experiments to determine a person's capability to follow simple instructions, with a small electric shock being administered if the person followed the instruction incorrectly. They were assigned the task of the 'teacher' and had to administer these small electric shocks to the 'student' who was situated on the other side of a pane of glass, the two being separated by a contraption described as an 'electric shock machine'. The arrangement is shown in Figure 3.1.

Figure 3.1

Milgram's famous experiment

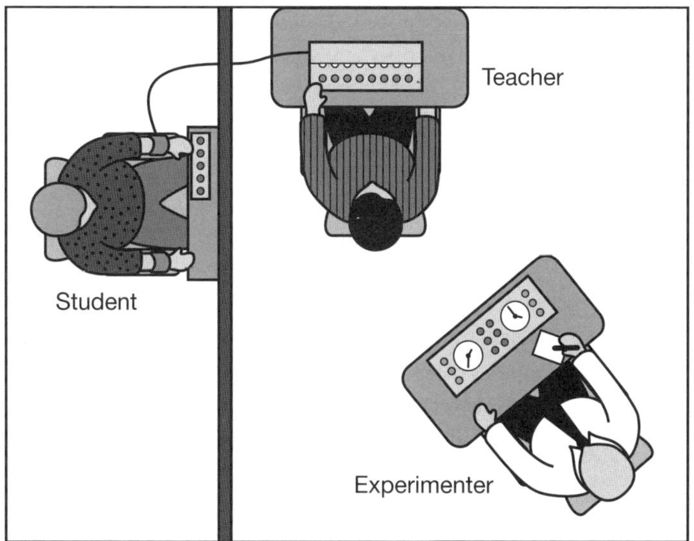

In fact there were no electric shocks and the real subjects of the experiment were the 'teachers' who were being asked to administer what they believed to be increasingly severe electric shocks to the 'students' (who were in fact actors) for no other reason than that they had got the answer to a simple question wrong. As the 'shocks' increased the 'students' displayed increasing amounts of distress. Milgram's 'teachers' were accompanied by authority figures in white coats (the experiments were conducted at Yale University in the US) to whom they frequently appealed during the experiments for permission to stop. Always, however, the answer came back calmly but firmly to proceed with the administration of the 'electric shocks'. Milgrim was interested to test how far people would go in following instructions from an authority figure. The results were extraordinary. Very high percentages of the subjects (sometimes up into the 70 per cent bracket) would proceed to administer what they believed to be lethal electric shocks to the 'students'. This led Milgram to his chilling conclusion: 'A substantial proportion of people do what they are told to do, irrespective of the content of the act and without limitations of conscience, so long as they perceive that the command comes from a legitimate authority'. (*Source*: www.stanley milgram.com/quotes.php)

If Milgram's experiment dealt with people's propensity to follow orders, then the experiments conducted by another American psychologist named Solomon Asch graduated more towards people's willingness (or otherwise) to speak out in a group when they believe that something is wrong. Asch sat his single subjects in groups with 11 others, all of whom knew the true purpose of the experiment, with only the subject unknowing. A group would be shown different images of lines of differing lengths and were asked to state which line was longer, which was shorter, etc. Each member of the group would state his or her opinion in turn. The subject was always in the latter half of those asked, such that the majority in the group had already given their opinion by the time it came to the subject. The differences in the line lengths were quite obvious. For a couple of rounds in each group, the majority of those asked 'Which was the longer line?' gave the correct answer, as did the subject. However, at a certain point the majority gave wrong answers and, again, in surprisingly high numbers the subjects would agree with the majority even though the evidence of their own eyes was telling them quite clearly that the opposite was true.

These two experiments demonstrate what most of us have probably already experienced: that in organisations people tend to do as they are told and are, by and large, very reluctant to speak out when they receive an instruction which they believe to be 'wrong'. Applying this to an AML/CFT culture it becomes easy to see how such a culture would be weak and ineffective unless senior management is not only '*talking* the talk' but also '*walking* the talk', i.e. insisting upon adherence to necessary standards, even where that may mean giving up a short-term revenue gain.

Example

The case of the rising star

In one financial institution there was a policy which stated very clearly that: 'In case of doubt we do not hesitate to reject potential customers or terminate business for AML concerns, even if it means losing profitable business. Consequently we accept from staff a critical attitude with regards to new customers.' A young relationship manager, aware of the policy, was publicly criticised by his manager in team meetings when he raised concerns about certain new customers and the origin of their wealth. He was told, 'Go and join the Compliance Department, you'd fit in better there than you do here,' and he was overlooked for promotion and received a lesser bonus than some of his colleagues. He raised the matter privately with the Compliance Department who, after getting nowhere with the business manager concerned, escalated the matter to the CEO, explaining that in its view it was essential that the business manager should get a clear message from the CEO that the AML policy was meant to be followed in practice. The business unit run by the manager was, however, performing extremely well. Its revenues were at record levels and undoubtedly the manager was partly responsible for this.

In spite of several subsequent requests, the CEO took no action, choosing rather to issue a generally worded memo to all staff about the importance of the AML policy. A month or two later, another manager in the business unit informed Compliance that the manager had treated the matter humorously in a subsequent team meeting, quipping that the CEO needed him more than he needed the Compliance Department. The second manager said, 'Everyone knew what had happened and everyone knew what the outcome had been. From that moment on nobody was in any doubt that, whatever the AML policy said, the view of their manager, backed by senior management at the highest level, was that whenever the policy jeopardised profits, it could be overlooked.'

Gaining senior management support

Genuine support from senior management is so essential that nothing good or effective will be achieved without it. There are some obvious things that you can do on a personal level to foster support from senior managers, such as:

- communcating with senior managers regularly, both orally and in writing
- regularly sharing information with senior managers about different aspects of AML/CFT compliance (but don't become a bore)
- inviting senior managers to contribute to discussions about AML/CFT compliance (e.g. at department meetings or training sessions)

- ensuring that news of positive developments reaches key senior people, whilst also ensuring that any 'bad surprises' are flagged up as early as possible, together with options and recommendations for resolution
- developing good relationships with regulators whose views senior management must take note of.

However, AML/CFT compliance officers must appreciate that it is insufficient simply to write lots of memos and other communications pointing out what the laws and regulations say. To achieve *real* commitment and all the good things that flow from it the AML/CFT function must adopt an approach that is business-focused, one that casts AML/CFT compliance as something that is there to help the business *succeed*, rather than as a 'blockage' to be got around or ignored.

The foundation stone for your business-focused approach should be a desire to *achieve* (or, if a great one exists already, to *maintain*) the right culture within the organisation. This will not be a culture in which the business views compliance as being the Compliance Department's problem, but rather a culture in which the business takes *ownership* of compliance for itself and incorporates it seamlessly into its business processes, with the support and help of the CEO and senior management team and the Compliance Department. This type of culture is typically achieved by:

- a business-owned governance structure that puts a heavy emphasis on business responsibility for compliance
- a complete set of policies that can be 'seamlessly' integrated into each business unit's operating procedures and that apply in practice as well as on paper
- adherence to current best practice, demonstrating a commitment to anticipate and keep pace with a rapidly developing regulatory environment
- IT systems designed to assist the organisation in fulfilling its obligations and in meeting its AML/CFT objectives
- a continuous training and communication programme emphasising the importance of AML/CFT compliance and equipping staff so they can comply with both organisational policy and national law.
- A proactive, business-friendly approach from AML/CFT Compliance Officers, with an emphasis on efficient and effective suspicion reporting management.

Business ownership

What practical steps can you, the Compliance Officer, take to embed responsibility for AML/ CFT compliance within the business itself? In terms of corporate governance there are a variety of possible measures, outlined below.

Policies

Corporate policies should state clearly that responsibility for compliance lies with business units. For example:

> **'Business heads are responsible for ensuring that procedures and controls commensurate with these standards and guidelines are in place for all units under their control.'**

Anti-Money Laundering Group (AMG)

It is not sufficient that business managers' responsibility for compliance should simply be incorporated within policy documentation. Managers will need reminding on a constant basis that responsibility is theirs. A good mechanism for achieving this is a regular AMG meeting, comprising the heads of the major business units concerned, briefed to discuss AML and CFT issues specifically. The AMG should be chaired by the chief executive or general manager and would consist of the heads of businesses, the Chief Operating Officer, the Compliance Officer and any other key personnel. An example agenda is shown below:

Example

AMG AGENDA

for the meeting to be held on [date] at [place]

1. Minutes and action points from last meeting on [date].
2. Update on Suspicious Activity Reporting (Compliance Officer) and 'live issues' from business units.
3. Progress on staff training and awareness and other initiatives within the anti-money laundering strategy (each Business Head).
4. Policies and procedures – any points arising.
5. Legal and regulatory update – including global/international developments (Compliance Officer/MRO).
6. A.O.B.
7. Next meeting.

Chaired by the Chief Executive Officer, or in his absence the Deputy CEO or Chief Operating Officer (COO).
For attendance – Heads of Businesses, COO and any other key personnel agreed.

Link to performance

Responsibility for AML/CFT compliance should also be built into the organisation's performance management framework, thus ensuring that observance of AML/CFT good practice is one of the measures against which managers' work performance is assessed. Specific AML/CFT objectives can be included within a business manager's overall personal performance objectives. Similar provisions can be cascaded down into the objectives of more junior staff. This will highlight the importance of AML/CFT compliance and signals clearly that bonuses may be at risk if compliance performance objectives are ignored. An example for a senior business manager might be as follows:

Example

Anti-Money Laundering objectives

During the assessment period, actively to assist the bank's drive against money laundering and to provide business leadership on money laundering prevention by:

- attending and contributing at the senior management AML meetings
- implementing action points agreed upon and decisions made at AML meetings
- attending and, where appropriate, introducing staff training sessions on AML
- achieving a score of 18 or more in the 20 questions AML self-assessment test administered by compliance.

Compliance Champions

It is rare that an AML/CFT function will have sufficient resources and personnel to have an employee present in each business unit. Even if it did, as representatives of the Compliance function such employees may be viewed as separate from the business. A 'Compliance Champion' therefore is an employee who sits within the business and undertakes certain specific activities such as:

- distributing information (e.g. articles or briefing notes) about a particular topic received from the AML/CFT Compliance Officer
- helping in the organisation and delivery of formal training sessions and training programmes on AML- and CFT- related topics, in conjunction with the Compliance Department
- providing the AML/CFT Compliance Officer with direct feedback on the effect of certain policies and procedures on the business, and making suggestions for improvement
- periodically meeting up with the AML/CFT Compliance Officer and Compliance Champions from other business areas to discuss compliance issues and problems and recommend practical solutions which will work at the point of business
- delivering short, informal briefings on compliance-related topics at, for example, business team or management meetings.

Because of their proximity to the business, Compliance Champions are unable to undertake any kind of independent assessment of compliance standards. This must be done either by the Compliance Officer or the Audit Department in accordance with the three-line defence model discussed earlier.

Communication of requirements

Setting up a business ownership structure as outlined above requires communication – from the Compliance Officer to the Chief Executive, and from the Chief Executive to business heads. Shown below are examples of the documents that might have a role to play in such a strategy, based around the three themes of:

1. creating a 'culture of compliance'
2. embedding responsibility for compliance within business units
3. the development and maintenance of sound AML and CFT policies and procedures.

Clearly the Compliance Officer should discuss their overall approach with the CEO beforehand and obtain their support for the approach, but otherwise these memos are practical documents which, when taken in conjunction with a senior management presentation and a staff briefing, for example, could form the basis of an effective communication strategy to explain the business ownership approach advocated here.

Example

MEMO TO CHIEF EXECUTIVE OFFICER RECOMMENDING ACTION STEPS ON MONEY LAUNDERING RISK

To: [ ], Chief Executive Officer
From: [ ], [Compliance Officer][Risk Officer][Title]
Date: [ ]

Re: Money laundering risk – Action going forward

1. I refer to our discussions regarding the above, and now set out formally, as requested, my observations on how [Name] Bank should best deal with the management of money laundering and terrorist financing risk going forward.
2. In common with other regulated banks and financial institutions in [Country], we have been complying with [Central Bank] regulations regarding the opening of customer accounts, the mandatory reporting of certain transactions and the reporting of unusual or suspicious transactions for some time. However, in view of international trends in relation to money laundering prevention, which clearly indicate:

Example continued

- a significant tightening of regulatory standards
- a significant increase in the reputational damage likely to be suffered by defaulting banks, and
- a significant increase in likely penalties to be imposed upon defaulting banks – including possible denial of access to the financial system in key areas such as the US, EU etc.

I believe we (the senior management team) now need to adopt a **strategic approach** to this issue, and to formalise the general increase in awareness which we have all felt, into a concrete and comprehensive plan of action which is visible to staff, customers and regulators alike. The medium- and long-term aims and benefits of doing this will be substantial and will include:

- a reduced risk of use of our bank by criminal elements
- in the event that such use does occur against our best efforts, a much greater ability to defend ourselves from criticism, due to our having initiated voluntarily a programme of best practice measures which complement the minimum regulatory requirements
- as a result, a strengthening of our overall risk management capability.

3. I believe that our strategy should concentrate on three broad and complementary areas or 'themes' of action, and I outline what these are below, together with some of the practical measures which we can implement to bring them to life.

THEME 1: BUILDING 'A CULTURE OF AWARENESS' AMONGST STAFF IN RELATION TO MONEY LAUNDERING

In best practice benchmark organisations, all staff – but particularly those in key areas – are aware of the risks posed by money laundering and terrorist financing, and of the steps which are expected of them in trying to prevent and/or to identify it. This means much more than just making the relevant laws and policies (see below) available to staff. It means imbuing them with an instinctive vigilance which they, whilst remaining hungry for business, then apply to all customers and all transactions. Actions to achieve this objective would include:

- regular training (suited to job, grade, etc.)
- regular distribution of relevant materials and resources
- periodic surveys to measure awareness
- periodic assessments to test knowledge
- suitable treatment of the issue during the staff induction process
- 'stress testing' of vigilance in, for example, branches
- overt and unequivocal senior management support for the anti-money laundering message.

Example continued

THEME 2: EMBEDDING RESPONSIBILITY FOR ANTI-MONEY LAUNDERING COMPLIANCE WITHIN BUSINESSES

In organisations where the primary responsibility for ensuring anti-money laundering compliance is seen to rest with the Compliance/Risk function, businesses never fully accept their role in preventing money laundering. Management time is wasted as businesses and risk functions adopt 'us and them' postures. Risk is increased as, freed from responsibility for the ultimate outcome, businesses attempt to accept business which they may be less than sure about. Genuine revenue opportunities are lost as compliance/ Risk functions, feeling pressured and under attack, veto business which might otherwise be accepted.

In best practice benchmark organisations, however, primary responsibility for compliance lies with the businesses, where such compliance is seen as an integral part of the business cycle. Actions to achieve this objective would include:

- specific CEO memorandum to business heads, setting out their responsibilities [see 'BusinessACMem.doc']
- policies and procedures which specifically include statements of business responsibility and accountability [see 'Policy'.docs (various)]
- ensuring that policies and procedures are observed day-to-day, by rewarding compliance and punishing non-compliance
- the launch of a senior management group, called the Anti-Money Laundering Group (AMG) to oversee [Name] Bank's overall anti-money laundering effort [see 'BusinessACMem.doc]; such group to include heads of businesses
- inclusion of a specific anti-money laundering objective in the personal job objectives of business heads and all other staff, with performance against this objective being included in a person's annual appraisal
- during anti-money laundering training, a continuous emphasis on the personal responsibility of staff for the prevention and identification of money laundering
- the appointment of specific people at a more junior level within businesses to act as 'Compliance Champions' (this role to be 'double hatted' with their existing roles), assisting the Compliance Officer/Risk Manager with various tasks such as training and the dissemination of relevant materials and resources.

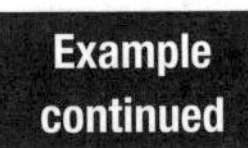

THEME 3: THE [DEVELOPMENT OF] [MAINTENANCE AND ENHANCEMENT OF OUR] ANTI-MONEY LAUNDERING POLICIES AND PROCEDURES

We must [develop] [maintain and enhance our] policies and procedures in key areas connected with the fight against money laundering, so as to ensure that [Name] Bank's position on anti-money laundering is clearly spelled out, and that staff have clear standards to follow. These must be adapted to be specifically relevant to each type of business and should [be updated to] cover the following issues:

- screening against international, regional and national 'blacklists'
- customer identification and risk assessment
- 'know your customer/business' procedures, according to risk
- account monitoring, according to risk
- records retention
- identification of suspicious transactions
- reporting of suspicions
- handling of customers under suspicion
- use of 'material deficiency' findings
- internal auditing and compliance monitoring
- pre-employment screening
- staff education and training.

4. Our policies and procedures must be living documents, which are updated regularly so as to remain relevant to new products and risk areas, and which are an integral part of the way in which each business is run.
5. The three themes complement each other. A strong culture of awareness amongst staff will make it easier for businesses to assume responsibility for compliance, just as the assumption of that responsibility will help develop the desired culture. Clear, relevant and up-to-date policies and procedures will help – and be helped by – both.
6. If you are in agreement with the above, the next step would be for us to have discussions with the business heads concerning this new strategy, before convening the first meeting of the AMG to agree a more detailed plan of how and in what order to launch and implement the various initiatives.

Sincerely, etc.

Example

CEO's MEMO RE: BUSINESS RESPONSIBILITY FOR ANTI-MONEY LAUNDERING COMPLIANCE

To: All Business Heads [and e.g. COO]
From: [ ], Chief Executive Officer
Cc: [ ], Compliance Officer
Date: [ ]

Re: 1. Business responsibility for anti-money laundering compliance
2. Launch of Anti-Money Laundering Group (AMG)

The purpose of this note is to outline the responsibilities which you and your businesses bear in relation to the prevention and detection of money laundering and terrorist financing in [Name] Bank in [Country] , and to set out the terms of reference for a new senior management group which I have decided to form, to be called the Anti-Money Laundering Group (AMG), to assist in the planning and implementation of a comprehensive anti-money laundering strategy for [Name] Bank in [Country].

1. Business responsibility for anti-money laundering compliance
Primary responsibility for compliance lies with the business, and not with the compliance officer/risk manager. As discussed with each of you individually, I view your responsibilities as follows:

- To oversee the devising and implementation of anti-money laundering and counter-terrorist financing policies and procedures suitable for your business, and to keep them updated and relevant to new products and changes to local laws and circumstances and international conditions.
- To ensure that these policies, procedures and laws are observed day-to-day, for example by rewarding compliance with them, and by punishing non-compliance.
- To ensure that a specific anti-money laundering objective (in the form attached at the Appendix) is included within your own personal job objectives, and that suitably adapted versions appear within the objectives of other key identified staff, with performance against this objective being included in annual appraisals.
- To ensure that anti-money laundering and counter-terrorist financing training is undertaken for all relevant staff, with a repeated emphasis being placed on the personal responsibility of staff members for the prevention and identification of money laundering.
- To appoint, in consultation with the compliance officer/risk manager, a specific person within your business, to act as a 'Compliance Champion' (this role may be 'double hatted' with their existing role), assisting the Compliance Officer/Risk Manager with various tasks such as training

and the dissemination of relevant materials, information and resources in relation both to money laundering and to compliance generally.

- To ensure that relevant staff, when considering customers, business and transactions, give due consideration and weight to money laundering and terrorist financing risk. In particular, that they do not abdicate their own personal responsibility for ensuring the suitability of business.

2. Launch of Anti-Money Laundering Group (AMG)
The AMG will be the senior body within [Name] Bank in [Country] for the management of money laundering and terrorist financing risk. Comprised of the heads of businesses, [the chief operating officer (COO)], the compliance officer/risk manager and myself, it will have the following terms of reference:

- The broad objective of the AMG will be to implement an anti-money laundering strategy, specifically:
  - to help create a 'culture of awareness' amongst staff within [Name] Bank in [Country], in relation to money laundering risk;
  - to help embed responsibility for anti-money laundering compliance deep within the businesses of [Name] Bank in [Country]
  - to help [develop] [maintain and enhance] effective anti-money laundering policies and procedures in [Name] Bank in [country]
  - to help ensure that [Name] Bank in [Country] takes considered and appropriate action in response to [Name] Bank, national or international issues arising in connection with money laundering.
- The AMG will meet at least once every two months, or more frequently should it be required.
- The standard agenda for AMG discussions will be as per the document entitled AMGAgenda.doc, but other topics may be included as required.

The first meeting of the AMG will take place on [date] at [time], when we will attempt to establish priorities and timings for the various initiatives.

In conclusion, I cannot over-emphasise the devastating effect which even inadvertent involvement in a money laundering and/or terrorist financing scandal would be likely to have on our business and reputation [in the current environment]. Nor can I overstate the critical importance of your providing firm leadership on this issue within your respective businesses [and functions]. I know I can count on you to work with me to ensure that our anti-money laundering strategy is a success.

Sincerely, etc.

Example continued

APPENDIX – FOR INCLUSION IN STAFF PERFORMANCE OBJECTIVES

During the assessment period, actively to assist the Bank's drive against money laundering and terrorist financing, and to provide business leadership on money laundering and terrorist financing prevention by:

- attending and contributing at the senior management AMG meetings
- implementing action points agreed upon and decisions made at AMG meetings
- punishing mistakes of non-compliance appropriately
- attending at and, where appropriate, introducing, staff training sessions on money laundering
- achieving a score of 80 per cent or more in the money laundering self-assessment test administered by compliance/risk management.

AML/CFT policies, procedures and systems

With the assistance of the AML/CFT Compliance Officer, businesses will need to implement complete policy, procedure and system solutions to the AML/CFT risks which they face. The precise scope and content of these polices, procedures and systems will be influenced by local law and regulation, but in order to comply with international standards they will need to deal with at least the following areas:

- *Customer acceptance and black list screening*. How the organisation takes on a new client and determines that the client is not on any international black lists.
- *Client Due Diligence (CDD) and risk assessment*. How the organisation checks that clients are who they say they are and how they determine the level of money laundering and terrorist financing risk posed by each client (see Chapter 4 for more detail).
- *Know Your Customer (KYC)*. How the organisation builds its knowledge of each customer's transaction and business pattern so as to be able to discern any unusual activity.
- *Monitoring*. How the organisation monitors its clients' accounts for unusual and potentially suspicious activity.
- *Suspicious transaction reporting*. How the organisation detects and reports (internally and externally) transactions or relationships which are potentially suspicious (including its policies to deal with customers who are under suspicion).
- *Mandatory reporting*. If the law requires this, how the organisation reports transactions of a certain type or above a certain threshold to the authorities.

- *Record keeping*. How the organisation creates and stores customer records in accordance with national and international legal and regulatory requirements.
- *Ongoing screening*. How the organisation screens its existing client base on a regular basis to ensure that it is free of individuals and entities named on relevant lists of proscribed persons.
- *Training*. How the organisation raises awareness of AML/CFT risks and provides staff with the knowledge and skills necessary to combat them.
- *Material deficiency findings*. How the organisation detects, responds to and implements the findings of relevant international bodies (e.g. FATF, UN) in relation to areas or geographies of AML CFT risk.
- *Staff screening*. How the organisation screens key staff ahead of their employment for AML/CFT risk.
- *Audit and assurance*. How the organisation assures itself that the AML/CFT compliance function and policies and procedures are operating effectively.

AML/CFT BEST PRACTICE

The World Bank and the IMF have produced a guide to best practice, grounded in the original FATF recommendations and in the Basel Committee on Banking Supervision's international standards and this text is based on its consequential guidelines. In addition there is relevant guidance from other industry-specific bodies and relevant sources including IAIS (insurance), IOSCO (Securities), the Wolfsberg Group (international and private banking), the Joint Money Laundering Steering Group (UK consultative body) and the US Department of Treasury Anti-Terrorist Financing Guidelines (re charities), summarised in composite form below.

Customer identification and due diligence

The global KYC standard outlined here derives from the World Bank and IMF guidance and from the FATF recommendations together with associated regulatory guidance issued in countries such as the UK and US. The standard can be used as a benchmark for the banking sector, as well as a best practice reference point for other financial sectors.

How far should the KYC policy extend?

Whatever regime is introduced at the headquarters of an institution must be applied to its branches and to any majority-owned subsidiaries, both domestically and internationally, unless it clashes with local law in that jurisdiction.

If there are differences in regulatory standards between home and host countries, then the more comprehensive/stronger of the two should be applied.

Who is a customer?

Banks need to establish at the outset whether the person with whom they are dealing is acting on their own behalf, or whether there is a beneficial owner of the account who may not be identified in their paperwork. If a bank suspects the customer is representing a third party, it must carry out due diligence on that third party as well.

Third parties may be organisations or legal entities as well as individuals. It can be particularly difficult to establish who the beneficial owner is when 'tiered ownership' is involved, with a whole pyramid of companies controlling one another and in some cases a parent company at the top. Again, appropriate due diligence is necessary in such a situation to find out the precise identity of the parent entity.

Customer acceptance procedures

It is necessary for banks to be able to identify which potential new customers represent a high risk in terms of money laundering and the financing of terrorism, by developing high-risk profiles against which they can be measured. Standard risk indicators for money laundering will include factors such as:

- the customer's country of origin (e.g. from a country notified by the International Cooperation Review Group (ICRG) of the FATF, or a country habitually associated with the production, transit or processing of illegal narcotics)
- the type and country of business activity (e.g. arms, casinos, diamonds, jewellery, money exchange)
- any linked accounts, and whether or not they have a high-profile position and/or are 'politically exposed'
- the kinds of products which the customer wishes to use, and whether they are of particular use to someone wishing to launder money (e.g. no notice restrictions on withdrawals).

As regards terrorist financing, it simply is not possible to produce a meaningful profile for an individual terrorist financier, but clearly issues surrounding the general profile of an account will be relevant, such as:

- known connections with a conflict area or country associated with terrorism
- business interests in or with such countries/areas
- frequent money transfers to and from such areas and travel to and from them (such as with associated charities and non-profit organisations)
- complex ownership structures leading back to individuals or businesses with connections to such places.

Senior management approval

The risk-based approach generally means that the bank can afford to exercise reduced due diligence with low-risk customers. The IMF/World Bank guidance recommends that the rigidity of the acceptance standards should be in proportion to the risk profile of a potential customer. However, when new customer business deemed to be 'high risk' is up for consideration, the onus should be on the *senior* management to make the decision as to whether or not such business is appropriate for the bank to take on.

Customer identification

Bank staff should verify any new customer's identification to their satisfaction before an account is opened. Customers are not allowed to open accounts in fictitious names, and nor are numbered accounts permitted unless the usual customer ID procedures and supporting documentation are used as a matter of course.

Once they come to request identification documents, banks should ask for those that are hardest to forge. For individuals the most suitable are official documents such as passports, driving licences, personal ID cards or tax identification documents. An institution's procedures should specify which of these or other documents might be acceptable for different individuals. For legal entities the suitable documents specified might include a certificate of incorporation, the business's registered address, its tax identification number and whatever other proof of the business's legitimacy as an entity is required.

When an intermediary – for example a trustee, financial adviser or nominee – is opening an account or carrying out a transaction on behalf of an individual or a corporate customer, then unless legally sanctioned 'passporting' procedures apply (e.g. as in the EU, where business introduced by other EU-regulated entities may be assumed to have been correctly identified already), the financial institution needs to take steps to verify the identification of the beneficiary. This will include the following information:

- the name and legal form of its organisation
- its registered or legal address
- the names of the directors and the principal beneficiaries
- the details of the agent acting on behalf of the organisation and the organisation's account number with the agent
- the regulatory body to which the organisation answers.

There are sometimes legitimate reasons why a customer may not be able to provide preferred identification such as a passport or driving licence.

Since the purpose of customer identification is not to exclude legitimate customers from having access to financial services, an institution's identification procedures should therefore include some alternative means of identifying customers to a satisfactory standard.

Detecting forgery

Particular care needs to be taken with the risk of forged identities, since this is a mechanism known to be used increasingly by terrorists, as well as criminal groups. For example:

- When dealing with a new customer face to face, it is important to check that the photo supplied is of the person actually opening the account, and that the date of birth given is realistic in the light of their appearance (an obvious point, but one easily missed in a frenetic retail environment).
- If bank statements from two financial institutions are presented as supporting evidence, check that the two show different transactions (one known method is to 'cut and paste' transactions to manufacture a second statement).
- Does the ethnicity of the name seem to match that of the customer?
- Is the content of each document consistent throughout (e.g. do the dates match)?
- Are the document margins straight? (Crooked margins are a red flag for forgery)
- Are there any other signs that the document has been tampered with?

Originator and beneficiary information on funds transfers

Funds transfers of any description should be accompanied by accurate and meaningful originator and beneficiary information – including name, address and account number – and that information should remain with the payment all the way along the payment chain.

Maintenance of KYC information

Knowing your customer is an ongoing exercise, which means that banks have to put some effort into keeping records up to date – for example if there are material changes in the way an account is run, or in the event of significant transactions being made on the account.

Low- vs high-risk accounts and transactions

As discussed above, the risk-based approach requires financial institutions to assess the AML and CFT risks attached to different types of customer profile. Similarly, financial institutions need to weigh up the potential for different kinds of product to be misused for criminal activities. For instance, a wire transfer service is a more obvious choice than a 90 days' notice deposit account in this respect, (though long notice accounts can have their criminal uses too).

For lower-risk categories of customer (e.g. public companies or government enterprises) financial institutions may be able to scale down or simplify the due diligence requirements, for example by requiring fewer details about the business relationship or expected transactions. Nonetheless *all* customers, even lower-risk ones, should be required to prove and verify who they are. For higher-risk categories, banks should take additional precautions when they carry out customer due diligence. We look more closely at the various types of higher-risk customers, products and services in Chapter 4.

Record-keeping requirements

Minimum periods

As we have already seen, when intelligence services or regulatory authorities are tracing the evidence trail behind a money laundering or terrorist financing discovery, the availability of customers' financial records (current and/or historic) can be a significant help in the detection and prosecution of the individuals involved. Moreover, the very fact that records are kept as a matter of course is believed in some cases to deter would-be criminals from their original illicit plans.

FATF Recommendation 11 sets a minimum international standard for the period over which banks and other financial institutions must retain records of the identification data obtained from customers (at least five years beyond the end of the customer relationship) and records of the customers' transactions (at least five years beyond the date of the transaction). National regulation and institutional policy must therefore enforce this or a higher standard of record keeping. The regulators of any country may, of course, choose to extend the minimum five-year holding period for institutions based in their jurisdiction.

Type of information retained

The information retained by banks as a matter of course should include:

- a customer's name, address and account number
- the date and nature of each transaction
- the currency and amount involved
- any other information that is routinely recorded by the bank and could be relevant in piecing together a criminal evidence trail.

Reporting obligations

Suspicious Transaction Reports (STRs)

STRs are the mainstay of anti-money laundering programmes. They place the onus on financial institutions to spot suspicious or anomalous activities among the daily flood of transactions, and despite the difficulty in detecting financing activity at the front end of the terrorist financing chain, they have their place in countering terrorist financing, too. As FATF puts it:

> **'If a financial institution suspects or has reasonable grounds to suspect that funds are the proceeds of a criminal activity, or are related to terrorist financing, it should ... report promptly its suspicions to the financial intelligence unit.'**

Source: www.fatf-gafi.org

However, a financial institution should, under no circumstances, alert the customers under scrutiny to the fact that their behaviour has been monitored and reported to the authorities.

Characteristics of suspicious activities

'Suspicious activities' can take numerous forms, but many will share certain broad-brush characteristics. Most obviously, as far as money laundering in particular is concerned, they tend to involve transactions out of step with the usual patterns seen on the account in question. So any complex or unusually large deals, or unusual transactions without any obvious commercial or lawful purpose, should be viewed as potentially suspicious and reported internally and, if appropriate, thereafter to the relevant authorities.

As far as terrorist financing is concerned, a variety of indicators may give cause for concern, ranging from problems with identification documents through to, for example, unusual signing arrangements, evidence of ulterior control by undisclosed parties, and wire transfer activity which shows signs of manipulation or structuring in order to evade reporting requirements or disguise ultimate sources of funds information.

Extent of reporting duties

How far does the reporting organisation have to go in its reporting duties? An STR simply comprises of the factual details of a transaction or series of events; there is generally no reason why the reporting bank, insurer or other financial institution should necessarily know anything about *what* it thinks may be wrong, only that it thinks that something *may* be wrong. Given that a United States' Office of the Comptroller of Currency (OCC) guide identified more than 200 predicate crimes for money laundering, of which terrorist funding is just one, anything else would be an unrealistic expectation. In any case, anything more than initial attempts to try to clarify details by asking leading questions of the customer could amount effectively to a tip-off that their account was under scrutiny. Financial institutions' obligations to report are therefore based on nothing more concrete than suspicions, and once they have filed an STR then any further investigation is generally left in the hands of the authorities, although reporting institutions may cooperate with the authorities in order, for example, to further their investigations and, hopefully, bring about successful prosecutions.

Currency transaction reporting

Given the enduring attractions of cash for money laundering or terrorist financing purposes, which in many ways goes against the global trend towards the use of plastic and the electronic movement of money, there is arguably a case for reporting any cash transaction above a certain threshold, on the basis that if everybody does it, such mass data can then be used for the purpose of trend analysis. The FATF Forty Recommendations go no further than suggesting that countries should consider the feasibility and utility of implementing such a regulation. Some jurisdictions have taken this step (including the US, Russia, and the countries of Eastern Europe and the former Soviet Union), but others have not, notably the UK and some other Western European Nations.

For example, the US requires that financial institutions record and report to the authorities any currency or bearer instrument transactions of $10,000 or more as a matter of course, and Australia has a similar A$10,000 threshold. The UK regime is entirely suspicion based, and has no automatic reporting threshold, although KYC procedures are required for one-off transactions above a €15,000 limit. The EU Third Money Laundering Directive extends this to cover other non-financial businesses such as casinos and estate agents, as well as anyone selling goods for which more than €15,000 is paid in cash.

Reporting obligations for transactions involving cash do apply across the board where same-day multiple transactions – known as 'smurfing' – occur. This process is used by money launderers as a means of avoiding a designated reporting threshold by breaking up the movement of cash into many smaller transactions. If smurfing is suspected, financial institutions need to report the entire series of transactions to the authorities, even though individually they do not breach any reporting threshold that may exist. Additionally, a single transaction could also be suspected on the grounds that the customer was trying to evade the reporting requirements, if it was for slightly less than the relevant reporting threshold. Again, in such cases the bank should look more closely at the transaction and file a report if it is suspicious.

Duty of confidentiality vs duty to report suspicion and/or other transactions

An important consideration as regards the whole principle of filing reports to the authorities on customer transactions is the concept of what are known in the US as 'safe harbour' laws. These are laws that protect financial institutions and their staff from criminal or civil liability arising from the alleged breaking of confidentiality or secrecy laws, provided they report suspicious transactions *in good faith*; that is, without malice.

Controls and independent audit

All organisations covered by a country's AML and CFT laws need to set up their own internal policies and procedures to protect themselves against the risk of being criminally exploited in either way. A critical aspect of these internal controls is an independent audit function (whether based within the firm or brought in from outside), which is separate from the AML/CFT compliance function and therefore able to test objectively the adequacy of the overall compliance arrangements.

Staff training

Equally significant is the requirement for ongoing staff training. Whilst regular training programmes on how to recognise potential money laundering activity and what action to take have become a well-established feature of fully compliant financial institutions, much less attention is paid to the specifics of terrorist financing within the formal financial system. In the words of one (anonymous) senior compliance figure in the EU banking industry: 'There's not sufficient focus on terrorist financing generally. Banks should be able to point to specific CFT action that staff should take and training which they have undergone.'

Name screening

Prior to 9/11, the sanctions lists produced by international or national authorities focused mainly on specific countries or regimes, with the aim of prohibiting fund transfers to the sanctioned country and freezing the assets of the government, businesses and residents; or else they targeted known political figures (e.g. Slobodan Milošević). Since that date, the composition of the lists has changed, as thousands of individuals and organisations suspected of having terrorist links have been added to the lists.

Accessing and making effective use of the lists is a challenging operational requirement for all financial institutions. There are many sanctions lists available. The UN produces a broad global list, applicable to all member states, while the EU consolidated list comprises names featuring in the annexes to various EC regulations. In addition, individual countries may have their own domestic sanctions regimes.

For the US financial sector, the sanctions authority is the Office of Foreign Assets Control (OFAC). The OFAC list should include names listed under the UN sanctions regime, but it will not necessarily contain EU sanction targets. Use of the OFAC lists as well as the national and UN sanctions lists is necessary for all foreign financial institutions dealing directly with the US, and for this reason is generally undertaken by all large banks and indeed should be undertaken by any bank undertaking dollar business.

Pre-lists

In addition to these formal sanctions lists, from time to time the authorities issue warning lists of names deemed to be a source of concern to those institutions where those people are believed to have accounts, even though there are no legally binding sanctions attached at this stage. The purpose of the warning lists is to enable financial institutions to move immediately to freeze the target assets if or when these names are subsequently added to formal sanctions lists.

Initial and subsequent screening

Financial institutions are required to run all new accounts of any sort against the current updated versions of the relevant lists, and similarly to screen all existing accounts on a regular basis. Wire transfers should also be screened as a matter of course (see below) to establish that no person or entity whose name appears on a list is the recipient of the funds. It is a key operational responsibility for the AML/CFT Compliance function to decide which lists their organisation must watch and how often. This latter point will be a matter for each firm's internal policy, and a reflection of its size and character. For instance, a small insurance firm might choose to scan its database monthly, whereas an international bank opening 10,000 to 20,000 new accounts each day would need to scan on a daily basis. Effectively this means that such institutions must have systems and software that can do this for them and there are a multitude of solutions on the market. Use of such systems is not mandatory under the EU Third Directive, although it *is* required of banks in the US.

Name match vs target match

Lists should contain any alternative name spellings and aliases used by the suspects in question, but of course it is not possible to conclude that just because someone has a name that features on a sanctions list, that they are the wanted individual. There is a distinction between a 'name match', where the organisation has matched the name of an account holder with the name of a target included on a list, and a 'target match', where the organisation is satisfied that the account held is that of the actual target of the financial sanctions, that is, the suspected 'bad guy'.

Action when information is inconclusive

Full details of any target matches should be reported to the authorities and any affected accounts frozen immediately. However, it has to be said that target matches are a relative rarity. It is more likely that a name on the database will match with an entry on a sanctions list but there will be no conclusive evidence that it is the same person or organisation. In that case it is the financial institution's job initially to look more closely at the KYC information and customer profile on record, and to assess it against the details available on the list. If it is not possible either to confirm or to clear the customer's name on the basis of available information the financial institution may be able to seek guidance from the sanctions authorities, but in the meantime it is faced with the intractable problem of how to treat the customer's account. Given the consequences and penalties of making a mistake, many financial institutions will take the view that they have no choice but to adopt the somewhat brutal policy of blocking an account until they have satisfied themselves that they do indeed only have a name match. They will prefer to deal with the customer's lawsuit rather than a regulatory enforcement action or a criminal prosecution.

It is in these circumstances that the importance of painstakingly and diligently collected KYC information becomes all too clear, not to mention software programs that can analyse such data against list information and, for example, produce 'target match' probability scores.

Effective compliance with name screening requirements

As well as conducting the screening process on all new accounts, on existing accounts as often as is necessary and on wire transactions and one-off non-customer transactions, financial institutions need to establish and maintain an effective programme to ensure compliance with the sanctions authority in question. This should include:

- the existence and observance of written procedures for checking transactions against the relevant lists
- open communication lines between internal departments
- regular staff training
- an annual, in-depth audit of the compliance function.

Other considerations include arrangements for maintaining current sanctions lists and distributing them throughout every subsidiary or branch office, both domestically and overseas.

False positives

As well as situations where the available facts are inconclusive, there are also those situations where financial institutions will actually determine, erroneously, that their customer is the person named on the list – the dreaded 'false positive' scenario.

In such circumstances it is essential that financial institutions should be capable of demonstrating that even if the outcome was wrong, they followed their full and correct procedure and carried out checks with any other parties involved (e.g. with a remitting bank). It is vital to keep clear records of the decision-making process leading up to any action taken.

BEST PRACTICE IN HIGHER-RISK PRODUCTS AND SERVICES

As discussed earlier, one of the fundamental tenets of a risk-based approach is that financial institutions should make judgements about the risks of misuse attached to each relationship and should then focus the greater part of their attention in those areas where the greater risks lie. In this regard, specific attention should be paid to the following.

International correspondent banking accounts

Correspondent accounts may be maintained between banks, for use in making transactions for customers or between themselves. They are overwhelmingly above board, but certain cross-border correspondent arrangements are at risk of misuse by money launderers and terrorist financiers (the assumption being that due diligence and KYC will be dealt with by the respondent bank in the country of origin). Such accounts maintained with banks based in lightly regulated countries are particularly vulnerable, as they may offer a route for people or organisations to access the global financial system while sidestepping more rigorous checks.

As the IMF/World Bank guidance points out, before entering into such a cross-border arrangement, any financial institution should make an assessment of the respondent bank in question, establishing:

- its location
- the nature of its business
- the purpose of the proposed account
- the bank's reputation
- the quality of its supervision
- the extent of its in-house AML/CFT policy and training provisions.

The importance of the above cannot be over-emphasised in the training provided to relevant staff. If 'payable-through accounts' are to be used, then the financial institution needs to ensure that the respondent bank will verify the identity of its customers and carry out ongoing due diligence on them.

More generally, the respective responsibilities of the banks should be established and documented beforehand. Correspondent banking is another area where senior management should take responsibility for approving the business relationship before it actually gets going.

Banks should not set up correspondent banking arrangements with organisations located in certain FATF designated high risk jurisdictions, nor with so-called 'shell' banks (banks which are unconnected with any effectively regulated financial system and which are incorporated in a jurisdiction where they have no physical presence or actual staff operations).

Electronic banking

There has been a rapid and dramatic expansion in non-face-to-face business as a result of the development of financial information services and product delivery via electronic means, including ATMs, telephone and internet banking. Although there is no inherently greater risk involved in applications received by phone or internet than in, say, applications by post, a combination of other factors typically aggravate the risks involved.

For example, it is possible to make an application instantaneously, at any time and from any location; it is also easier to make multiple fictitious or anonymous applications without any additional risk and with less danger of detection. Physical documents are not typically required as part of the application process, therefore making it relatively easier to apply by using a stolen identity. All these factors increase convenience for criminals or terrorist groups, and correspondingly, the risks to financial institutions. However, FATF leaves it to individual jurisdictions to work out and put in place appropriate regulatory measures for their financial institutions.

The updated guidelines on customer identification provided by the UK's Joint Money Laundering Steering Group (JMLSG) are an interesting example of the approach being adopted in some quarters. The JMLSG takes the view that:

> 'The extent of verification in respect of non face-to-face customers will depend on the nature and characteristics of the product or service requested and the assessed money laundering risk presented by the customer …
>
> The standard identification requirement (for documentary or electronic approaches) is likely to be sufficient for most situations. If, however, the customer, and/or the product or delivery channel, is assessed to present a higher money laundering or terrorist financing risk – whether because of the nature of the customer, or his business, or its location, or because of the product features available – the firm will need to decide whether it should require additional identity information to be provided, and/or whether to verify additional aspects of identity.

> Where the result of the standard verification check gives rise to concern or uncertainty over identity, or other risk considerations apply, so the number of matches that will be required to be reasonably satisfied as to the individual's identity will increase.'
>
> *Source*: www.jmlsg.org.uk

The guidance goes on to provide examples of the additional checks that institutions might use to mitigate, in particular, impersonation risk, but leaves it to the institution to determine how and when these will be applied Additional checks could take the form of, for instance (again, depending on the perceived risk presented by the customer), electronic checks as well as documentary evidence, or a written communication to the customer's verified home address, or requiring a form to be completed and returned by post.

Wire transfers

Electronic transfers pose particular concerns for financial authorities and regulatory bodies. FATF's Recommendation 16 and the Interpretive Note thereto sets out in detail the steps that financial institutions should take when sending money electronically:

- Subject to *de minimis* thresholds (which cannot be higher than US$/€1,000) cross-border and transfers should contain the names of both the originator and beneficiary and their account numbers used for processing the transaction (or a unique transaction reference number, if accounts are not used in processing), plus the originator's address or national identity number or customer identity number, or date and place of birth.
- When a single originator bundles a number of transfers destined for various beneficiaries in another country into a single file, and sends them all together, there is no need to include full originator information on every transfer, provided that the batch file contains all the relevant originator and beneficiary identification details, as above.
- Domestic transfers must also include all the originator information, as above, unless the originating bank is capable of providing this on demand, in which case all that needs to accompany the money is an account number or some other effective means by which to identify the originator. 'On demand' means within three days of the originating bank receiving the request for information from the receiving bank or the authorities, as the case may be.
- Ordering, intermediary and beneficiary financial institutions all have responsibilities for ensuring that the requirements of R16 are met and for identifying and dealing appropriately with wire transfers which do not contain the necessary information.

Private banking

Private banking relationships are set up not only by wealthy individuals and Politically Exposed Persons (PEPs) but also by law firms, investment companies, investment advisers and trusts. Particularly with regard to money laundering, private banking is viewed as a potentially high-risk sector of the banking universe for various reasons – not least because of the typical levels of wealth, the complexity and sophistication of financial services available (in particular, so called 'secrecy' products), and the number of advisers and intermediaries that may be involved in a client's financial affairs. Often, too, the very purpose of starting a private banking relationship is to hide wealth and put it out of reach (whether from corrupt authorities, probing journalists or a vengeful spouse) – a process which is just as effective for criminal proceeds as it is for legitimate funds.

On the other hand, private bankers are likely to have more proactive and personal relationships with their client than would be the case in retail banking, and may therefore have additional insights into anomalous account activity. In this regard it is important to remember that the wealthy client issuing execution-only instructions for transfers of funds between various investments and offshore vehicles could just as easily be a terrorist sympathiser and financial donor, as a genuine client, or a criminal money launderer. Because private banking relationships can be so complex, it is also important that there are effective systems in place within each bank to monitor and report suspicious activity, and that this can be done based on a client's total activities.

Standards for private banking have been largely driven in recent years by the Wolfsberg Group of international banks, which has drawn up a set of best practice guidelines for global private banking. These set out as the basic principle for client acceptance the requirements that banks will accept only those clients whose sources of wealth and funds can be reasonably established as being legitimate, and whose beneficial ownership is clear. It is the responsibility of the individual sponsoring private banker to make sure this is the case and, indeed, to be alert to suspicious activities on an ongoing basis. Importantly, say the Wolfsberg principles: 'Mere fulfilment of internal review processes does not relieve the private banker of this basic responsibility.' (www.wolfsberg-principles.com)

In addition, the principles address other key areas, as follows.

Client identification and due diligence

Crucially, client identification requirements under Wolfsberg extend beyond the actual named client to the beneficial owners of account assets. The private banker is expected to understand the structure of companies and trusts sufficiently to establish who are the main players involved, and they must make a judgement as to whether to carry out further due diligence on the individuals and companies concerned. Due diligence must include:

- the client's reasons for opening the account
- the client's expected levels of account activity
- details of the business or other economic activity that has generated the client's wealth and an estimate of net worth ('source of wealth')
- details of the sources of funds to be paid into the account upon opening.

References or other corroboration of the details are also required, where this is possible, and it would normally be expected that a client would meet their banker face-to-face before opening the account.

Enhanced due diligence for higher-risk accounts

Extra caution is necessary, as would be expected, in cases where a client's money was sourced in high-risk or lightly regulated countries, or where the client is involved in an area of business known to be susceptible to money laundering activities, or where the client is known to send funds to countries associated with terrorist activity or where the client donates to causes in such countries.

PEPs (who tend to favour the bespoke nature and privacy of private banking arrangements) also require additional due diligence (see below), and senior management must approve any new relationship with a PEP. Suspicious transactions (which may include large cash transactions, any account activity out of line with the customer profile, or 'pass-through' transactions) might be identified in a number of ways beyond the usual monitoring of the account. Suspicions might be triggered, for example, through third-party information from the media about a client, meetings with the client, or personal knowledge about factors such as the political situation in the client's country. The onus, according to Wolfsberg, is on the private banker to keep abreast of the 'bigger picture', as well as gaining and maintaining a thorough knowledge of the customer and their situation.

Specific counter-terrorist financing principles

The Wolfsberg Group supplemented its original principles, which focused on money laundering and other financial crimes in relation to private banks, with a further statement on best practice dealing with countering terrorist financing. This highlights the importance of name screening:

> 'The proper identification of customers by financial institutions can improve the efficacy of searches against lists of known or suspected terrorists [applicable to that jurisdiction].

To that end, it expands on existing identification, acceptance and due diligence best practice. Banks need to implement name-screening procedures and report any matches to the authorities; in addition they need to look at ways of speeding the retrieval of information about a customer if it is required.'

Source: www.wolfsberg-principles.com

Enhanced KYC policies should be in place for any customers involved in business sectors widely misused by terrorist groups, such as alternative remittance systems. Due diligence should be more extensive and rigorous on new business applications from such customers, and monitoring should be increased on both existing accounts and on those new accounts that meet the acceptance criteria. As a basic principle, banks should limit their business relationships with remittance businesses, exchange houses, bureaux de change and money transfer agents to those which are subject to appropriate AML/CFT regulation.

The Wolfsberg statement recognises that there is little chance that account monitoring will be able to identify individual transactions linked to specific terrorist attacks, but it emphasises the importance of continuing to look for and report suspicious transactions on the grounds that such information could provide leads for intelligence services. In particular, it highlights the need to scrutinise more rigorously the account activities of any customer involved with business sectors known to be a conduit for terrorist funds, and the need for banks to try to spot patterns and trends in terrorist financing.

Unusual/purposeless transactions

As well as monitoring the various higher-risk categories of business outlined above, the World Bank/IMF guidelines emphasise the need for financial institutions to be alert, across the spectrum of their customer accounts, to any complex, unusually large transactions, and to unusual patterns of transactions without any obvious lawful purpose.

They are instructed to look more closely at such transactions to establish as far as they can what is going on and why, and to keep a record of their findings. If they cannot obtain the information they want, or if their findings leave them still suspicious, they should consider turning the business away, and if necessary filing an STR.

Just as some kinds of financial services products are more likely than others to be exploited for illicit ends, so financial institutions are also expected to take a view on the likelihood that particular types of customer will pose a higher risk of involvement in criminal activity (including terrorist financing activity), and to adjust their due diligence, KYC and monitoring efforts accordingly.

Politically Exposed Persons (PEPs)

Among the categories identified by FATF, increased due diligence with regard to money laundering would be expected in the case of accounts for PEPs (senior people in prominent public positions and their families or close associates). Bank staff would be expected to identify the PEP and their sources of wealth and funds; any new account in the PEP's name would have to be approved at senior management level, and more rigorous monitoring of the account would be required.

However, as the World Bank/IMF notes observe, 'Actually finding out whether a customer is a PEP is often the biggest challenge for a financial institution.' There is no official list of world PEPs to consult, for example, though 'rich lists' and other compilations are produced and updated commercially.

Business through intermediaries

Another potentially troublesome scenario involves clients introduced to financial institutions by intermediaries or other third parties, when the financial institution itself does not carry out the usual customer due diligence. In such instances, the IMF/World Bank guidance recommends that banks should make sure that the agent who brought the new business is obliged by the relevant regulator in the agent's home country to perform customer due diligence, that they have in fact collected sufficient information about the customer in question, and that the information can be made available promptly if it is required.

Financial institutions need to be particularly careful when business is introduced to them by an agent based in another country. According to the IMF/World Bank commentary:

> **'Several countries ... require that the introducer should be an individual or an institution that is subject to AML controls, is supervised by a regulatory body with responsibility for compliance with AML controls, and is located in a country that complies with FATF standards.'**
>
> *Source*: Schott, P.A. (2003) *Reference Guide to Anti-Money Laundering and Combating the Financing of Terrorism*, World Bank/IMF, Chapter VI.

WWW

(Note: a film account of a proposed transaction involving these issues can be previewed at http://www.antimoneylaunderingvideos.com/player/offshore_trusts.htm.)

Customers from high-risk geographic locations

It is most important for financial institutions to be able to identify customers and transactions coming from high-risk parts of the world. They should exercise heightened caution dealing with countries branded by FATF as higher risk in the fight against money laundering and with countries in which there is terrorist-inspired conflict or where those who support such conflicts raise funds. Transactions with such countries are not necessarily prohibited, but they are considered to carry higher risks and should be scrutinised accordingly. Again, if a bank has any doubts that a transaction with such a country is above board, it should think about declining the business and also consider filing an STR under its suspicion-reporting obligations. Additionally, the national security or regulatory authorities may have identified specific jurisdictions as being of particular concern, as may the management of the financial institution itself, if it has effective procedures in place for tracking the release of such information.

Banks and other financial institutions should also bear in mind that as the global marketplace becomes increasingly interconnected, it may become necessary to extend greater due diligence practices to other groups beyond their direct customers, particularly if there are higher-than-average risks attached to the relationship. These groups might include, for example, customer employees, correspondent banks as well as agents and suppliers working for their customers. (Note: a film account of a money laundering scheme involving a high-risk jurisdiction can be previewed at http://www.antimoneylaunderingvideos.com/player/brokerage_accounts.htm.) **WWW**

Charities and NPOs

Charities and non-profit organisations (NPOs) may be open to abuse by terrorist groups, often by diverting funds originally raised for humanitarian purposes. It is therefore crucial that financial institutions should carry out enhanced due diligence to ensure that they 'know their charity'.

Senior management should approve any new relationship, and should bear in mind that there could be high risk attached to the business. A bank representative should visit the charity premises, meet the leaders and prepare a report on the visit, including such details as:

- the organisation's legal type and the activities for which it is licensed, its sources of capital, the number of staff employed, number of years established at the present and previous addresses, the nature of its present activities and its geographical location
- personal details for the directors/owners, and information about their powers
- any involvement of a PEP
- typical size and sources of donations
- whether the charity is licensed to receive donations locally or overseas.

Financial institutions with charitable or NPO customers also need to monitor their accounts closely, and to be aware of potential red flags, such as the following:

- corporate layering or 'routing' – transfers between the charity's bank account and those of its directors or staff for no clear reason
- wire transfers by charities or NPOs to beneficiaries based in countries known to be bank or tax havens, or countries of concern for terrorism purposes
- lack of apparent fundraising activity (in other words, a lack of small cheques or typical donations) that would normally be connected with charitable bank deposits
- transactions with no logical economic purpose (e.g. no link between the activity of the charitable organisation and other parties involved in the transaction).

Voluntary best practice guidance for charities issued by the US Department of the Treasury is also worth mentioning. This guidance includes a section on financial accountability and practices which may impact on charities' dealings with financial institutions holding their accounts, at least insofar as it shapes the typical NPO account activities and profile that a bank with charitable accounts might expect to see. These guidelines state that:

- The charity should have an annual budget, overseen by the board.
- There should be one individual appointed as the finance officer, with responsibility for day-to-day control over the charity's assets.
- Charities with annual gross income over a $250,000 limit should bring in an independent accounting firm to audit the accounts and produce a financial statement each year.
- Full records of all money received and spent (including salaries and expenses both domestic and international) should be kept by the charity, with details of every charitable disbursement including the name of the recipient, the sum given and the date.
- As soon as money received has been recorded, it should be deposited in the charity's bank account.
- Cash in particular should be paid in promptly.
- If possible, money to be disbursed should be sent by cheque or via a wire transfer rather than in currency.
- When the money is going to areas without normal financial services and there is no option but to send currency, funds should be provided in smaller increments for short-term needs, rather than large lump sums for longer periods.
- The charity should also keep detailed records of such currency payments.

IT SYSTEMS

IT systems can be expensive and AML/CFT systems are no exception. Particularly in an emerging markets environment where valuable corporate money is already being spent on policies, procedures, personnel and training, the temptation may be to skimp on systems expenditure. This is a mistake. It is almost impossible to comply with international best practice unless you have some minimum capability to do certain key things and systems are now effectively an essential part of your organisation's capability to do this. Set out below are different types of systems plus their capabilities and ideas on how Compliance departments can get 'smart' information on constrained budgets.

Name check portals/filter systems

These are systems that will screen the names of customers against regularly updated lists of prohibited persons, in order to comply with the international requirements referred to earlier. There are various subscription products such as World-check and Thomson Reuters to which financial organisations subscribe. Names of proposed customers are input to the system, either manually or automatically (see 'Combined systems' later on) and the system then compares the name with a composite list of various proscribed persons, typically drawn from the United Nations list, the US OFAC (Office of Foreign Asset Control) list and any national list in force in the country where the financial organisation is located. If there is a name match the system produces a report which can then be investigated in the manner described earlier. Such systems are also used for determining whether or not a customer is a PEP, and hence whether enhanced due diligence should apply to them. They are also used by financial institutions to sweep the entire customer base periodically to check that existing customers have not become either proscribed or politically exposed during the interim period.

Suspicion reporting systems

The function of these types of systems is to detect transaction patterns or individual transactions which are unusual. Information describing expected account habits is input into the system at the start of the relationship. Categories of information typically cover such items as expected account turnover, expected largest single payment, expected largest cash payment, identities of major customers and suppliers and their banks and countries of operation, expected highest monthly balance, etc. This information is obtained from the customers themselves. The system then monitors the accounts for transactions or patterns of transactions which fall outside the expected profile contained within the system, and produces an exception report if there is a variance above a given range, which can be specified by those running the system (e.g. exception reports to be produced at variances greater than 30 per cent, 40 per cent, 50 per cent, etc.). In practical terms, the challenge for Compliance Officers is always the same; namely, to set the variance levels at rates which are not so high as to produce no exception reports at all, and yet which are not so low as to produce hundreds or even thousands of reports, which then have no prospect of being analysed for potential suspicious activity, as described in the example below

Example

In the first decade of the twenty-first century, many US financial firms faced fines and regulatory sanctions from the Federal Reserve Bank and other regulators for failing to implement transaction monitoring systems correctly. It had become a requirement that banks should implement such systems, but a problem was that having done so, the banks were not prepared in terms of staffing and skill sets to analyse the exception reports produced by the systems. In one instance, a reputable international bank's New York office had installed a transaction monitoring system which was producing many hundreds of exception reports. However, only one person was available to review and analyse the reports and that person had many other responsibilities.

It follows that such systems can also be used for the purposes of mandatory reporting, should regulations require it. The mandatory reporting thresholds or transaction descriptions are input into the system, which then recognises transactions above the thresholds that then need to be reported to the national financial intelligence unit, whether manually or automatically, direct from system to system.

Beyond the more simple, rule-based systems described above, it is possible to purchase so called 'intelligent' systems that use 'fuzzy logic' and databases drawn from very wide pools of customer data to predict account behaviour patterns for certain classes of customer. For example, in circumstances where transactions have occurred on an account which do not fall outside the set parameters within the rule-based system (and which, hence, will not produce an exception report) an intelligent system will be able to detect that, nevertheless, whatever the customer has told you to expect, this particular transaction pattern is unusual for other customers of that type.

Combined systems

The largest institutions will have global systems which combine all the different capabilities described above in one all-encompassing package which is linked to the organisation's main banking system and which has been specifically tailored to the organisation's own anti-money laundering policy. These combined systems can cost upwards of $20 million to $30 million and provide a complete system solution for client screening, black-list checks, new customer acceptance, transaction monitoring, mandatory reporting, exception reporting, records retrieval, transaction blocking and account freezing.

Figure 3.2 shows an intelligent transaction monitoring system. Figure 3.3 shows a processed flow for a combined system capable of accepting or rejecting new clients and allocating different intensities of monitoring activity in accordance with a risk-based approach.

Spending many millions of dollars on AML/CFT systems may still be well outside the budgetary constraints of many emerging markets' financial institutions. This means, therefore, that AML/CFT Compliance Officers in those countries must often seek to do the best they can with what is available, identifying the highest-risk areas and concentrating on those whilst also seeking and fighting for additional resources at opportune times.

Probably the highest-risk area in the current environment is that of proscribed persons – the terrorist lists. As a financial institution grows it becomes increasingly difficult to accomplish name screening effectively without a system and this is, therefore, the essential place to start. A simple, limited user subscription to one of the available databases will provide a level of protection against taking on or retaining clients on proscribed lists and will also assist in identifying potentially higher-risk clients such as PEPs.

If the organisation's core banking system is already handling mandatory reporting requirements, then a discussion with the IT department ought to enable a Compliance Officer to access additional information which is relevant. For example, again using a risk-based approach, it ought to be possible for a Compliance Officer to data-mine the core banking system for the following types of relevant information:

- large transactions
- daily account opening
- turnover reports
- foreign currency remittances above a certain amount, in and out
- remittances to and from countries of money laundering or terrorist financing concern.

By accessing such information from the organisation's core banking system, a Compliance Officer can also learn a lot about the money laundering and terrorist financing risk profile which the various businesses are assuming in practice.

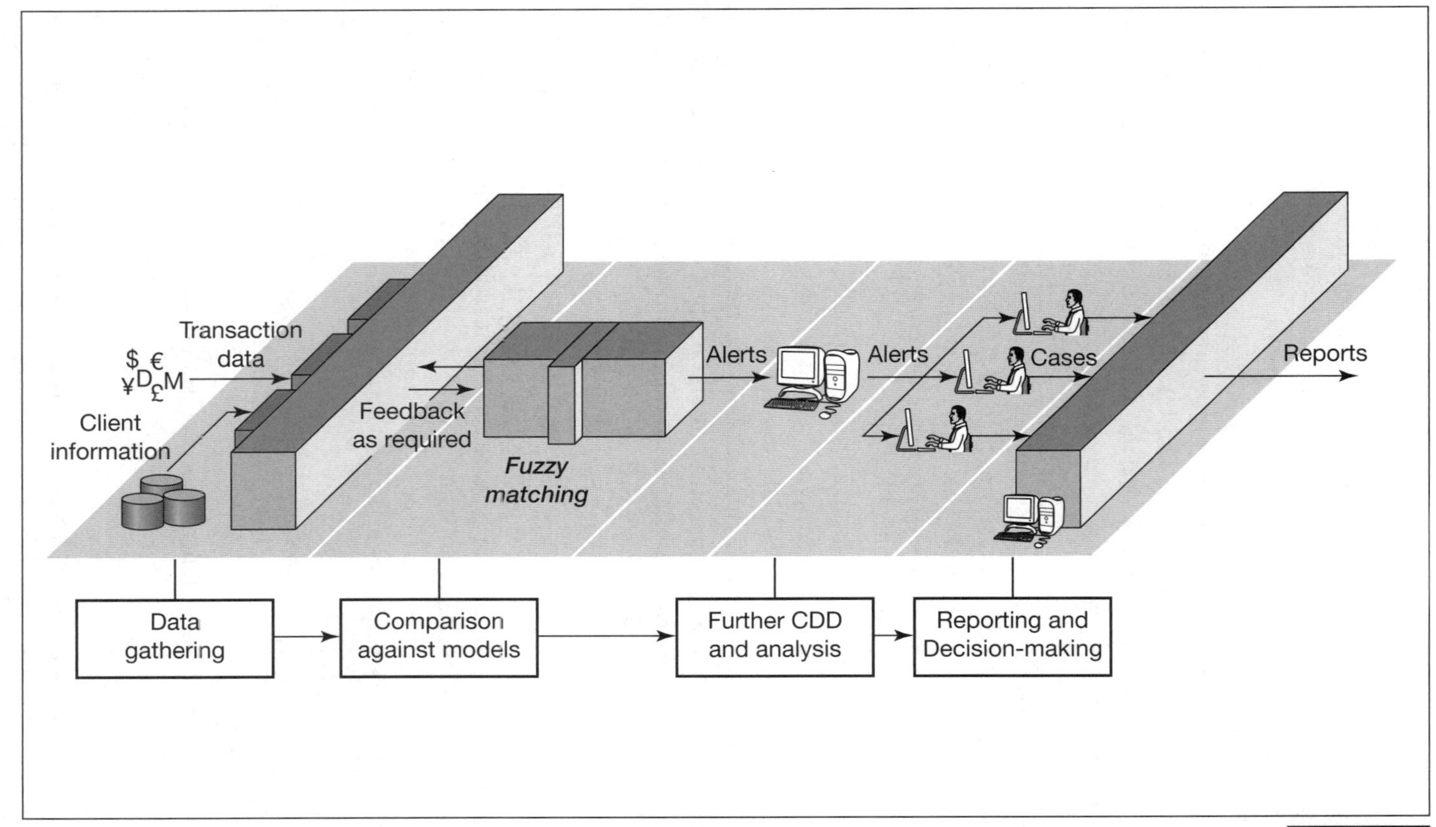

An 'intelligent' AML system

Figure 3.2

Client acceptance process flow **Figure 3.3**

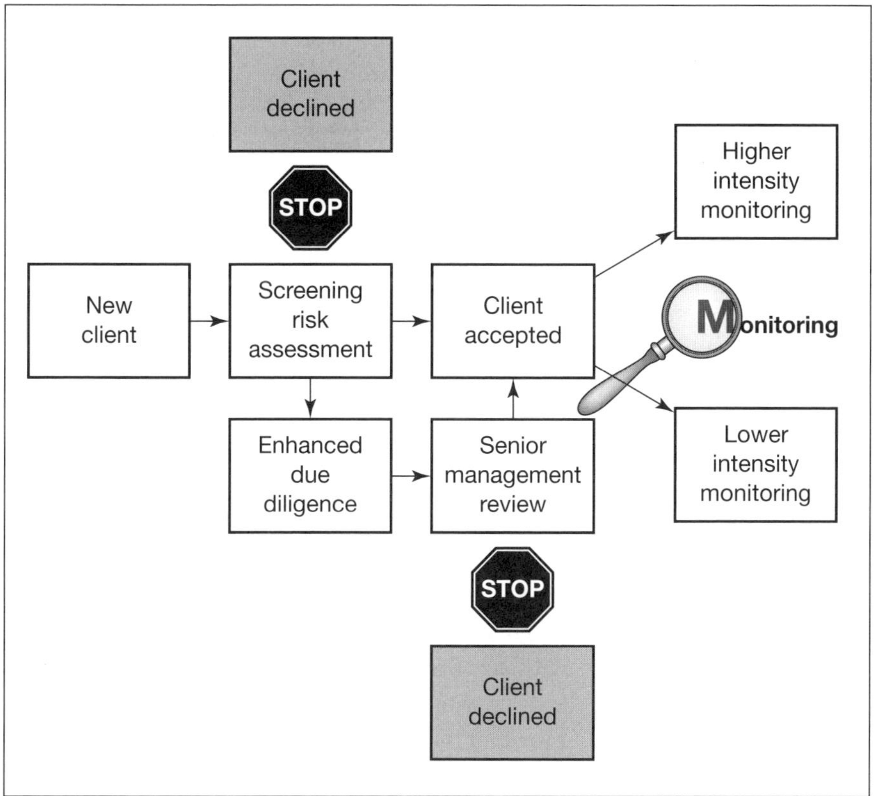

TRAINING AND COMMUNICATION

Training is an essential component of the Compliance Officer's role. Unfortunately it is also something that tends to be ignored when more pressing operational requirements weigh in upon the Compliance Officer. Such an outcome should be avoided at all costs since not only is training a regulatory requirement in most countries, it also helps to generate the culture of awareness amongst staff which is such an important part of the organisation's overall AML/CFT effort. It is unlikely that you will be able to train everybody in everything which they need to be trained in, immediately. It is more likely that, with limited resources, you will have to prioritise. In order to prioritise you need to be able to assess the most important requirements and then select accordingly. To do this, you will need to conduct a Training Needs Analysis (TNA).

Training Needs Analysis (TNA)

What is a TNA? It is a simple, logical system used by training and development professionals to enable training needs to be established within an organisation and thereafter to set priorities. The processes are outlined below:

Stage 1 – Establish previous provision

The first stage of a TNA is to work out what training has already been done in the organisation within a given period (e.g. the past two years). Relevant questions are:

- How long ago was the training done?
- To whom was it given (e.g. which businesses, which job roles within those businesses)?
- What was the content?

For example, look at the information on previous training provision across business and job functions shown in Figure 3.4.

Of all the jobs listed across the businesses shown in Figure 3.4, you might find that the only training which has been done is for account opening staff and bank tellers; those dealing with account opening documentation requirements and mandatory cash reporting thresholds, respectively. This would mean that no other training had been provided for any of the other job descriptions.

Stage 2 – Establish current and future requirements

Having worked out what training has been done and for whom, it is now necessary to cstablish what training needs to be done going forward. This entails a degree of enquiry by the Compliance Officer. What training is required by the law of the country? Have there been any poor internal or external inspection reports within specific business areas which are indicative of a training need?

Figure 3.4 **Previous training provision**

Training and communications

Previous provision

- Corporate relationship managers
- Private banking relationship managers
- Retail sales and investment advisers
- Account opening staff ✓
- Tellers ✓
- Back office payments operations
- Treasury dealers

Are there any upcoming reviews or inspections (e.g. a central bank inspection or a review by a US or EU correspondent bank)? Are there any particular business risks which have raised their profiles recently? Does the organisation's own AML policy require certain types of training, and if so in what? Have there been any disasters or 'near misses', indicating that further training needs to happen (e.g. nearly opening an account for someone on a terrorist list)?

Stage 3 – Establish the gaps in provision and prioritise

Having worked out what training has already been done and having established what training *needs* to be done, the Compliance Officer should now be in a position to map the existing provision against the current and future needs in order to arrive at a list of training requirements. But this on its own will not be enough. Unless the Compliance Officer is blessed with enormous resources, there will simply not be the time, people or money to achieve everything which needs to be achieved straight away. Therefore, the Compliance Officer will need to prioritise and create a training schedule accordingly. Here, it is better to be realistic rather than over ambitious, and it is absolutely necessary to have very clear training objectives with 'do by' dates attached to them. For example, referring back to the example box above, the Compliance Officer in that organisation might decide that they need to address the most basic requirements first, whilst also ensuring that their current highest business risk is also covered. They might therefore decide on the following training prioritisation:

By 30 June 2012:

- all staff to have received 'basic training'
- 100 per cent record in induction training
- all payments staff to have received specialist training on suspicion indicators in funds transfers.

Risk-based approach to training

This is a risk-based approach to AML/CFT compliance training. It demonstrates to regulators, potential overseas correspondents and stakeholders generally that the AML/CFT Compliance function is organising its training carefully, thinking about the issues and creating prioritised training to address the key risks. Training to address less-important perceived risks can then follow. The important thing is for the Compliance Officer to be able to show not only that they are undertaking training, but also that they are targeting the training efforts to make them as effective as possible when matched against the risks which the organisation is confronting.

Wide approach to training

There is a temptation to think that training only counts if it is people sitting in a classroom listening to a person (e.g. the compliance officer) talking and showing slides. This is too narrow an interpretation of the activity. The wider phrase 'training and communications' encompasses any method used to convey knowledge, teach new skills, change attitudes and encourage staff to do what is required.

Beyond classroom training, an organisation's AML CFT training programme is limited only by resources and need. Below are some of the other methods that can be deployed:

- e-learning – the use of web-based learning and knowledge testing applications accessed via users' PCs and tablets
- self-study – the distribution of books, notes and pamphlets for people to read in their own time
- videos – hard hitting and informative DVDs or online videos dealing, for example, with relevant law and the methodologies used by money launderers and terrorist financiers
- poster campaigns – posters can be sited at key locations (e.g. by lifts or water coolers) containing key messages, for example in relation to KYC.
- email campaigns can be run over several weeks or even months, with each email prepared in advance and designed to deliver key messages.

Sometimes organisations may not just wish to train their staff, but to prove to the outside world that those staff have achieved a certain standard of knowledge and competence. They may therefore wish to obtain independent accreditation for the learning achieved with a certificate that counts as more than a certificate of attendance, typically after the passing of some exam.

The largest global financial institutions will tend to adopt a blended approach to AML/CFT training, mixing classroom with distance learning techniques (techniques in which the learner is not physically present with the teacher in a classroom). E-learning tends to play an important role, given the need to train large numbers of people in the same way across vast distances. Such systems will often have self-certification built in, i.e. the user takes a test and if successful, the system produces a certificate confirming that they have passed the test, which is then centrally recorded by the system. Systems of this type can also be constructed as a series of discrete 'chapters' or 'modules' which are relevant to different people in different businesses and/or in different countries and using different languages. The most advanced systems are sophisticated in this respect and consequently quite expensive, although the per person training cost over time can be greatly reduced. An example is shown in Figure 3.5.

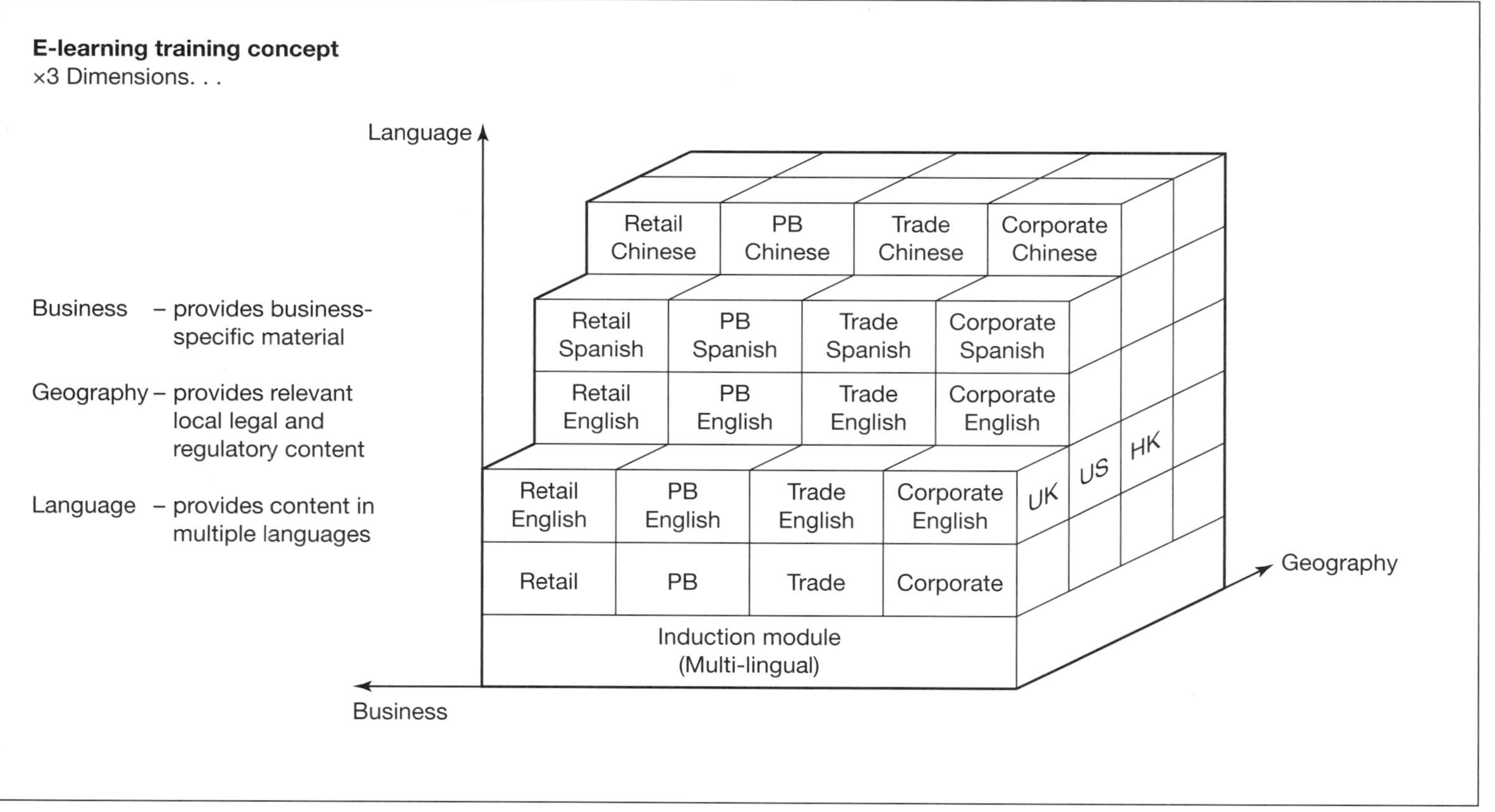

E-learning training concept **Figure 3.5**

A word about CFT training

To many Compliance Officers, the idea of training staff in CFT is a difficult concept to grasp. After all, what on earth can you train people on? Everybody knows by now that, without a tip-off from the security services, terrorist financing is all but impossible to detect. Not much can enhance an organisation's capability to detect sub-$10,000 transactions when they are within the normal transactional range on the account or relationship in question, and when there are no other features marking them out as 'suspicious'. Tie this in with other known truths concerning source of funds or source of wealth (which are not necessarily criminal where terrorist financing is concerned) and the need to keep records readily available for when the security services come calling (essential), and, so the argument goes, training on CFT can be confined to the following points, inserted succinctly at a time or place of your choosing within an existing AML programme:

- Terrorist financing is like money laundering, except it's often in reverse, i.e. using legally derived funds for an illegal purpose.
- The amounts used to fund terrorist attacks are too small to make traditional AML tools much use, so all efforts should focus on effective customer identification, efficient name-screening, excellent record-keeping and unfailing cooperation with law enforcement in the investigation of suspects and their accounts.
- And ... that's it.

If the above is essentially what your CFT training says – and if that is pretty much all it says – then you could be selling the risk short within the overall context of your AML or wider financial crime training programme. Why? First, because training on CFT should take place within the context of a discussion about terrorist financing, *not* one on money laundering. Though they share many of the same characteristics, the two are essentially different activities undertaken by different people for very different purposes. A failure to recognise this and provide appropriate treatment to terrorist financing within the overall AML/CFT programme risks a charge that you have conducted 'by-the-way' training (as in 'Oh, and by the way...') and failed to educate staff at a basic level.

Secondly, suspicion recognition training for terrorist financing isn't the total non-starter which it may at first seem, especially if you distinguish between the financing of terrorist movements generally (what we may refer to as *Type I* terrorist financing) and the funding of individual attacks (*Type II*). It is of course true that, given the relatively modest amounts required to fund individual attacks, systems and people are unlikely to detect specific funds and fund movements earmarked for those attacks. But fund-raising activities further back up the chain have detectable characteristics that staff need to be made aware of so that they can identify them and take appropriate action. This will become even more relevant now that FATF is expanding its remit to include proliferation (of WMD) financing and the various typologies associated with it.

Thirdly, whilst some might say that a good 'test question' for the CFT elements of the overall AML/CFT training programme should be *'Are there any suspicion indicators that are exclusive to terrorist financing which staff wouldn't otherwise be aware of from the AML part of the programme?'*, this is too restrictive an approach and moreover is definitely not the approach which would have been adopted had money laundering and terrorist financing both arrived as issues on the financial services scene at the same time (instead of money laundering coming along first.) Rather, what organisations should be doing for *both* subjects is providing ongoing training which, apart from the legal basics, is rich in case study, example and explanation, and which *over time*, enables the relevant workforce to construct internal reference frameworks for a wide range of situations and their potential causes; situations which they can compare with events and information that they encounter in their daily work. A workforce that has been educated in this way will be familiar with the underlying methodologies, preferences and structures of both non-terrorist and terrorist criminal groups and is likely to offer the organisation better levels of overall AML/CFT compliance and protection.

Designing and structuring the CFT elements of the AML/CFT training programme: training review

As with anything else, training should be geared around the risks that the organisation faces. If you are concerned that your existing training programme may not be hitting the mark as far as CFT is concerned, perhaps because it had been inserted by a predecessor as an 'add on' to an existing (and maybe longstanding) AML training programme, or because you do not think that it is detailed enough, then you should conduct a training review. Not only will this help you frame the relevant programme content, it will also help demonstrate that your training has been constructed intelligently, and not just thrown together to tick a box on an internal auditor's checklist.

A training review is, in essence, no different from a Training Needs Analysis (TNA) in that its purpose is to assess actual versus required training provision, to link training needs to specific individuals (e.g. on a role or business basis) and to set priorities. Remember, the basic structure of a TNA is designed to answer a series of questions about your organisation's training, and to plan further training accordingly:

- Establish current provision levels. (What training has been/is being done? To whom? Covering what?)

- Establish the organisation's needs. (What are the areas of highest business/product/country risk? What are the legal/regulatory requirements? What corporate events have taken place (e.g. key personnel changes, business acquisitions, regulatory or operational 'near misses', etc.) which raise the risk profile?)
- Map the needs against the provision to produce a training plan.

Ideally, the training review should occur as an integral part of the wider, regular business risk review, although if it has been omitted from that process it should still be undertaken. The training plan should, of course, be specific about who is going to be trained, what the training will cover and the desired outcomes (e.g. enhanced awareness of use of wire transfer networks by payments staff; or enhanced awareness of use of opaque structures and agent-consultants by corporate and private banking relationship managers, etc.).

Contents of a CFT training programme

Based upon the results of the exercise described above, different organisations will end up with different ideas about how best to segment the various potential content combinations, but it is possible to conceive of the following type of structure, accommodated as an integral yet distinct element within the wider AML training framework.

Foundation

The foundation elements of the CFT training programme would deal with the core issues of general relevance to most people who have been assessed as requiring AML/CFT training. These issues would encompass areas such as:

- *Background* – definitions of 'terrorism' and 'terrorists', and the difficulty in reaching international agreements on this; the effects of terrorism (human, economic, political); the link between terrorism and terrorist financing; and the nature of the obligations of financial firms to combat it.
- *The legal and policy framework* – the essential elements of the international regime put in place including key items such as: the 1999 UN Convention for the Suppression of the Financing of Terrorism; UNSCR 1373; the FATF Recommendations; and details of regional (e.g. EU) and national legal and regulatory requirements such as the Terrorism Act 2000 and the Bank of England Consolidated List (in the UK).
- *Origins of terrorist funding* – basic methodologies for collecting finance used by different terrorist groups (e.g. Al-Qaeda, Provisional IRA, Jemaal Islamiyah, Tamil Tigers) involving, donations from sympathisers, collections by religious and cultural bodies, diversion of funds from legitimate charities, business takeover, fraud, organised crime, etc.

- *Personal obligations and internal reporting* – linking in with AML structures, MLRO, SARs, etc.

Additional

The additional elements of the CFT programme would contain more detailed information relevant to front line, customer-facing, operations and managerial staff designed to raise their awareness of how terrorist financing is conducted and would encompass items such as:

- *Factors informing the risk assessment* – e.g. business area (conflict zones involving terrorism), customer type (charity and NPO customers with operations in conflict zones involving terrorism, trading companies, money remittance businesses, cash intensive businesses in areas of ethnicity connected with conflict zones involving terrorism), product type (wire transfers, trust and nominee accounts, off-street cash conversions and forex purchases, single premium insurance products).
- *Detailed examples of terrorist financing: typologies and structures* – for example cases involving:
  - payments and receipts unrelated to the provision of legitimate goods or services
  - unusual and repetitive wire transfer activity
  - charities with unusual donation profiles
  - unusual signing arrangements on accounts
  - account takeover of student accounts by terrorists
  - credit card fraud used to fund terrorist operations
  - medical insurance fraud used to fund terrorist operations
  - terrorist financing through early redemption of policies
  - dormant accounts
  - structured payments.

Specialist/specific

The specialist/specific elements of the CFT programme would contain items of specific operational relevance to particular sections of staff conducting certain activities relevant to some important aspects of CFT operations, such as:

- *Know Your Customer (KYC) and Customer Due Diligence (CDD)* – for staff opening accounts and checking identification, training and examples showing how the operation of the UN blacklist enhances the importance of customer identification and verification data quality.
- *Identity theft and fraud* – for staff opening accounts and checking identification, training and examples showing how terrorists have used identity theft to gain access to the financial system, and the enhanced importance of correct application of measures to deter and detect identity theft.

- *Dealing with blacklist problems* – for staff conducting client acceptance checks and others involved in dealing with new business, training and examples showing how the organisation handles issues such as name matches and false positives (where a customer or potential customer's name matches that of a proscribed person, but where there is uncertainty over whether the identities actually match).

Taking such a structure as a starting point, it ought to be possible to construct powerful combinations of training that would be relevant to particular business units or job types. During the course of either a training review or a wider CFT business risk assessment, AML/CFT Compliance officers may find that certain combinations suggest themselves, which can then be incorporated as distinct elements within the overall programme.

However such a programme is constructed, gone should be the days when CFT is the 'by the way' item at the end of your AML training.

A 'PRO-BUSINESS' APPROACH

The Compliance Officer performs one of the most critical risk control functions within the organisation – namely the safe and effective management of the analysis and reporting of unusual and/or suspicious transactions to the national authorities. They also have additional responsibilities which require a real understanding of and empathy for the businesses they serve.

General approach

Compliance Officers must approach their duties from the perspective of a commercial banker committed to the commercial success of the organisation, combined, however, with an essential objectivity and a deep commitment to preventing the use of the bank's services by criminals, and to cooperating with the national authorities in the successful investigation of actual or attempted instances of money laundering. Each of these perspectives in the overall approach is as important as the other.

Compliance Officers need to remain sensitive to the commercial objectives of the organisation, otherwise they risk creating unnecessary and counter-productive friction with the businesses they serve. They must remember that the organisation's objectives are primarily concerned with the provision of excellent services to customers at a profit. There is no legal duty on the bank to become a detective in the prevention and detection of crime, nor to marginalise its own commercial objectives in the fight against crime. Forgetting – or even appearing to forget – these realities, makes the Compliance Officer appear detached from the business, and reduces their credibility and effectiveness. Compliance Officers can demonstrate their alignment with business objectives by:

- showing an interest in business performance
- maintaining regular contact with business managers
- attending key business presentations and events (e.g. product launches)
- exploring, rather than dismissing, views which contradict their own
- spending 'as much time listening as talking…'.

In doing so, Compliance Officers are likely to learn more about the various businesses within the organisation, and thus enhance their ability to make judgements on reported transactions. In particular, the objective of any investigation is always to decide whether a transaction is suspicious and whether it has to be reported, not to prove that the Compliance Officer's initial 'gut instinct' is always correct, in all circumstances.

Equally, Compliance Officers must be wary of accepting explanations for transactions from business managers or customers which are unconvincing and which will not withstand detailed scrutiny. They must have the strength of character and the determination to challenge such explanations, and to dig deeper in search of the truth. At times, Compliance Officers may find themselves subjected to great pressure – particularly where a customer is a good source of revenue for the organisation – to adopt a less searching attitude towards that customer's transactions. They must resist such pressure, retaining the essential objectivity and independence which is so essential for their role.

In conjunction with the CEO, Compliance Officers should do their utmost to ensure that businesses and business managers adopt due responsibility for assessing the suitability of customers and proposed account purposes at the time when accounts are opened, discussing any uncertainties with the Compliance Officer before account opening takes place. Otherwise, a mentality can develop in which businesses see their role solely in terms of bringing business into the bank and maximising revenue from the account, rather than accepting a joint responsibility with risk functions such as the Compliance Officer for the overall quality of the bank's business. Disengagement by businesses from this task can result in a wastage of resources as Compliance officers spend their time investigating transactions that should have been refused upfront. In the worst cases, the reputation of the bank is placed at risk as suspect business which should have been prevented at source is allowed into the bank.

MANAGEMENT OF INTERNAL SUSPICION REPORTING

For audit purposes the Compliance Officer should adopt effective procedures for the management of internal reporting of suspicious and/or unusual transactions. Three files should be maintained:

1. 'Suspicious Transactions – Initial Reports' (File 1)
2. 'Suspicious Transactions – No Action Taken' (File 2)
3. 'Suspicious Transactions – Reports Made to Authorities'. (File 3)

File 1 is the ongoing operational file containing reports that have been made by the businesses and that are being investigated prior to a decision being made on whether they warrant the filing of an external report. Following the making of a decision on external reporting, File 2 is the repository file for those cases in which the Compliance Officer decides that the transactions in question are not suspicious, and that no external report is required. File 3 is the file containing those cases in which reports are filed with the relevant authorities.

In each case following the making of a report by a member of staff, a written record must be kept of the further investigations conducted by the Compliance Officer and of the reasons behind the decision either to report externally or not to report, as the case may be. The purpose of this system is to achieve full, auditable transparency regarding the reporting and decision-making process. It is particularly important that the reasons for any decision *not* to report a case to the relevant authorities are clear and fully documented, so as to avoid any justifiable criticism of the organisation's actions in not filing such a report.

Compliance Officers should periodically remind staff about the importance of reporting unusual or suspicious transactions, and should take steps to facilitate such reporting, such as the provision of standard suspicious transaction reporting forms.

Once a report has been filed by a staff member, the procedure for the investigation and subsequent reporting and filing is as shown in Figure 3.6.

For cases in which a decision to report is made, the report itself should be submitted to the relevant authority in the format (if any) prescribed by such authority, and a copy of it retained in File 3 'Suspicious Transactions – Reports Made to Authorities'. A copy of the report should also be sent to the CEO and the customer's file should be removed from the 5 year document destruction cycle, so as to prevent key historic transactional information being automatically destroyed.

Complete records of investigations leading to a decision (whether to report or not to report) must be maintained, including details of:

- staff members and any other persons spoken to, and the outcome of interviews/conversations

STR investigation process

Figure 3.6

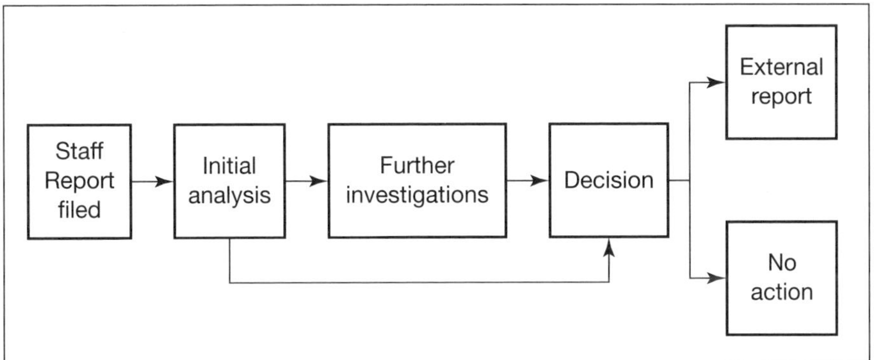

- documents reviewed
- explanations offered or discovered in respect of the reported transaction or transactions.

Full correspondence records with the relevant authorities and with any other parties must be maintained following the filing of a report, along with clear records of any actions taken or permitted.

Full cooperation must be extended to the relevant authorities in relation to any investigation which they make into the reported case, including, but not limited to:

- provision of required information
- provision of required copy documents
- access to staff and premises
- liaison during regulatory visits and interviews
- access to administrative and communications facilities during visits.

Deciding whether to make a report

The critical factor in deciding whether or not an external report is required is whether or not the transaction or transactions brought to the Compliance Officer's attention are 'suspicious'. No definition of 'suspicious' can be exhaustive. In its normal everyday context the word means 'mistrust – the imagining of something but without proof' and compliance officers are expected to use judgement and experience in deciding whether a transaction is suspicious or not, taking into account all the circumstances of the case. Specifically in a money laundering context, however, transactions are likely to be suspicious:

where there appears to be no convincing explanation for them, *and* where:

- they are inconsistent with the stated or apparent purpose of the customer's account; *and/or*
- they are inconsistent with the history of previous transactions on the account; *and/or*
- they are otherwise suggestive of activity known to be undertaken by money launderers.

The purpose of any initial investigation into a matter which has been reported internally is not to prove or disprove conclusively whether a suspicion is justified. Rather, it is to establish that there are no known facts that contradict the suspicion which has been raised, or which otherwise suggest that the fears about the customer or transaction are groundless.

Chapter 6 explores the concept of suspicion in greater depth, with the use of a wide range of examples.

4

KYC and the Risk-based Approach

Background to the risk-based approach

Components of the risk-based approach

Mitigating controls

Regulatory environment

Special categories: PEPs

Constructing a risk-based approach for your organisation

The core components of CDD

CDD processes and tools

Example risk assessment frameworks

Constructing a CDD framework for financial institutions

Constructing a CDD framework for retail/consumer banking business

Constructing a CDD framework for private banking

Excerpts from Recommendations 1 and 10 of the FATF 40 Recommendations (February 2012) and the Interpretive Note there to:

'countries should apply a risk based approach to ensure that measures to prevent or mitigate money laundering and terrorist financing are commensurate with the risks identified.' **(R1)**

'Financial Institutions should be required to apply each of the CDD measures ... above ... but should determine the extent of such measures using a risk based approach (RBA)...' **(R10)**

'There are circumstances where the risk of money laundering or terrorist financing is higher and enhanced CDD measures have to be taken. When assessing... money laundering and terrorist financing risks [relevant factors are] types of customers, countries or geographic areas, and particular products, services, transactions or delivery channels.' **(R10 Interpretive Note)**

BACKGROUND TO THE RISK-BASED APPROACH

The requirement for a 'risk based approach' has generated probably the most radical overhaul in AML/CFT strategy to have been seen since the inception of global standards shortly after FATF was formed in 1989.

The so called risk-based approach, having been initially adopted within the economically developed nations which originally formed the Financial Action Task Force (FATF) is now a general global requirement. It may be helpful for Compliance Officers in emerging markets (where AML and CFT standards may only have been adopted very recently) to understand not only the principles of its operation, but also its background. In doing so, they may better understand the industry and other pressures that are likely to confront the AML and CFT regimes put in place in their own countries.

Historically the various AML measures required by the original 40 Recommendations were not welcomed with open arms by the financial community. They were seen as bureaucratic and cumbersome, costly to maintain, not user friendly and hostile to good customer relations. In particular there were concerns regarding the ability of inflexible AML standards to distinguish between different types of customer, and it is this concern especially which the development of a risk-based approach has been designed to address.

For example, non risk-based principles would require a financial institution to treat a retired state pensioner in her seventies in the same way as a businessman in his forties receiving large funds from a country known for the production of blood diamonds. That is to say that, if one did *not* weigh the differences between these individuals, then the same identification, Know Your Customer (KYC) and account monitoring principles would apply to both of them, even though it is clear from a risk perspective that their profiles are entirely different.

Faced with the risks, what most countries and financial institutions ended up doing was applying a 'one size fits all' approach, which was viewed as being exceedingly harsh on the vast majority of customers who actually posed very slight money laundering risks. It also meant that scarce resources were not being applied as effectively as they might be in tackling higher-risk customers and relationships. By spreading the effort equally over *all* customers, it was argued that 90 per cent of that effort was in effect being wasted on the 90 per cent of customers who were very unlikely to have any involvement at all with crime or money laundering, with only 10 per cent of the effort being directed at the higher risk accounts (see Figure 4.1).

AML: the traditional approach **Figure 4.1**

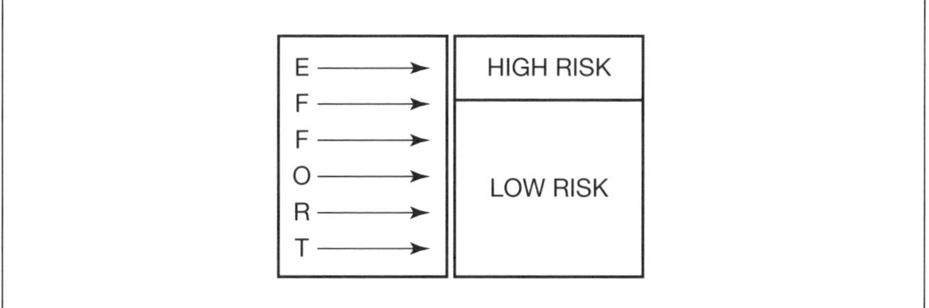

Would it not be better, so the argument went, if a risk-based system could be introduced which reversed these odds and enabled financial institutions to apply *90 per cent* of their available resources towards the *10 per cent* of their business which actually constituted the most serious risk? This would mean less bureaucracy, less paperwork, less form filling and of course a more welcoming experience for most customers (see Figure 4.2).

AML: the risk-based approach **Figure 4.2**

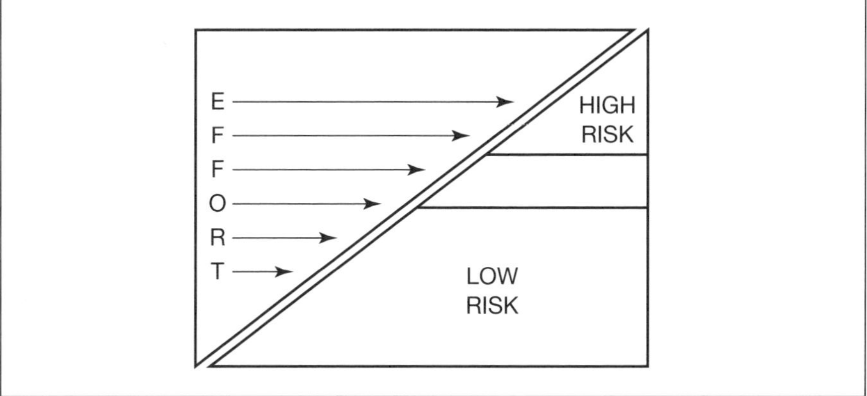

It is of course the case that higher-risk customers tend to be (but are not always) wealthier, more international and worth more on an individual basis as customers. It is important to note, therefore, that from a business perspective the risk-based approach requires a considerable degree of finesse in its application to these higher-risk customers, so that they do not end up feeling that they are being discriminated against.

Pressure from the financial services industry within the developed economies led, in the early part of this century to discussions regarding a risk-based approach. These discussions manifested themselves first as proposals and then as revised recommendations and standards. Risk-based principles have now been embodied not only in the FATF 40 Recommendations, but also in other standards and in laws and regulations such as:

- the EU Third Money Laundering Directive
- the revised Wolfsberg principles
- the revised standards of the Bank for International Settlements (BIS)
- the national Regulations of all EU member states
- the USA Patriot Act, as amended.

COMPONENTS OF THE RISK-BASED APPROACH

Risk indicators

How do you decide whether a customer is high or low risk from a money laundering perspective? The FATF Recommendations refer to 'customer risk factors', 'Country or geographic risk factors' and 'Product, service, transaction or delivery channel risk factors' and then go on to list some relevant factors which create 'potentially higher-risk situations'. From a practical perspective, a key requirement is a series of questions in relation to a number of important areas.

Type of customer

- Individual or business?
- High income or low income?
- Politically exposed or not?
- Introduced or brand new?
- Anomalous circumstances (e.g. geographic distance between financial institution and customer)?
- Non-resident?

- Corporate asset holding vehicle for an individual?
- Company with bearer shares or nominee shareholders?
- Complex ownership structure?

Type of business

- Which sector (industrials, trade, import/export, diamonds, arms)?
- Cash intensive?
- Does the business act solely for itself or does it represent others (e.g. investment or professional firms)?
- Type/identity of counterparties – which third parties is the customer doing business with and what is its risk profile?

Geography

- Where is the customer located (modern, developed country with advanced laws, or developing country with a developing legal system)?
- Is the customer a non-resident?
- In what other countries does the customer do business or have contacts?
- Is cash the normal medium of exchange within the country in which the customer is doing business?
- Is it a country known for the production of drugs or other high levels of criminal activity?
- Is it a country experiencing conflict or high levels of terrorist activity or insurgency?
- Is the country subject to sanctions or identified by credible sources as providing funding or support for terrorist activities?

Type of product and distribution channel

- What products is the customer using and how is access to those products being provided?
- Are those products more attractive or unattractive from a money laundering perspective (e.g. do they provide anonymity, such as with cash)?
- Do the products allow immediate access to funds?
- Do they allow for instantaneous international transfer of funds (e.g. SWIFT and telegraphic transfers)?
- Do they allow deposits to be made by third parties?
- Does the product facilitate the disguise of customer identity and transaction ownership (e.g. special use accounts, omnibus accounts, bearer instruments, beneficiaries, etc.)?

- Is the product distributed directly to the customer by the financial institution's branches, or via a network of independent salespeople/intermediaries?
- Does the product attract customers without face-to-face interaction (e.g. via the internet)?
- Does the product provide enhanced levels of discretion and security (e.g. private banking)?

Transaction types

- Are transactions on the accounts typically in very high amounts?
- Is there an especially high transactional volume?
- Are they 'payable through' transactions (i.e. where the account is neither the originator nor the ultimate beneficiary)?
- Are the economic reasons for the transactions clear and justifiable (e.g. bill payment, purchase of goods, etc.)?

All the above indicators will affect a particular relationship's susceptibility to money laundering and terrorist financing. Under the risk-based approach, what financial institutions then need to do after risk analysing their customer relationships, is to design and implement management and operational controls that are appropriate for and commensurate with the level of risk identified.

MITIGATING CONTROLS

In management and operational terms there are various aspects of policy and control that can be adjusted according to perceived risk levels, with more stringent, enhanced controls being applied to higher-risk relationships and less stringent, simplified controls being applied to lower-risk categories.

Identification requirements

For lower-risk relationships, a single form of identification and address verification may be appropriate. For higher-risk relationships, a greater degree of background research (and corresponding supporting documentation) as to identity, history, residence and other aspects of a customer's identity may be deemed necessary.

Management approvals required for customer acceptance

If a customer is categorised as low risk, there ought not to be any need for senior management approval before they are accepted as customers. For higher-risk customers, however, the approval of more senior management may be appropriate and necessary and for the highest-risk customers, it may even be appropriate for the board of directors to sign off on the account.

Due diligence and KYC information

If a customer is in a lower-risk category, there may be very little point in making extensive enquiries about their background, the nature of their income and their activities and operations. For higher-risk customer groups, however, these types of enquiries make a great deal of sense because they increase the financial institution's understanding of the customer and hence its capability to detect unusual and potentially suspicious behaviour. Enquiries might relate to, for example, further information on the nature of the business relationship, source of wealth, the reasons for intended and performed transactions, etc.

Frequency and depth of account monitoring activity

For lower-risk customers it may be appropriate to do virtually no monitoring at all. For higher-risk categories more frequent monitoring is required, the depth of which may also vary according to perceived risk. For example, sample sizes can be increased and transaction thresholds reduced to provide closer monitoring. In the highest-risk cases it is possible to conceive of 24/7 monitoring, but at those extreme risk levels one would have to query whether a relationship should exist at all.

Audit/independent testing

The audit level of the three-line defence model described in Chapter 3 should be adjusted according to risk. For example, higher-risk businesses should be audited with greater frequency and to a greater width and depth of sampling than lower-risk businesses.

Communication, training and awareness

Within the overall control environment it would be appropriate to focus greater resources on training and awareness within higher-risk business units at the justified expense of those businesses deemed to be lower risk, provided that all statutorily required basic training requirements for the organisation have been covered.

REGULATORY ENVIRONMENT

The risk-based approach effectively represents a trade-off between regulated firms and regulators. In return for a more business focused, less bureaucratic form of regulation, financial institutions have accepted a greater burden to analyse risks effectively and act accordingly. The implication is that if they fail to do this then the censure and punishment they face will be even greater than before.

Table 4.1 shows an example of what one particular financial institution considered to be high-risk characteristics from an AML perspective. Read the categories and then take a moment to consider how appropriate it is for your own organisation. Consider whether there are any items that you would add or delete from any of the columns with regard to your own business.

Table 4.1 **High-risk characteristics**

Customer/ business types	Geography	Product/delivery channel	Transaction types
Politically Exposed persons. Non-residents. Money service businesses. Gaming and betting. Real estate brokers. Jewellery businesses. Car, boat, and aircraft equipment dealerships. Charitable organisations and NPOs. Law and accounting firms. Pawnbrokers. Phone or debit card companies. Off-shore trusts.	Sanctioned countries. High-risk countries (e.g. 311 USA Patriot Act and FATF).	Private banking Trusts. Retail involving high net worth individuals and their corporate interests with high levels of personal service. Internet delivery. Nominee accounts. Prepaid stored valued cards.	Offshore. Foreign wire transfers, money instruments and cash. 'Omnibus' and 'concentration accounts'. E-bill payment services. Correspondent bank clearing. Payable through accounts.

SPECIAL CATEGORIES: POLITICALLY EXPOSED PERSONS (PEPS)

A category of high-risk customer that receives particular attention in the various international standards and guidelines (FATF 40, BIS, Wolfsberg, EU Third Directive, USA Patriot Act) is that of Politically Exposed Persons (PEPs). PEPs are defined in the FATF 40 recommendations (interpretative notes section) as follows:

> 'Foreign PEPs are individuals who are or have been entrusted with prominent public functions in a foreign country, for example heads of state or of government, senior politicians, senior government, judicial or military officials, senior executives of state owned corporations, important political party officials. Domestic PEPs are individuals who are or have been entrusted domestically with prominent public functions, for example heads of state or of government, senior politicians, senior government, judicial or military officials, senior executives of state owned corporations, important political party officials.
>
> Persons who are or have been entrusted with a prominent function by an international organization refers to members of senior management, i.e. directors, deputy directors and members of the board or equivalent functions.
>
> The definition of PEPs is not intended to cover middle ranking or more junior individuals in the foregoing categories.'

Source: www.fatf-gafi.org copyright © FATF/OECD. All rights reserved.

Why are such figures considered higher risk from an AML perspective? The reasons stem mostly from the high profile that such individuals hold. They tend to attract a great deal of interest from business people, some of whom may have criminal connections or may even be criminals themselves. They often have substantial decision-making powers (or, in democratic states, the prospect of obtaining these powers through the political process) including the power to allocate vast state funds to particular companies through the award of government contracts. This therefore makes them vulnerable to bribery and corruption. In the worst instances, they may even themselves be of a criminal disposition whereupon they will be well placed to misappropriate public funds. Finally, of course, by virtue of their positions they are likely to be in possession of sensitive non-public information which could enable them to benefit in a criminal manner at the expense of others (e.g. insider trading), should they choose to use it that way. And because PEPs are aware of the scrutiny which their activities are likely to be subject to, they may use family members, associates and, completely unknown 'fronts' as conduits through which to conduct their transactions and escape scrutiny.

Recommendation 12 requires that financial institutions should, in relation to both foreign and domestic PEPs, and in addition to performing normal due diligence measures, have appropriate risk management systems to determine whether the customer is a PEP. Once such a determination has been made, then in relation to all foreign PEPs and in relation to domestic PEPs whom they have assessed as being higher risk, financial institutions should:

- obtain senior management approval for establishing business relationships with such customers
- take reasonable measures to establish the source of wealth and source of funds, and
- conduct enhanced ongoing monitoring of the business relationship.

Clearly, the capability of an organisation to determine whether a prospective customer is a PEP is an important one. But how do you determine whether an account holder is a PEP? There are various methods available:

- Seek information directly from the individual.
- Review sources of income including past and present employment history and references from professional associates.
- Review public sources of information (e.g. databases, newspapers, microfiche records, etc.).
- Check the Central Intelligence Agency (CIA) online directory of 'Chiefs of State and Cabinet Members of Foreign Governments' (www.odci.gov/cia/publications/chiefs/index.html).
- Check the Transparency International Corruption Perceptions Index.
- Check private vendor sources (e.g. World Compliance/Regulatory DataCore (RDC), Factiva and WorldCheck).

CONSTRUCTING A RISK-BASED APPROACH FOR YOUR ORGANISATION

Basic model examples

The risk-based approach (as described above) is already a regulatory requirement in many jurisdictions and will progressively spread to all jurisdictions, as they move towards full compliance with international AML and CFT standards. Care needs to be taken that risk-based solutions which are in keeping with international standards are nevertheless still consonant with national regulatory requirements.

Conceptually, it is helpful to think of the process of designing risk-based controls in terms of having two dials, X and Y. The X dial is connected to antennae capable of gathering relevant information and it records risk according to the various criteria discussed above. The Y dial is adjustable and sets control levels. It can be calibrated, according to the risk information received from the X dial, so as to provide the optimum control environment for the institution. This model is depicted in Figure 4.3.

Risk-based approach assessment and control model

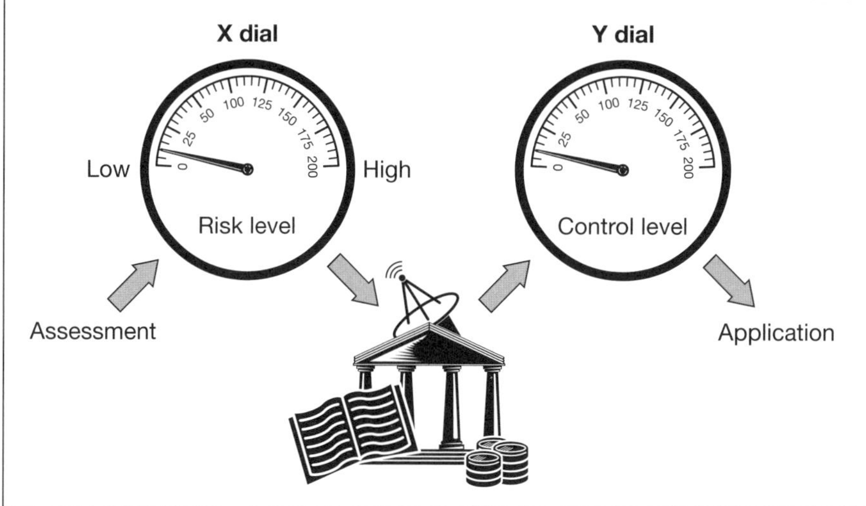

In terms of risk assessment, clearly organisations must be able to harness as much high-quality information as possible in order to make a meaningful assessment of risk. Questionnaires, therefore, for completion by the customers themselves or by bank staff, paper-based or electronic, will be an important medium through which information about the customer is acquired. Other important data-gathering media include well structured interviews, background research (where this is justified) and, in extreme cases, private vetting via investigations agencies (more on this in Chapter 5, which deals with the subject of reputational risk).

Information about the customer needs to be married with an assessment of the product risk and country risk, as discussed above.

Product risk assessment – test your instincts

What makes a product more or less risky from an AML and CFT perspective? We looked at some of the features earlier on and now we will try to put these into practice. Below are some product descriptions from different areas of financial services. Look at these descriptions and for each product assess whether you consider that product to be either higher or lower risk.

Banking

Product: Personal current account – *high or low risk*?

Product: Personal current account

Description: Ordinary account for daily living

Surrender/withdrawals: Yes

Payment methods: Cash, cheque, draft or transfer

Third-party payments: Yes

Additional payments: Yes

Minimum periods: None

Complex structures: Possible

International: Possible

Other controls: Identification requirements on account opening

This product may be high risk for placement and layering activity, but will only normally be considered high risk if the amounts going through it are large. It satisfies many of the launderer's requirements. It can receive money, in cash if needs be, and from third parties, and send it anywhere in the world to other third parties. There are no limits to the amounts which can be put through it (subject to staff suspicions) and no minimum periods or lock-ins.

Product: Letter of credit/documentary credit – *high or low risk*?

Product: Letter of credit/documentary credit

Description: Trade finance product through which bank pays exporter for goods and reclaims funds from importer

Surrender/withdrawals: Yes, value is exchanged at the point where bank accepts reimbursement from importer

Payment methods: Cheque, draft or transfer

Third-party payments: Yes

Additional payments: No, but multiple credits possible for single clients

Minimum periods: None

Complex structures: No

International: Yes

Other controls: Fraud controls on import/export documents

These products are lower to medium risk within the banking sector due to the fact that a customer will have to undergo intrusive scrutiny (e.g. credit checks) to discover whether it is a proper trading company, or through a registered office visit to verify that the business is as it claims to be. Letters of credit can be and are used for money laundering (typically layering), despite being vulnerable to discovery from vigilant trade clerks who may e.g. recognise that the import documents are fake.

Product: Credit card – *high or low risk*?

Product: Credit card

Description: Running credit account based on point-of-sale credit transactions, with balances and/or interest repaid monthly

Surrender/withdrawals: Yes, value is exchanged at the points where (1) goods and services are purchased, and (2) debit balances incurred are repaid

Payment methods: Cash, cheque, draft or transfer, but amounts are usually small, less than €5,000.

Third-party payments: Yes, but would be considered unusual

Additional payments: Yes, payments are made monthly

Minimum periods: None

Complex structures: No

International: Yes

Other controls: High predictability of profile on most accounts allows easy identification of unusual card usage

Credit cards are lower risk because they are not as flexible as, say, a current account (you can do fewer things with them.) But they can be used by criminals at the integration stage – particularly at the platinum end of the market – for unlimited spending, with funds of criminal origin used to repay the card. Credit card frauds can also be used to finance terrorist attacks.

Product: Corporate treasury foreign exchange services – *high or low risk*?

Product: Corporate treasury foreign exchange services

Description: Conversion and transfer of currency deposits, both for trade/commercial purposes and as part of speculative/trading strategy. Often large sums involved (more than €1 million)

Surrender/withdrawals: Yes

Payment methods: Cash (rare, given amounts), cheque, draft or transfer

Third-party payments: Yes

Additional payments: Yes

Minimum periods: None

Complex structures: Often

International: Yes

Other controls: Services often offered only to limited pool of well-known institutions

These products are higher risk, given the large sums involved and the international nature of the business, allowing substantial cross-border payments to be made to and from an account. The Risks can be mitigated by limiting availability, as above.

Fund management

Product: Hedge funds – *high or low risk*?

Product: Hedge funds

Description: Non-discretionary investment for sophisticated investors with high-risk appetite (e.g. may involve derivatives trading and short selling)

Surrender/withdrawals: Yes, but usually a lock-in for a set period (e.g. five years)

Payment methods: Bank draft or electronic transfer

Third-party payments: Yes

Additional payments: Yes

Minimum periods: Five years and beyond

Complex structures: Yes

International: Yes

Other controls: No

These products, are higher risk, due to the fact that they allow a diverse range of investors, as well as the use of complex investment structures and some offshore tax havens with a lower degree of regulatory scrutiny.

General insurance

Product: Personal household insurance – *high or low risk?*

Product: Personal household insurance

Description: Household insurance for contents and buildings insurance

Surrender/withdrawals: Upon a claim

Payment methods: Monthly or annually

Third-party payments: By the broker

Additional payments: For increases in contents liability

Minimum periods: Annually

Complex structures: No

International: Possibly, subject to permissions in the overseas country

Other controls: Fraud claims. If payment stops so does policy.

This would be low risk, due to the fact that payout only occurs after assessment. Also a police crime reference number has to be provided. If premiums cease so does the cover. Fraud controls will also be in place.

Adjusting product controls to the overall level of the relationship risk

As we have seen, AML and CFT risk is about more than just the product. It also encompasses the type of customer, geographic issues and business issues. In order to make the risk-based approach work, organisations need to construct methodologies for applying particular control regimes to a particular type of risk – assessed relationships. At a basic level, one can imagine a process as follows:

- consider product, distribution channel, customer and domicile
- consider whether high-risk elements shift the relationship into a higher-risk category (e.g. a high-risk customer using lower-risk products)
- adopt increasing control strengths according to whether a relationship has been assessed as either 'low', 'medium' or 'high'. For example:

  Low risk = A + B (i.e. minimum legal requirement of customer identification (A) and address verification (B))

  Medium risk = A + B + C (i.e. identification plus address verification plus source of funds check (C), i.e. where the funds have originated from – e.g. bank, private account)

  High risk = A + B + C + D (i.e. identification, address verification and source of funds check as above, plus source of wealth check (D), i.e. what economic activity has generated the customer's wealth?)

Monitoring activities are also adjusted accordingly, such that very limited monitoring takes place on low-risk accounts, more monitoring takes place on medium-risk accounts and very frequent monitoring occurs on high-risk accounts.

It is important to note that a low-risk product could be placed in a higher-risk category if the customer is perceived as a high risk (e.g. a politically exposed person using a credit card).

Relationship risk classification – test your instincts ...

Using the above methodology, we can now review some relationship examples and try to ascribe a risk assessment rating (low, medium or high) and a corresponding control regime (A + B; A + B + C; or A + B + C + D) to each example. Note that at this stage we are not using a consistently applied calculating mechanism (that comes later). Rather, we are exploring how different combinations of customer, product and geographic risk factors affect our assessment of risk and the different control responses required accordingly,

Scenarios

Scenario 1

An individual customer from a FATF member country wants a credit card, which will be repayable from their current account at an EU regulated financial institution. The predicted average monthly spend on the card will be around €800.

This scenario involves a low-risk product, a low-risk customer, a low-risk jurisdiction, with low regular payments from a regulated financial institution in a low-risk jurisdiction = a low-risk relationship. So A + B would be appropriate – identity check and address verification, with the least intensive monitoring.

Scenario 2

A government official from a highly corrupt country wishes to open a numbered deposit account with your private bank, with the initial funds being transferred from the accounts of nominee companies owned by him in various offshore locations, some of which have been associated with tax evasion. The initial expected receipt is for US$2 million.

This scenario involves a high-risk product, a high-risk customer, a high-risk jurisdiction, a very large initial deposit (given the applicant's occupation) = a high-risk relationship. In fact, even allowing for A + B + C + D (identification, verification, source of funds and source of wealth checks) – query whether you should be doing this business at all unless you can get some compelling evidence on the legitimacy of the applicant's source of wealth.

Scenario 3

A trading company wishes to open letters of credit for products being exported from a FATF country to a neutral country (i.e. neither FATF nor ICRG). Payments under the credits are to be received from the importer's local bank. The products in question are perfume and certain other fancy goods.

This scenario involves a low to medium-risk product, a low-risk customer, and a medium-risk counterparty (the paying bank) from a medium-risk jurisdiction = a medium-risk relationship. So A + B + C would be appropriate – identity check, address verification and source of funds check. You would also need to conduct due diligence against the importer's bank.

Scenario 4

An established institution from a FATF country wishes to make a medium-sized investment in one of your property funds (an investment fund containing a portfolio of commercial property and producing income from rental streams and profits on sales from properties located in the EU, the US and Hong Kong; investment range from US$10m to 25m)

This scenario involves a relatively low-risk product, a low-risk customer, low-risk jurisdictions and a moderate investment sum = a low-risk relationship. A + B only are appropriate – identity check and address verification, with minimal monitoring

Scenario 5

A previously unknown firm of investment consultants from an offshore tax haven states that it represents a group of international private investors with a high-risk appetite and a very large amount of money for investment in your best performing hedge fund.

This scenario involves a high-risk product, a high-risk customer, a high-risk jurisdiction and large investment amounts = a high-risk relationship. A + B + C + D is required – identity check, address verification, source of funds check and source of wealth check.

Taking it to the next level of detail

Figure 4.4 Digging deeper for information

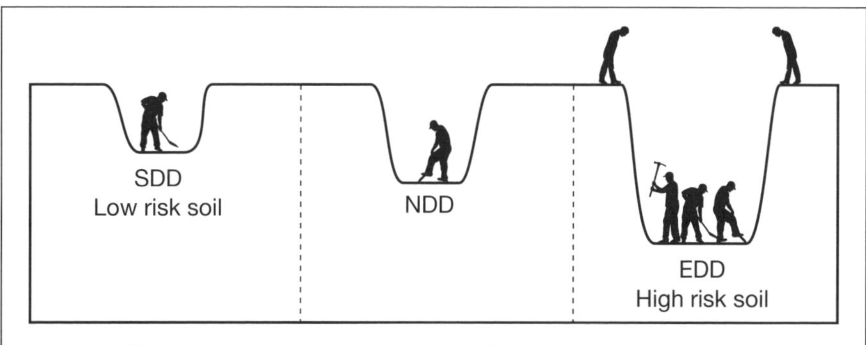

Building upon the principles outlined in this chapter, you should think of due diligence as a process of digging for information (see Figure 4.4). If a relationship is very straightforward and low risk, then you're not expected to dig very deep and a simplified form of due diligence (denoted as Simplified Due Diligence – SDD Figure 4.4) will be appropriate, involving only a restricted number of the information elements listed above. Depending on the business profile of your institution, this may actually be a relatively small minority of the overall number of customer relationships. There will then be those customers and relationships where the risks are of a medium nature with much more digging required in many more of the key information elements listed above (designated as Normal Due Diligence – NDD). Again, depending on the specifics of the institution's business profile, this category may turn out to encompass a significant majority of its overall customers and relationships.

Finally, there will be those relationships which are classified as high risk, for the various reasons that we identified earlier on in this chapter. These will require the greatest depth of digging. The purpose of this digging is not just to increase the chances of identifying information and previously unknown risks that may affect your decision to take the customer on or affect your treatment of them, if you are already in a relationship with them; The digging *also* ensures that you can demonstrate to the world at large that you took greater precautions when you perceived higher degrees of risk. For these high-risk relationships the full range of information types outlined above would need to be collected. This level of quite intensive 'digging' is designated as Enhanced Due Diligence (EDD in Figure 4.4).

THE CORE COMPONENTS OF CDD

Information collection

Whatever risk assessment framework you are operating, the due diligence which your company undertakes will comprise the base level elements of information collection and information verification.

The type of information which it may be relevant to collect for due diligence purposes is wide ranging. Details could be required, for example, in relation to any or all of the following.

Personal information

- Name – including any aliases, shortened versions and variations in the order of the words in the name (e.g. 'John Vey Atta', also known as 'Atta John' or 'Vey John').
- Address – including alternative addresses where these exist.

- Date of birth.
- Nationality.
- Occupation.
- Source of funds – i.e., the location (country/city) and bank or other institution from which funds entering the account have originated.
- Account purpose – the reason why the account is being opened (e.g. to receive salary; to purchase a new car; to set aside funds for investment, etc.). This is a critical piece of information which, all too often, is completed by relationship managers in insufficient detail. Answers which the author has seen on customer acceptance documentation have included 'general', 'N/A' and even 'bank account'.
- Anticipated account activity – i.e. the types, size, volume or frequency of transactions anticipated to take place on the account.
- Source of wealth – the economic activity which has generated the funds or other assets which the institution is handling for the client (e.g. inherited wealth, wealth from the sale of a business, investment income, etc.).

Personal information of a corporate nature

It is not just for personal accounts that you may need to obtain personal information. Individuals obviously hold or perform key positions and functions in corporations and other legal entities, in which case the following information may be required:

- Names and identities of directors and partners.
- Names of registered and beneficial owners holding (25 per cent or more significant percentage of the shares or voting rights in an entity) ('Beneficial owners' may not appear on share registers, and are natural persons – not corporate entities – who ultimately own or control the entity, or for whose benefit or on whose behalf transactions are conducted).
- Names of all authorised signatories.
- Names of settlers, trustees and beneficiaries.

Corporate (non-personal)

Finally, there is information about the customer entity itself when it is an artificial person, such as:

- Name.
- Registered number/tax identification number.
- Type of entity – e.g. private corporation, public/state-owned entity, partnership, etc.

- Registered office.
- Business address (if different).
- Country of incorporation.
- Purpose of account.
- Anticipated account activity.
- The nature of the business – i.e., the business sector in which the entity is involved and any specialist products or services it provides.
- Countries where the entity conducts business – this would include, for example, export destinations and import origination, as well as details of overseas offices and branches, with special reference to high-risk countries and countries which are a subject of sanctions.
- In case of financial institutions, information on internal AML and CFT policies and controls.
- Details of reputation in terms of corporate activity.
- Quality of supervision.
- Reason for opening account.
- Source of wealth.

All of the above adds up to quite a lot of information and would impose significant burdens on most institutions if all of that information had to be collected in each and every case. Thankfully, because of the application of risk-based principles, this isn't necessary.

Verification

What do we mean by 'verification'? Verification refers to the process by which we provide proof or reassurance that a piece of information is true.

If your institution has account opening discussions with a representative of a company who tells you that the name of the company is Bertoli Communications Ltd, how do you prove it? Because remember, if you didn't prove it and the company was actually a different company or, more likely, non-existent, then money could be laundered through its accounts, those accounts could be emptied, everybody would disappear and there would be nothing left to go on.

If the representative of the company tells you that its business is the import and export of mobile phones and other electronic communications equipment, how do you prove it? If you don't, then it's possible that it could be a shell company and that all the activity on its account represents money laundering.

If the representative tells you that the beneficial owners of the company are Mr X and Mrs Y, how do you prove it? Because if you don't, how can you say that the company *isn't* owned by an organised crime syndicate or a corrupt politician?

Verification doesn't stop accounts and relationships being used for money laundering, but it is an important barrier, an inconvenient additional hurdle which criminals and launderers must overcome if they are to achieve their objectives.Verification involves the collection and retention of evidence in the form of official documentation (e.g. passports, constituent documents of companies and other artificial legal persons, print-outs from websites), certification (e.g. certifying copies as being true copies of originals which have been sighted, and stamping documents as such, obtaining official letters from embassies, notaries, solicitors or attorneys regarding the truth and reliability of documents and copies of documents), reportage (e.g. a report prepared by a relationship manager of a visit to an address, confirming that the company is actually operating a business from that address) and electronic data (with the emergence of the data-driven economy over the past 10 or so years, increasingly now in a growing number of countries there are reliable, independent databases which can serve as a means of electronic verification of, for example addresses and telephone numbers against names and dates of birth).

The extent of information verification will, like the collection of the information itself, be undertaken on a risk-sensitive basis. The higher the perceived level of risk, the more extensive the degree of verification that is required. As we shall see, in the highest-risk relationships involving, say, politically exposed persons or companies operating in very high-risk sectors or countries, the required information and verification levels may be quite extensive and will involve asking lots of questions and checking the answers against a wide range of documents such as trade agreements, financial returns, solicitors' letters, press articles, business sale agreements and property deeds. There are also multiple sources of publicly-available information which can be used to check the consistency of information which has been provided to you, though it should be remembered that the easier it is for the information provider to manipulate such sources, the less reliable they are. Examples include:

- company website and literature
- Google
- newspapers and other media (including their websites)
- industry magazines and websites
- local and industry contacts and other third parties
- subscription information services such as WorldCheck.

In certain situations (which we explore in more detail in Chapter 5), it may prove necessary to instruct external agencies and consultants to conduct investigations against individuals and companies in order to establish their *bona fides*.

Long gone are the days when it was acceptable to 'take a gentleman at his word'.

CDD PROCESSES AND TOOLS

In the wholesale/corporate, financial institution, retail/consumer and wealth management/private banking example processes which follow, I have suggested a common framework and some common tools with which to inform a tactical approach to implementing the broad principles of the risk-based approach. This framework is shown in Figure 4.5.

Figure 4.5 **Example CDD process**

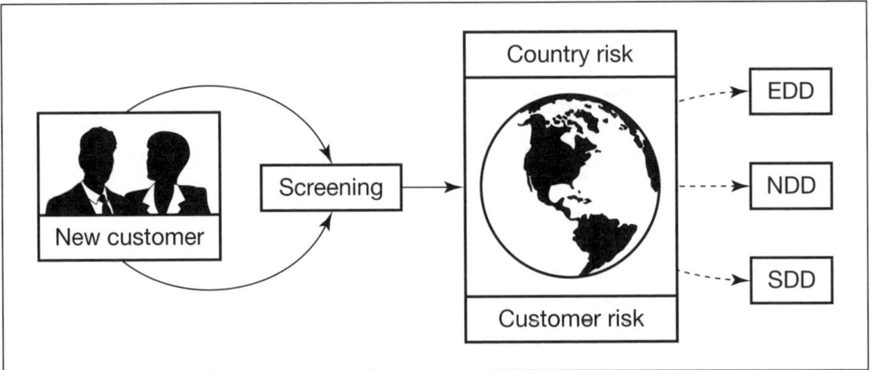

Figure 4.5 echoes the earlier generic client acceptance process flow described in Chapter 3. At various stages, systems, procedures and controls must be in place to enable your institution to:

- screen applicants for business against a company watch-list of prohibited entities and prohibited account or relationship types
- reach meaningful assessments of country, customer and product risk
- classify relationships into one of three categories which I have designated as simplified due diligence (SDD), normal due diligence (NDD) and enhanced due diligence (EDD)
- calibrate information, verification, approval levels, account monitoring and audit intensity according to the level of perceived risk
- review relationship activity on an ongoing basis (again, risk-sensitive) and recalibrate where necessary.

Unacceptable clients and relationships tool

Apart from your institution's alert-list requirements, a key tool during the screening stage of the process will be your list of unacceptable accounts and relationships. This will be based upon both generally accepted practice and your company's own risk appetite based upon its own experience (things which have gone badly, gone well or could go well if they were managed differently, etc.).

Here is an example of one such list:

Institutional list of unacceptable accounts/relationships

Example

- Proscribed entities
- Shell banks
- Unlicensed banks
- Unregulated money service businesses
- Customers with known or suspected involvement in money laundering, terrorist financing, WMD proliferation or tax evasion
- Anonymous or numbered accounts

In other words, this is your institution saying to the world: 'We are not even going to go to the trouble of assessing risk here, we simply will not do this business – ever.'

Country risk list tools

Clearly you cannot rely on individuals or business units to make their own assessments of money laundering and terrorist financing risks in different countries on an *ad hoc* basis. They will need a list, updated regularly, which designates every country in the world as either low risk, medium risk or high risk for money laundering, terrorist financing and, latterly, for international tax compliance and proliferation financing. There are companies and commercial websites selling consultancy services and collated publicly-available information that can assist you in determining which category a country should fall into. This is also something which you and your institution should spend some time thinking about. Relevant factors include:

- economic sanctions
- presence on the FATF ICRG list
- offshore status (and if so, current status on the OECD managed tax information exchange agreement process)
- any Moneyval, WorldBank or IMF mutual evaluations or assessments of the strength or otherwise of the country's AML regulatory regime

- membership of bodies such as the FATF or its regional sub-groups
- membership of the EU
- political unrest, war, insurgency or terrorist threat
- whether a producer or transit country, for example, narcotics, people trafficking or smuggled goods such as weapons, alcohol and tobacco
- any specific features of its financial services industry which make it higher risk (e.g. tax advisory, nominee/trust companies, private banking)
- any institution specific incidents or beliefs relating to that country (e.g. based on knowledge of local business practices).

Country risk lists, particularly those from governmental or regional institutions, are obviously immensely useful in assessing the comparative risks of different jurisdictions. However, the fact that a country is listed on a 'low risk country' list is no guarantee that business within that country is automatically low-risk. For example, in the EU a 'Doctrine of Equivalence' applies to all member states. In effect what this means is that member states are assumed to have common AML and CFT standards and are therefore entitled to be labelled as 'equivalent' jurisdictions. If a jurisdiction is labelled as an 'equivalent jurisdiction' then this is usually taken as a heavy pointer towards lower risk assessments for customers based in that country, with all the attendant benefits (cost and time-wise) of lower due diligence levels. Indeed, most EU-based financial institutions carve out a special place in their country risk assessment lists for EU equivalent jurisdictions. But it's important to remember that just because a country is an EU member state doesn't automatically mean that financial institutions will necessarily be rating it as 'low risk'. For example, for different reasons, a number of financial institutions rate Luxembourg and Greece as 'high risk', even though they are EU member states and equivalent jurisdictions. Likewise, most financial institutions rate Russia as 'high risk' even though it is a member country of the FATF. People form their own judgements and so should you and your institution.

Table 4.2 shows a sample example a country risk-assessment sheet, followed by a list of equivalent jurisdictions in Table 4.3.

Business sector risk tool

Again, your business units will need policy guidance on this, as individual perceptions of risk will differ. What makes a business high- or low-risk for money laundering and terrorist financing purposes? To answer that question one must look at how attractive certain business types are for those who wish to launder money or finance terrorism. Clearly cash-based businesses are attractive for the reasons we have identified earlier, as are any businesses involved in the transmission of money for other people. Import and export

Table 4.2

An example country risk tool

High risk	Medium risk	Low risk
Afghanistan	Angola	Armenia
Albania	Aruba	Australia
Belarus	Bahrain	Belgium
Burma	Cambodia	Botswana
Haiti	Cayman Islands	Brunei
India	China	Canada
Indonesia	Hong Kong	Chile
Iran	Hungary	Czech Republic
Iraq	Ireland	Finland
Liechtenstein	Jersey	France
Luxembourg	Kazakhstan	Germany
Macau	Malaysia	Ghana
Nauru	Malta	Greece
Nigeria	Mauritius	Iceland
Pakistan	Philippines	Israel
Paraguay	Singapore	Italy
*Republic of Bissan**	Togo	Japan
Russia	Turks & Caicos Islands	Lithuania
Sao Tome and Principe		New Zealand
Switzerland		South Africa
Ukraine		

*used in examples later (not a real country)

Table 4.3

An example jurisdictions tool

EU member states		
Austria	Belgium	Bulgaria
Cyprus	Czech Republic	Denmark
Estonia	Finland	France
Germany	Greece	Hungary
Ireland	Italy	Latvia
Lithuania	Luxembourg	Malta
Netherlands	Poland	Portugal
Romania	Slovakia	Slovenia
Spain	Sweden	United Kingdom
EEA member countries		
Iceland	Liechtenstein	Norway
Switzerland		
Non-EU FATF member and observer countries*		
Argentina	Australia	Brazil
Canada	Hong Kong	Japan
Mexico	New Zealand	Singapore
South Africa	United States of America	

*Observers may not always be regarded as equivalent under JMLSG guidance.

companies with a valid business reason for remitting and receiving large sums in their normal course of business will also be high risk for their 'cover' potential for money launderers, and we know that the real estate sector also offers attractive opportunities for money laundering. Religious organisations, charities and non-profit organisations (NPOs) are high-risk for terrorist financing.

In terms of medium risk, these would be business types which have some potential for money laundering and which, whilst not offering the same level of attraction as the high-risk business sectors above, nevertheless are known to have been involved in money laundering schemes, such as the construction industry, certain categories of business consultancy and professional services (lawyers, tax accountants, company formation agents, etc.) and the sale of computer equipment, mobile phones and technology.

Lower-risk sectors would be those which are not immediately and obviously attractive, or known in the past to have been associated with money laundering activity. As with country risk, consultancies will sell advisory services on business sector risk assessment for AML/CFT purposes. There is also publicly-available information on business sector risk. In terms of how you go about creating the business sector risk list, there is no point in re-inventing the wheel. The best place to start is with the business type lists which your institution already has in place for credit assessments and other forms of business risk and opportunity analysis. An example is shown in Table 4.4.

Source of wealth information checklist tool

There will be occasions when, typically as part of enhanced due diligence (EDD) enquiries, business unit staff will be required to seek information to prove a customer's source of wealth. Although at first sight this may seem to be a fairly straightforward task of asking and obtaining information from the customer, experience suggests that, in practice, staff – particularly in sales and relationship functions – need to be pushed to do it properly. They often feel that they are putting the overall relationship (and the revenue which comes with it) at risk by asking questions which may be deemed by the customer to be too intrusive. This is particularly so when dealing with the types of wealthy and high-profile clients who are precisely the kind of people from whom such information should be obtained (lest it should turn out that the significant sums which have been entering and leaving their accounts on a regular basis have come from illegitimate rather than legitimate sources). For this reason, such reluctance by staff must be overcome and a good practical way in which to do this is to provide firm and detailed guidance on the questions which they should be asking, as well as more skills-based guidance and training on how to solicit relevant information during the course of normal social interaction. There is more on this in Chapter 5, which deals with reputational risk.

Table 4.4

An example business type risk tool

HIGH RISK (sample)	
Antique dealers Art dealers Auction houses Computer and computer software/ peripheral stores Foreign exchange brokers and dealers (money service bureau – MSBs) Gambling/gaming related services General importers and exporters Manufacturing of weapons and ammunition Motor vehicle dealers (new and used) (retail) Other credit granting Other monetary intermediaries Other recreational activities	Precious metals dealers Real estate development – commercial Real estate development – industrial Real estate development – retail Real estate development – residential Real estate development – others Religious organisations Restaurants and bars Retail sale via stalls/markets Retail wine/alcohol stores Sale of used automobile and other motor vehicles (wholesale) Wholesale wine/alcohol Wholesale and retail of gems and jewellery
MEDIUM RISK (sample)	
General/special trade construction of buildings and civil engineering works Construction – residential Construction – industrial buildings Construction – commercial buildings Construction – retail buildings Construction – others Business consultancy Highway, street, bridge and tunnel construction Water, sewers, gas, pipeline construction Construction of dams and water projects	Communication and power lines construction Construction of railways Other heavy construction Other building completion works Other building installation activities Retail sale of pharmaceutical and medical products Renting of construction or demolition equipment with operator Sale of motor vehicle parts and accessories (retail) Maintenance and repair of motor vehicles
LOW RISK (sample)	
Land reclamation works Grain farming Oil palm Oil seeds or oleaginous fruit Tobacco farming Rubber plantation Sugarcane farming Cotton farming Manufacture and/or distribution of industrial products Vegetables, horticultural and nursery products	Cocoa plantation Coffee plantation Tea plantation Other fruits, nuts, beverage and spice crops necessary Livestock farming Other animal farming, production of animal products Agricultural and animal husbandry service activities IT consulting

An example of a source of wealth checklist is shown in Table 4.5.

Table 4.5 **An example source of wealth checklist**

Source of wealth generated from business ownership
Nature of business and operations Significant products and/or services? Market penetration? Geographic trade areas? Number and identity of locations? Number of people employed? Details (percentage) of applicant's ownership of the business? Ownership of the business Names of other owners and their percentage ownership? Estimated annual sales volume? Estimated annual net income? Length of time during which applicant has been involved with business? Are there significant revenues from government contracts? *Business history* How long has the business been in operation? How long has the applicant been in this particular business? How was the business established? Is the company publicly traded?
Source of wealth derived from a senior executive position
The individual What is the person's position in the company (e.g. managing director, chief executive officer, chief operating officer, etc.)? Length of time at the company? Area of expertise? Details of compensation (salary, bonus, share options, etc.)? (Note: look out for any differences between total stated and apparent net worth and compensation × number of years.) *The company* What is the business of the company? (Note: a good degree of detail should be provided. General answers such as 'financial services' or 'manufacturing' are insufficient. There should be a reasonably detailed description of what the company specialises in, unless it is a well-known global brand.)

Source of wealth derived from a profession (e.g. accountant, lawyer, doctor)
What is the profession? Are there any areas of specialism? Any previous employment history prior to joining the profession? Practice licence details? How is wealth derived from the profession? (For example, charge-out rate per hour/day × number of hours/days per year less estimated costs = net income, multiplied by number of years with appropriate reductions for lower earnings.) Strength of business reputation? (For example, prominent clients, details of academic/professional publications, advertisements, membership of professional bodies and position in local society – e.g. Round Table and other associations.)
Source of wealth derived from PEP status
Elected or appointed? Number of years in office or position? Any available public information (particularly negative information)? (Note: refer to Chapter 5 on reputational risk for a more detailed checklist on this issue.) Main responsibilities (including responsibility for specific business sectors such as construction, transport, power, etc.)? Any known associations or interests in business entities?
Source of wealth derived from inheritance
From whom were the assets inherited? When were they inherited? What was the type and value of the assets inherited? How have the assets been dealt with since the time of inheritance (e.g. public and private investments, property, business venture)? (Note: you should be able to relate current wealth, by means of calculation, to any originally-inherited wealth plus whatever has been earned from other sources such as employment or investment. Significant gaps between the amount originally inherited and current wealth need to be explained.)
Source of wealth derived from investments
List all assets by name, type (e.g. shares, bonds and other securities, fund and hedge fund investments, insurance policies, stakes in private businesses and franchises), value and growth in value since the investment was made. What was the original source of wealth for the investments (see above)? Any significant/high-profile transactions (e.g. private equity acquisition and disposal, involvement in hostile takeover, disposal of significant stake)? Estimated annual income from investments? Length of time client has been an investor?

CDD documentation tools

The requirement in the FATF standards is that financial institutions should undertake customer due diligence measures against their customers when establishing business relations and when carrying out occasional transactions which fall within certain parameters. This immediately raises a practical issue. There is a large array of different types of customers of varying legal compositions. It's possible that your company might have to conduct CDD against any of the following:

- individuals
- smaller companies in the private sector
- more well-established, substantial private sector companies
- publicly listed companies
- governments
- state-owned corporations
- regulated financial institutions and correspondent banks (dealt with in the next section)
- partnerships
- trusts and foundations
- non-government organisations
- charities
- clubs, societies and unincorporated associations
- entities conducting one-off transactions above certain financial thresholds
- if you are a large international group, introductions from other business units in other countries.

Your procedures will need to be very clear in terms of what information and documentation is required in relation to each in different circumstances, and the verification methods used. For these purposes you will require a detailed set of tools which show staff what types of documents must be obtained from customers and about different types of customers during the CDD process, for each of the different due diligence risk classification levels (SDD, NDD and EDD).

All such tools are not reproduced in detail here, but would basically comprise the legally required identification and verification documents for each of the above categories of customer.

The following example shows a CDD documentation tool for corporate customers, showing the different documentation requirements depending on whether the customer is classified as SDD, NDD or EDD.

CDD documentary requirements for corporates

Example

Simplified Due Diligence (SDD)

Identity and due diligence information:

- Company number
- Registered office in country of incorporation
- Business address
- Purpose and reason for opening the account or establishing the relationship (unless obvious from the product)
- The expected type and level of activity to be undertaken in the relationship (e.g. total account turnover, largest expected balance (CR/DR)).

Verification:

1. Evidence of listing of publicly quoted companies (e.g. copy of relevant internet page published by the regulated market). Evidence of existence of government entity (e.g. copy of web page from government website).
2. The majority ownership status of any subsidiary.
3. The licensing and regulatory regime status of the company (e.g. letter from regulator confirming that the company is regulated).
4. Authority of authorised signatory(s) to open and operate the account (e.g. board resolution/mandate or government authorising document).

Normal Due Diligence (NDD)

Identity and due diligence information:

- Full name
- Company number or other unique identifying number assigned by government to the entity (e.g. taxpayer identification number)
- Registered office in country of incorporation
- Business address
- Purpose and reason for opening the account or establishing relationship (unless obvious from the product)
- The expected type and level of activity to be undertaken in the relationship (e.g. total account turnover, largest expected balance (CR/DR))
- Names of all directors, partners, proprietors
- Names of all beneficial owners
- Names of shareholders owning at least 25 per cent of the shares or voting rights
- Names of all authorised signatories

- Nature and details of the business
- Whether the customer conducts business with any countries subject to national or international sanctions
- Source of funds
- Copies of recent financial statements.

Verification:

1. Identity of business (e.g. relevant company registry search, or certified copy of certificate of incorporation/partnership deed/business registration certificate (or equivalent) or other equivalent independent and reliable sources. The guiding principle is that the documents used have been issued by a government, government body or agency or accredited/regulated industry body. For corporate documents, certification can be by an appropriate authority of the customer (e.g. the company secretary).
2. Identity of one controlling director (e.g. managing director), partner or proprietor (see 'Officers of corporations', below).
3. Identities of all significant beneficial owners owning at least 25 per cent of the shares or voting rights.
4. Authority of authorised signatory(s) to open and operate the account (e.g. board resolution/mandate).
5. Where the shareholders are not natural persons, the structure should be investigated until the natural persons or a publicly listed company are identified. It should then be established whether any such natural person(s) hold a proportionate interest of 25 per cent or more of the customer or exercise management control over it (i.e. significant beneficial owners).
6. Companies with an unduly complex structure of ownership should be subjected to EDD. This generally means there are three layers or more layers of shareholding ownership between the company and the ultimate principal beneficial owners.

For company officers
Identity and due diligence information:

- Full name
- Current residential address
- Date of birth
- Nationality
- Identity document number
- Nature and details of the business/occupation/employment.

Verification:
The preferred document to verify identity would be a government issued document which contains the name, an evidencing photograph or similar safeguard and either the residential address or date of birth. For example:

- passport
- driving licence
- national identity card or
- Electoral ID card.

Enhanced Due Diligence (EDD)
As for NDD, except

1. Verify the identities of two controlling directors (or equivalent) that must include the managing director or CEO.
2. In addition, fuller investigations into the nature of the entity's business, and the legitimacy of its business activities and revenues/ sources of wealth and funding. (Corroboration of source of wealth could be from actual documents provided by the customer (e.g. the proof of a sale of a property), available public information surrounding the individual or, where appropriate, from a detailed due diligence report of the relationship manager that has included elements of external enquiry and detailed meetings with the customer.)

These tools are really nothing more than a more detailed, granular manifestation of the 'digging holes' graphic shown in Figure 4.4. If you look at it, you'll see that for SDD there is a relatively light amount of information and verification required, but that these requirements increase as the risk classification rises up through NDD and into EDD. Similarly, detailed tools should exist for each of the customer categories outlined above.

EXAMPLE RISK ASSESSMENT FRAMEWORKS

Constructing a CDD framework for corporate/wholesale banking business

Given the complexity of many modern financial transactions and structures, it may not be immediately clear to your staff who the corporate customer actually is, and so this is something which will need to be spelled out in your policy documents and your training.

Who is the customer? In the type of relationship depicted in Figure 4.6, the answer is straightforward. The customer is a company called XCo that is placing deposits with and taking loans from the bank. However, things may not always be so obvious, so here are a few examples of different types of financial transactions which could be included in policy documentation to guide staff on 'Who is my customer?'

Figure 4.6 **'Plain vanilla' banking relationship**

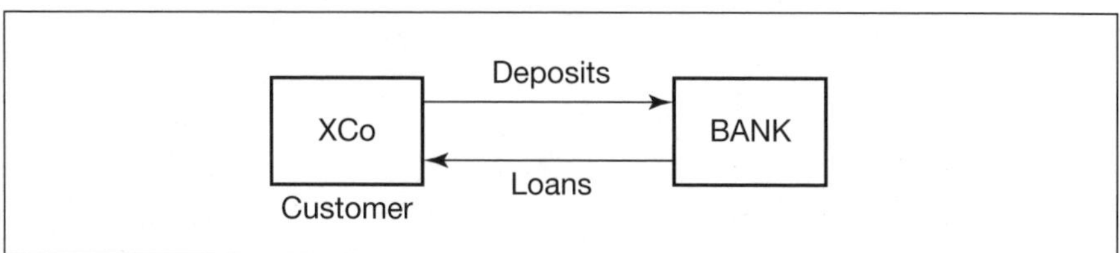

Examples

Case 1

AlnaBank buys from K Bank the loan portfolio of WonderTaste Limited, which is in financial difficulties and requires a debt restructuring which K Bank is not prepared to provide. According to the workout deal, in addition to acquiring the existing loans, AlnaBank is also to provide an additional credit line of $20 million.

KBank and WonderTaste are both clearly candidates for CDD. But which of these should the CDD be conducted against, or is it both?

The answer in this case is that CDD must be conducted against both counterparties, KBank and WonderTaste. AlnaBank is receiving and paying for financial assets from KBank, and WonderTaste will actually be opening accounts and (hopefully) repaying loans.

Case 2

The hi-tech fund of AlnaBank Growth Ventures Limited (AGVL), AlnaBank's private equity arm, receives funds from X Limited, Y Limited and Z Limited and invests them in Advance Software Limited, so as to acquire a 65 per cent stake.

The candidates for CDD then are, respectively, X Limited, Y Limited, Z Limited and Advance Software Limited. But against which one should AlnaBank conduct CDD?

The answer in this case is that CDD must be conducted against X Limited, Y Limited and Z Limited since they are the entities from whom funds are being received as part of the investment process. Normally there would be no requirement to conduct due diligence against investee companies such as Advance Software Limited, nevertheless AGVL would be wise to undertake integrity checks against Advance Software before making the investment (see Chapter 5 on managing reputational risk).

Example continued

Case 3

Joyful Bank, Beijing branch, sets up SWIFT and tested telex arrangements with AlnaBank in India, which are also to be utilised by Joyful Bank's New York and London branches. Joyful Bank is incorporated in the People's Republic of China.

The possibilities for CDD here, therefore, are the three different branches of Joyful Bank in Beijing, New York and London. Against which must AlnaBank conduct CDD?

The answer here (in the absence of more stringent local requirements or separate subsidiary status for each branch AlnaBank would need to check) is that Joyful Bank would constitute a single legal entity, and as such CDD need only be conducted against that entity, i.e. there would be no requirement to conduct individual due diligence against each of the overseas branches.

Case 4

AlnaBank sells corporate bonds issued by Timeless Textiles to Excel Investments Limited, an investment firm. AlnaBank purchased the bonds in the secondary market from Alpha Investments Co Limited.

AlnaBank could conduct CDD against Timeless Textiles, Excel Investments or Alpha Investments. So against whom is CDD required?

The answer in this case is that CDD must be conducted by AlnaBank against both Excel Investments and Alpha Investments, as the subsequent purchaser and initial seller, respectively, of the bonds in question. This is because there is a direct business relationship between AlnaBank and these two entities involving the receipt of funds (from Excel Investments) and assets with value (from Alpha Investments). There is no requirement for AlnaBank to conduct CDD against the initial issuer, Timeless Textiles, because there is no business relationship between the two.

Case 5

The Habibian Brandy Company in Yerevan, Armenia, is exporting brandy to Party Pubs Limited in Thailand. AlnaBank is advising a letter of credit issued by Thailand Bank on behalf of Party Pubs Limited.

CDD would be possible against The Habibian Brandy Company, against Thailand Bank and against Party Pubs Limited. Against whom should AlnaBank conduct its CDD?

The answer in this case is Thailand Bank, since according to the structure of such transactions, Thailand Bank will have instructed AlnaBank, which will be receiving funds from it. There is no customer or other business relationship between AlnaBank and either the Habibian Brandy Company or Party Pubs Limited which, although lying at the commercial heart of the transaction, are not customers of AlnaBank.

Example continued

Case 6

AlnaBank is the receiving bank on a rights issue being arranged by another bank on behalf of its client, Alpha Limited. In the opening stages of the issue, the following applications are received:

Applicant name	Amount ($)
X Limited	300,000
Y Limited	70,000
Mrs Z	9,000

CDD would be possible against all three of the above, but against whom should AlnaBank conduct it? The answer in this case would be X Limited and Y Limited, but not Mrs Z. Why? Because these are one-off transactions and if the issue were oversubscribed, AlnaBank would have to return X Limited's and Y Limited's subscription funds which in each case would be above AlnaBank's maximum threshold for conducting one-off transactions without undertaking customer due diligence (set under the FATF standards at $15,000). This, of course, would be an ideal form of money laundering.

CDD is not required in this case against Mrs Z, however, since the funds which would have to be returned to her in the event of an over-subscription would be below the relevant threshold.

In this case, no CDD would be required against Alpha Limited either, since according to the structure of such transactions, AlnaBank would have no direct business relationship with Alpha Limited as the issuer.

Note: had X Limited's and Y Limited's funds come from accounts which they held at regulated financial institutions in countries which AlnaBank deemed to have a good, strong AML regulatory framework, then it would be entitled in its policies to rely on the CDD conducted by those financial institutions (as permitted under Recommendation 17 of the FATF standards). However, AlnaBank would have to satisfy itself that copies of relevant documentation would be available immediately upon request. It should also bear in mind that, notwithstanding its operation of such 'reliance' provisions, it would still remain legally responsible for any negative outcome.

Case 7

AlnaBank is the lead manager in the syndication of a loan to Vessyan Textiles, a listed company. The other syndicate banks are Blue Bank, Green Bank and Yellow Bank.

CDD is possible against Vessyan Textiles and the syndicate banks, so against whom should it be conducted?

The correct answer is Vessyan Textiles, which is actually entering into a transactional relationship with AlnaBank. No CDD is required against the syndicate banks since, according to the structure of a syndicated transaction, they do not enter into a transactional relationship with AlnaBank.

Risk-classifying corporate clients: example methodology

Having decided against whom we need to carry out due diligence, before we can determine what level of information and verification is required, we need a practical methodology for classifying clients as either SDD, NDD or EDD. Such a system:

- should be policy-based, such that decisions made about individual relationships can be referred back to a policy document
- should be capable of being operated by the business units themselves, only requiring separate input from your AML specialists in circumstances required under the policy or in difficult or borderline cases where staff are unclear, and
- must be reasonably robust and flexible, in the sense that it covers multiple different scenarios and is responsive to business needs (whilst, of course, meeting the compliance standards which have been determined).

Corporate banking risk calculator tool

Applying the above, therefore, you need to have a methodology for calculating the appropriate CDD risk level in a relationship which is based on the principles which we have been discussing, and which utilises the country and business sector risk tools described earlier – see Table 4.6.

What the calculator does for business units, therefore, is to provide a systematised, process-driven way to arrive at a reasoned risk-assessment, *all else being equal*. This last caveat is important because other policy factors will need to be taken into consideration in arriving at the classification. These are dealt with below. It is also important to remember that such processes must be subject to human overview and the application of commonsense.

EDD factors checklist

The following example framework is robust, albeit quite simple (it is possible to construct more complex and sensitive frameworks). Under this framework, relationships are classified for business reasons in the lowest level possible for the perceived business risks which they present. The presence of one or more factors determines that some relationships *must* always be classified as EDD. These are:

- PEPs, or customers linked to PEPs (unless the PEP is a non-executive director from a low-risk jurisdiction and does not own or control 15 per cent or more of the customer)
- entities involved in gambling/casinos
- entities involved in the arms trade
- entities dealing with diamonds and other precious stones

Table 4.6 **A corporate banking risk calculator tool**

Country risk (country of incorporation or country that customer is operating in, whichever is higher)	Business type (see example business type risk)	Business age 0–1 years = High 1–5 years = Medium Over 5 years = Low	Risk category
High	High	H	EDD
		M	EDD
		L	EDD
	Medium	H	EDD
		M	NDD
		L	NDD
	Low	H	NDD
		M	NDD
		L	NDD
Medium	High	H	EDD
		M	EDD
		L	NDD
	Medium	H	NDD
		M	NDD
		L	NDD
	Low	H	NDD
		M	NDD
		L	NDD
Low	High	H	EDD
		M	NDD
		L	NDD
	Medium	H	NDD
		M	NDD
		L	NDD
	Low	H	NDD
		M	NDD
		L	NDD

- offshore trusts
- entities with complex ownership structures (e.g. three or more layers of ownership)
- entities that issue bearer shares (that is, shares of which ownership passes through physical possession of share certificates).

In other words, where any single one of the above features is present in the relationship, that relationship *must* be classified as EDD, notwithstanding the presence of multiple, other, low-risk indicators.

SDD factors checklist

Relationships which *can* be classified as SDD (unless any of the compulsory EDD features are present, or there is too great a preponderance of other high-risk features) are relationships with corporate entities that are:

- publicly quoted companies or their subsidiaries listed on a well regulated stock exchange
- companies subject to statutory licensing and industry regulation from low- or medium-risk jurisdictions
- government-owned and controlled bodies from low- or medium-risk jurisdictions.

Again, the presence of one or more of the compulsory EDD features in any of the above relationships would mandate an EDD classification.

In all other cases, according to this framework, you would use the corporate banking risk calculator, the country risk list and business sector risk tools described earlier, in order to arrive at the appropriate risk classification for customers. You would then use the relevant CDD documentation tool to designate in each case what the specific information and verification requirements were for each customer.

Matching information and verification intensity/depth to risk classification

As we saw earlier, the information-seeking and verification activity which you undertake on a relationship should become deeper and more intense as the perceived level of risk rises. The greater the risk, the deeper you need to dig.

We also looked at a range of different types of information relating both to natural persons in corporate roles (directors and officers of legal entities) and to the entities themselves, and the various methods by which such information could be verified.

The CDD documentation tool can be used in order to assign reasonable and appropriate information and verification requirements to the different risk classification categories (SDD, NDD and EDD) for corporate/wholesale banking customers.

Taking all of the above into account, you should now be able to assign a risk classification to different relationships and allocate appropriate CDD requirements to them. So here are some example cases on which to try out your CDD skills.

Case 1 – Ace Construction Limited

Ace Construction Limited is registered in your country and doing business there, specialising in so-called 'intelligent' buildings. Through a recently-won large new contract, it is also doing business in Nigeria. The company was founded six months ago by directors and shareholders (who are also the beneficial owners) David Harman and Peter Markin on the back of two initial, specialist, small office construction contracts undertaken for a Nigerian company which wants to use the technology in their new head office building. Herman Taylor, a local lawyer, holds a power of attorney and is also an authorised signatory.

What risk classification would be appropriate for this relationship and what CDD information and verification should be obtained?

The answer in this case is that this is an EDD classified relationship. From the facts, we can determine immediately that it cannot be an SDD account because it does not fulfil any of the criteria for SDD status that we outlined earlier (it isn't publicly-quoted, it isn't subject to statutory licensing and it isn't government-owned or controlled). We also know that it doesn't *have* to be EDD, because none of the features triggering mandatory EDD status are present (there are no PEP connections, the company is not involved in the gambling, armaments or diamond/precious metals trade, it is not an offshore trust, it doesn't issue bearer shares and it doesn't have a complex ownership structure, as defined). Since it cannot be SDD and need not be EDD, therefore, it *could* be either NDD or EDD and to determine this we refer to the corporate banking risk calculator. The relevant criteria for using this calculator are country risk (Nigeria = high: remember that the country risk will be the higher of the place of incorporation and place of business, if different), business sector risk (construction = medium) and business age (less than one year = high), according to which the overall classification using the calculator comes out at EDD, as shown in Figure 4.7.

In terms of the information and verification requirements, if we look at the CDD documentation tool we can see that the CDD requirements for this business in the EDD section would therefore be as follows.

Company information

- Full name
- Company number or taxpayer identification number
- Registered office

Figure 4.7

Application of risk calculator tool to Ace Construction Limited

Country risk (country of incorporation or country that customer is operating in, whichever is higher)	Business type (see example business type risk)	Business age 0–1 years = High 1–5 years = Medium Over 5 years = Low	Risk category
High	High	H	EDD
		M	EDD
		L	EDD
	Medium	H	EDD
		M	NDD
		L	NDD
	Low	H	NDD
		M	NDD
		L	NDD

- Business address (if different)
- Purpose and reason for establishing the relationship
- Expected account activity
- Names of all directors and beneficial owners owning or controlling 15 per cent or more of shares or voting rights
- Names of all authorised signatories
- Nature and details of the business
- Whether the company conducts business with sanctioned countries (Nigeria is not one, in 2011)
- Source of funds
- Copies of recent financial statements.

Verification of company information

- Certified copy of certificate of incorporation
- Certified copy of search at Companies Registry revealing identities of shareholders and directors
- Detailed investigation into the nature of Ace Construction Limited's business, the types and identities of contracts under which it has earned revenue (and the legitimacy of those contracts), i.e. source of wealth checks, corroborated by information from sources outside of, and independent from, the company.

Personal information

For each of the directors/shareholders David Harman and Peter Markin, and also for the power of attorney holder Herman Taylor, the following:

- full name
- current residential address
- date of birth
- nationality
- identity document number (passport, tax identification number)
- details of any other occupation or employment.

Verification of personal information

For each of the above individuals, sight of an original passport, driving licence or national identity card, with copies certified and retained on the file.

Case 2 – The Golden Export Company

The Golden Export Company is incorporated and registered in your low-risk country. Founded in 1989, it distributes a variety of general industrial products all over the region to low- or medium-risk countries. Its turnover last year was $10 million equivalent and it has a capital and asset base of approximately $25 million equivalent. The company provides generous funding for sports facilities in deprived local areas and desk research shows it to be well-established with a good reputation.

What risk classification would be appropriate for this relationship and what CDD information and verification should be obtained?

The answer in this case is NDD. None of the requirements triggering mandatory EDD status are present, so whilst it *could* be classified as EDD, it does not have to be. None of the factors permitting SDD status are present, so it cannot be SDD. If you look at the calculator, you can see immediately that the country risk is medium, the business type risk is low and the business age risk is low which, if you track it through, comes out at NDD (see Figure 4.8).

In terms of information and verification, again if you look at the requirements in the CDD documentation tool you can see that they are basically the same as for EDD, with the important exception that it is not necessary in this case to undertake the extensive fuller investigations into the nature of Golden Export's business and the legitimacy of its sources of wealth. It is also necessary to verify the identity of only one of its directors. (Indeed, for a company of this type – a well-established business with a good reputation and a sizeable balance sheet – some financial institutions might not require identity verification of any directors or officers at all.)

Figure 4.8

Application of risk calculator tool to the Golden Export Company

Country risk (country of incorporation or country that customer is operating in, whichever is higher)	Business type (see example business type risk)	Business age 0–1 years = High 1–5 years = Medium Over 5 years = Low	Risk category
Medium	High	H	EDD
		M	EDD
		L	NDD
	Medium	H	NDD
		M	NDD
		L	NDD
	Low	H	NDD
		M	NDD
		L	NDD

Case 3 – Aeglis Consulting Limited

Aeglis Consulting Limited (ACL) was founded in the UK in 1977 providing IT consulting services in the UK, Canada, Australia and New Zealand, primarily to government departments and public sector organisations. It was owned and run by the Merrit family until they sold the company in 2009 to Challenge Investments, a private equity group whose chairman, John Sandler, is married to a British cabinet minister, Sarah Patterson. Mr Sandler now sits on the Aeglis board. The ownership structure of the company is shown in Figure 4.9.

What risk classification would be appropriate for this relationship and what CDD information and verification requirements would apply?

The answer in this case is EDD. This is because notwithstanding the fact that the country, business type and business age risk are all low according to the corporate banking risk calculator, nevertheless the Aeglis Group is linked to a PEP (its chairman, John Sandler, is married to a UK cabinet minister) and PEP linkage is one of the triggers for automatic EDD status in the example policy framework outlined earlier. In addition, the ownership structure counts as a complex one, being four layers deep, and that is another trigger for automatic EDD status.

From a practitioner's perspective, however, there are at least a couple of features about this potential relationship which mark it out as a 'deceptor'. A deceptor is an account or relationship with many of the hallmarks of low risk, yet which is in fact high risk. The two features of particular concern here are:

Figure 4.9 **Ownership structure of Aeglis Consulting Limited (ACL)**

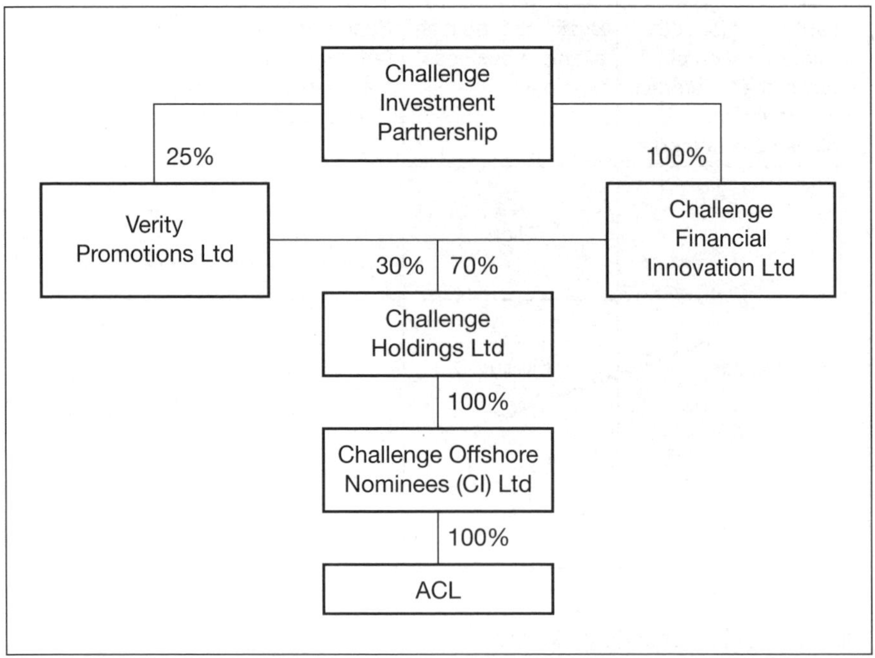

1 *A recent change in ownership*. Even a business which has been in existence for 35 years can be used for money laundering, if brand new owners decide that that is what they are going to use it for. The historic activities of the company in servicing government departments in and from low-risk countries might have become just that – historic – when the new owners took over in 2009.
2 *The ownership structure*. If you look carefully at the ownership structure you can see that the Challenge Investment Partnership does not actually own 100 per cent of ACL. Verity Promotions Limited actually owns 30 per cent of it, and Verity Promotions Limited itself is only 25 per cent owned and controlled by Challenge Investment Partnership. So who owns the remaining (majority) 75 per cent stake in Verity Promotions Limited? This would be an important question to answer since, without it, you would be taking on a relationship with an entity (ACL) with a 30 per cent beneficial owner about whom you knew nothing.

In terms of information and verification, therefore, not only would we require all the corporate and personal information and verification described in Case 1 for both ACL, the Challenge Investment Partnership and John Sandler, as well as his source of wealth, but also full details of the business activities and reputation of the Challenge Group and a CDD exercise against Verity Promotions Ltd.

Case 4 – Landisbourne Plc

Landisbourne Plc is an industrial components manufacturing group incorporated in England and registered and quoted on the London Stock Exchange. It has been in existence for more than 100 years. It has a significant export business, both to the EU and the US and to a number of developing countries including South Africa, Nigeria, Brazil and Indonesia.

What risk classification should apply to this potential relationship and what CDD information and verification should be obtained?

The answer in this case is SDD. Applying the framework outlined earlier, none of the criteria triggering mandatory EDD status are present, so the account could be either NDD or SDD. From that framework we also see, however, that SDD *can* be applied to, amongst others, publicly quoted companies or their subsidiaries on an approved regulated market. Since the London Stock Exchange is an approved, regulated market according to our regulated markets list, the relationship can therefore be classified as SDD unless the corporate banking risk calculator indicates EDD status. Checking the relationship against the calculator, you find a high-risk jurisdiction (Nigeria and Indonesia are high risk and would defeat the equivalent jurisdiction/low-risk status of the UK). But you also find a low-risk business type (manufacturer of industrial products) and a low-risk business age (over five years), so overall the level of risk comes out at NDD. EDD is not mandatory and SDD status *can* apply in this case, which means that you would arrive at an SDD classification.

In terms of CDD information and verification, reference to the CDD documentation tool reveals that for SDD no personal identification and verification of directors and officers is required. Instead, the following would be sufficient:

Corporate information

- Full name, nature and status of entity (public company)
- Company number
- Registered office in country of incorporation
- Business address
- Purpose and reason for opening the account or establishing relationship
- The expected type and level of activity to be undertaken on the relationship.

Corporate verification

- Copy of London Stock Exchange internet page showing the company as being listed
- Board resolution authorising the opening of the account and the authority of its authorised signatories.

CONSTRUCTING A CDD FRAMEWORK FOR FINANCIAL INSTITUTIONS

Despite the heavily regulated environments in which most of them operate, financial institutions are inherently risky to have as customers. This risk arises because they are not just taking care of their own business; they are taking care of other people's business as well. Like the Trojan horse, what matters about financial institutions is what's inside. A financial institution can have perfectly described AML policies, procedures and internal controls, yet if it has a high-risk customer, product and geographic profile, and a management with little regard for AML matters, cold comfort is had from this.

It is one thing to tick a series of boxes in a questionnaire, confirming that the AML policy of a financial institution business prospect includes provisions on customer identification, customer due diligence, staff training, the reporting of suspicions, etc. What is even more important is the culture and habits of the institution. For example:

- **How often are AML policy waivers applied?** Most AML policies will contain waiver provisions allowing accounts to be opened before the necessary CDD documentation has been contained; indeed the FATF standards permit this. But such waivers are only meant to operate in *exceptional* circumstances and for a *limited period*. Is that the case in the institution you are looking at? Or are waivers being given on multiple accounts on a continuous basis?
- **What is the record of senior management over-ruling Compliance?** In corporate governance terms most institutions are run by the board of directors, not the Compliance Department. When Compliance makes a recommendation, for example against opening an account, how often are they over-ruled?
- **Is there any evidence of management indifference or hostility to AML issues?** Some senior managers have been known to imply to business colleagues (but rarely in the presence of the Compliance Department) that when revenue and compliance policy conflict, revenue must always come first, if enough of it is at stake.
- **Is there evidence of a culture of secrecy?** For example, are there historic or ongoing issues relating to the management of accounts which no one is prepared to talk about?
- **Is there evidence of any recharacterisation of transactions?** One way of getting around a compliance or regulatory problem is to make something which is prohibited appear to be something else (something permitted) in the books and records of the institution. Typical examples include misrepresenting the origin of funds, the beneficial ownership of funds and the type and purpose of transactions. In problem insitutions

staff may know or suspect that there is a problem with what they are doing, but they may also take the view that it is simply 'the way things are done around here'.

- **Is there evidence of overly affluent senior management lifestyles or staff remuneration being significantly above the rest of the market?** This is a red flag for potential criminal associations in *any* business, and a financial institution is no different. Consider the following excerpt. It is based on information given to the author from an industry colleague in relation to a visit to a potential respondent bank.

> Our inspection revealed extremely poor levels of AML preparedness ... Staff had only the most basic levels of awareness. The AML policy was extremely brief and lacked detail and training appeared to be non-existent. Worryingly, no IT system existed for checking the status of proposed customers against internationally recognised lists of proscribed persons and there appeared to be no systematic monitoring of customer accounts, even relatively high-risk accounts such as non-residents, politically exposed persons and companies domiciled in offshore jurisdictions. Perhaps of most concern were the attitudes displayed by some of the senior managers with whom we spoke, who made no attempt to hide their ignorance of the new legislation and whose concerns revolved mainly around the business they believed they would lose as and when the new controls were applied.
>
> *Source*: Anonymous

Financial institutions, then, are one of the riskiest types of customers for another financial institution (e.g. your own organisation) to have. This is particularly so when the relationship between the two of you is that of respondent and correspondent (see Figure 4.10).

Correspondent/respondent banking relationship

Figure 4.10

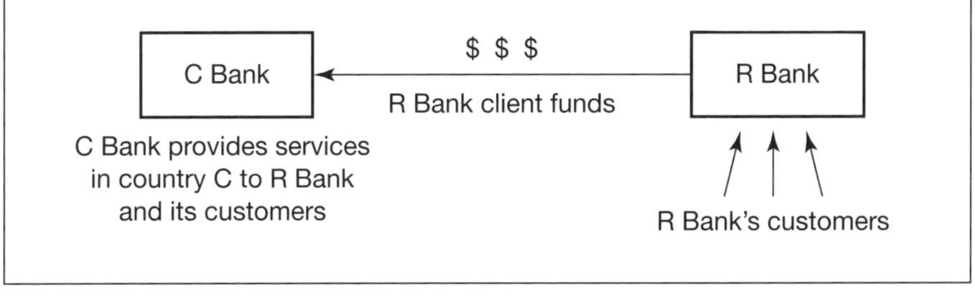

C Bank

$ $ $

R Bank

R Bank client funds

C Bank provides services in country C to R Bank and its customers

R Bank's customers

In the above correspondent banking relationship, C Bank is the correspondent providing services (e.g. clearing and payments services) to R Bank from Country R, which is the respondent bank in the relationship. R Bank is C Bank's customer and C Bank has an obligation to undertake effective due diligence against its respondent. As an industry colleague once commented memorably during an event:

> **'Health-wise, you have to remember that starting a correspondent banking relationship with a new respondent bank is a bit like starting a serious relationship with someone; if they're sleeping around without your knowledge, then you could be in big trouble'**

It's a situation, therefore, in which you really want to know as much as you can about your new client and the example policy framework which follows is designed to help you achieve that.

Example CCD policy framework for financial institutions

As was the case for the non-financial corporates just discussed, the task is to create a practical, robust system for the risk assessment of financial institution clients which can be implemented by business units directly, only seeking additional guidance in borderline cases or where certain aspects are uncertain.

The default position – EDD

Reflecting the significant areas of risk associated with financial institutions, the example framework described here is one in which the default position for a new financial institution client is a risk assessment classification of EDD. In other words, *all* financial institution clients will start out as EDD and can only achieve a lower risk classification through the elimination of certain key risk criteria to be described. The more of these criteria which are eliminated, the lower the level of risk classification until one arrives at SDD status, indicative of the lowest levels of risk.

Unacceptable relationships

As with all other customer types, however, the starting point for financial institution customers is unacceptable relationships. Here in our example policy we cite the following blockers, the presence of any of which will prevent the acceptance of the client (i.e. no risk assessment takes place because the client is simply rejected):

- shell banks
- unlicensed banks
- unregulated money service bureaux

- entities and individuals subject to UN sanctions
- where connections with money laundering or terrorist financing are suspected
- financial institutions that maintain accounts for customers which are anonymous or which are in obviously fictitious names
- financial institutions that issue bearer shares.

Mandatory EDD status

Under this example framework the presence of any of the following will mandate an EDD risk classification for the financial institution in question:

- There is to be a correspondent relationship with the financial institution (FI):
  - that is a 'downstream correspondent clearer' (i.e. it provides correspondent bank services itself to other financial institutions further down the chain), or
  - whose own customers will have direct access to its account with your bank, or
  - that is a private bank and conducts private banking as its only business. *OR*
- the FI is from a high-risk jurisdiction; or
- the FI is a money service bureau, or
- the FI is owned and controlled by a PEP.

If none of the above mandatory EDD factors apply, then in this example framework there are two situations in which an NDD rating is possible, as follows.

Potential NDD status

Situation 1 – No correspondent relationship

- Where there is to be no correspondent/respondent relationship between your institution and the FI under consideration, and
- the FI is regulated in a low- or medium-risk jurisdiction.

Situation 2 – Limited correspondent relationship

- Whilst there is intended to be a correspondent/respondent relationship between your institution and the FI under consideration, nevertheless none of the features triggering EDD status above, are present, and
- the FI is regulated in an equivalent jurisdiction.

Potential SDD status

Following on from the above, under this example framework business units are able to apply an SDD risk classification to a proposed relationship with a financial institution *only* if:

- there is to be no correspondent/respondent relationship between the financial institution and your bank, and
- the financial institution is regulated in an equivalent jurisdiction.

It will of course be possible to manipulate the above framework either to increase or reduce the risk appetite. For example, additional categories could be added to either or both of the prohibited and/or mandatory EDD lists or NDD could be permitted only in low-risk jurisdictions.

The important thing is that those responsible for CDD in business units are not left making individual, personalised judgements about different prospective accounts according to their own personal perceptions. Individual judgement is, of course, important – but only after an ordered analysis according to established, enterprise-wide principles.

Example cases

As we did earlier for non-financial corporates, let us now test-drive this example policy framework with some case studies. As before, your task is to use the policy principles above in conjunction with the tools in order to arrive at a risk classification, and CDD documentation and verification requirements for each case.

Case 1 – Ocean Bank

Ocean Bank wants to use your bank as its correspondent in your country. Ocean Bank is incorporated, registered and regulated in the Republic of Bissan (a made-up country). It is not a money service bureau, it conducts only wholesale corporate business and the largest shareholder is a UK pension fund with 12 per cent. It has no financial institution clients and its own customers will not have access to its accounts with you.

What risk classification is appropriate and what CDD information and verification requirements would apply?

The answer in this case is EDD. If you check the country risk tool you will see that the Republic of Bissan is classified as a high-risk jurisdiction and regardless of anything else, the incorporation of a potential FI client in a high-risk jurisdiction makes an EDD risk classification mandatory under the example policy framework which we are applying here.

In terms of CDD information and verification, you would look to your CDD documentation tool for financial institutions (EDD section) in order to obtain this. The typical types of requirements would be the following:

Corporate information

- Full name
- Registered number
- Registered office
- Business address
- Purpose and reason for opening account
- Nature of the financial institution's business
- Ownership details
- Assessment of AML controls
- Reputation and quality of supervision as well as details of ownership and executive management.

Corporate verification

- Either a copy of the internet page published by Ocean Bank's regulator, confirming its regulated status, or
- a certified copy of its licence.

No personal identification and verification would be required, given Ocean Bank's regulated status. However, significant due diligence would have to be undertaken concerning Ocean Bank's AML policies and controls, as well as its reputation and underlying business, its ownership structure and any natural persons with significant beneficial ownership or control, along with the names and reputations of its senior executive management.

In this regard, an important additional tool would be a questionnaire designed to elicit information regarding Ocean Bank's AML controls. Table 4.7 is an example of such a questionnaire, based on the questionnaire designed by the Wolfsberg Group

Case 2 – Haptan (TCI) Bank

Haptan (TCI) Bank, incorporated, registered and regulated in the Turks & Caicos Islands, wishes to open correspondent accounts with your bank. Haptan (TCI) Bank is a wholly-owned subsidiary of Haptan Bank, which is incorporated, registered and regulated in Bulgaria. Haptan (TCI) does not conduct private banking business, will not be allowing customers direct access to its accounts with your bank and will not have any financial institution clients of its own.

What risk classification would be appropriate and what CDD information and verification requirements would apply?

The answer in this case is NDD, but with a caveat. None of the criteria for mandatory EDD status is present, so Haptan (TCI) does not have to be classified as EDD. It cannot be classified as SDD because there will be

Table 4.7 **AML and CFT due diligence checklist for financial institutions**

Country:	
Client Name:	
Issue	Findings
	NB: Include reference to facts and/ or examples to corroborate your conclusions. Where relevant, the supporting documentation should be retained in the project files.
A. National Anti-Money Laundering and Counter-Terrorist Financing (AML/CFT) Laws and Regulations.	
1 Does the country have national AML/ CFT regulations? Do they comply with the recognised international standards (e.g. FATF Recommendations)? Are there secrecy or confidentiality laws that inhibit AML measures?	
2 What evidence do you have that national regulations as regards AML/CFT measures are properly implemented, and effective supervision is carried out?	
Client' Policies and Procedures: Does the financial institution …	
1 Know and comply with the letter and spirit of national AML/CFT regulations? What examples can you provide?	
2 Cooperate with the relevant authorities?	
Board Policies: Does the financial institution …	
1 Have specific anti-money laundering and counter-terrorist financing policies that have been approved by the board, supervisory board or equivalent?	
2 Have a committee of the board, supervisory board or equivalent, with responsibility for the institution's AML/ CFT policies and oversight (such as compliance or an audit committee)?	

AML/CFT compliance and internal controls: Does the financial institution ...	
1 Have specific AML/CFT procedures and internal controls? (A copy of the financial institution's policies and procedures should be retained in the project files.)	
2 Have a designated AML reporting officer? And to whom does the AML officer report internally?	
3 Produce an annual board report (prepared by the AML, reporting officer) on AML/CFT activities, results and conclusions (i.e. monitor compliance)? (A copy of the most recent reports should be retained in the project files.)	
4 Have an adequate programme for AML/CFT training and awareness raising among management and staff?	
5 Have procedures including an audit or internal control function testing the effectiveness of AML/CFT measures?	
Know your customer (KYC): Does the financial institution ...	
1 Have written KYC procedures and require reliable evidence of identity for all types of accounts, products and custody arrangements? In particular, do the procedures properly require:	
(a) Identification of the ultimate beneficial ownership of any customer?	
(b) Additional due diligence as regards high-risk counterparties (e.g. PEP trusts or other similar corporate vehicles that could be potentially misused to conceal the source of funds and their ownership, etc.)?	
(c) Assurance that correspondent banks have proper AM/CFT policies?	

(d) Effective application of KYC procedures to CFT measures, including checks against lists updated according to the resolutions of the United Nations Security Council and other competent authorities?	
(e) Understanding the nature of the business relationship (including adequate measures to prevent dealing with shell banks) and conducting ongoing due diligence as necessary?	
2 Allow third parties to do their customer due diligence for them or rely on due diligence performed by other financial institutions, and if so, in what circumstances?	
3 Conduct private banking as a sole business?	
4 Act as a downstream correspondent clearer?	
5 Provide services for shell banks?	
6 Maintain accounts for (a) prohibited or (b) designated high-risk client types, according to the Bank's procedures?	
Suspicious activities reporting and record keeping: Does the financial institution …	
1 Have reliable procedures for recognition and reporting of suspicious transactions?	
2 Have an adequate management information system to facilitate the identification and reporting of suspicious transactions?	
3 Have appropriate levels of suspicious transaction reporting in each of the past three years?	
4 Have adequate record keeping, providing an audit trail for suspicious transactions? (Note: you should review a sample of transactions as part of your due diligence.)	

Monitoring and review procedures: Does the financial institution ...	
1 Have a recently prepared independent review of AML/CFT policies and procedures?	
2 Have procedures to monitor AML/ CFT practices in foreign branches and subsidiaries, to ensure that the described policies and procedures are properly followed?	
Other issues	
1 Is there any evidence of a culture of secrecy?	
2 Is there any evidence of management indifference to money laundering risk?	
3 Is there any evidence of the client recharacterising the origin or purpose of funds being transferred?	
4 Is there any evidence of lack of knowledge of customers?	
5 Is staff remuneration in line with the local market?	
6 What improvements can/should be instituted?	
7 Is any further investigation required?	
Overall comments:	

a correspondent banking relationship if the account is accepted. Looking at the two situations for NDD, you can see that one of them applies, i.e. where the proposed correspondent/respondent banking relationship would not involve downstream correspondent clearing (Haptan (TCI) Bank has no financial institution clients) or access by Haptan (TCI)'s own customers to its account with your bank. Haptan (TCI) Bank is also regulated in Bulgaria which is an equivalent jurisdiction, being a member of the EU. The account would be eligible, therefore, for NDD status.

But should it be thus classified? If you look again at the fact pattern you can see that there are in fact several indicators of higher risk. If the animals of George Orwell's *Animal Farm* believed that 'all animals are equal, but some are more equal than others', then we, too, might note that, whilst in political terms all equivalent jurisdictions are equivalent, nevertheless for AML purposes, some are more equivalent than others. Notwithstanding the huge strides made by many EU accession states in bringing their AML laws into line with the standards required by EU membership (Bulgaria included), financial institutions are still entitled to draw their own conclusions and many would take the view that a risk premium should apply in the case of some accession states, as they continue their fight against organised crime and political corruption. The area of south-east Europe (the Balkans) of which Bulgaria forms a part has, in recent decades, developed an unwanted reputation for its associations with corruption and organised crime, particularly people trafficking for the sex trade, and the Turks & Caicos Islands are medium-risk rather than low-risk in the example country risk tool, as well as being an offshore jurisdiction. So you might want seriously to consider EDD status.

In terms of CDD documentation and verification, therefore, the same requirements would apply as in Case 1 above, with the exception that evidence of the majority ownership by Haptan (TCI) Bank would have to be obtained. It would also not be necessary to dig as deeply into the business, ownership and executive management, unless you decide that the higher risk factors above warrant an EDD rating.

Cases such as this prove the importance of standing back at the end of a standard process and actually *thinking* about the risks, rather than just applying a 'tick-box' approach and going with whatever result comes out. Ask yourself, despite the fact that the policy framework would permit you to accept the client on this basis, would you really be comfortable doing so?

Case 3 – Blossom Bank of Tokyo

Your bank is setting up bilateral, tested, telex arrangements with Blossom Bank of Tokyo, established, registered and regulated in Japan. Blossom Bank is not a money service bureau and does not have PEP ownership or control.

What risk classification would be appropriate and what CDD information and verification requirements would apply?

The answer in this case is SDD for financial institutions. None of the criteria for mandatory EDD status are present, the relationship is not to be one of correspondent/respondent and a look at the country risk tool reveals that Japan is an equivalent jurisdiction. So SDD is possible, and an overall look at the fact patterns does not reveal any other less obvious high-risk indicators, which means that an SDD risk classification would appear to be appropriate.

The CDD documentation requirement here would probably be: full name, registered number, registered office in Japan, business address and the purpose and reason for opening the account (although this seems pretty clear from the description provided). Verification would simply be to establish the regulated status of Blossom Bank in Japan by a recognised method (e.g. a printout from the relevant page of the Central Bank of Japan referring to Blossom Bank as a regulated entity). Note that with SDD there is no requirement to investigate the AML controls of the financial institution nor its business, underlying activities, customer base or ownership.

CONSTRUCTING A CDD FRAMEWORK FOR RETAIL/CONSUMER BANKING BUSINESS

In most institutions retail/consumer banking will constitute the business area in which the greatest volume of accounts are being analysed and opened. Potential customers include not only private individuals and family members, but also, in many institutions, small-to-medium enterprises (SMEs) which in some institutions may be managed by the consumer/retail business if they fall below certain corporate banking thresholds.

The purpose of this section is not to suggest how to deal with all possible combinations of eventuality. Rather, it is to get you thinking about how you can construct policy frameworks which allow business units to implement the risk-based approach in practice by utilising relevant criteria such as country risk, product risk and customer type risk.

Example retail/consumer risk assessment framework

Prohibited relationships and screening

As with all other types of business our retail/consumer risk assessment framework must begin with the need to screen all applicants against the institution's alert list of proscribed entities. There will then be those categories of relationship which it is your policy not to do business with. We shall assume for these purposes that the list of unacceptable relationships is the same as for the corporate side of the business, i.e. shell banks, unlicensed banks and unregulated money service bureaux, customers subject to UN sanctions or where money laundering or terrorist financing are suspected, and anonymous accounts or accounts in obviously fictitious names.

CDD risk classification principles

Generally, simplified due diligence is not appropriate for individuals and is not therefore permitted. Therefore, the risk classification categories that we are dealing with are EDD for the higher-risk accounts and NDD for lower-risk accounts.

Mandatory EDD status

As with corporate banking business, in this consumer/retail framework the following would trigger mandatory EDD status:

- all accounts linked to PEPs (except where the PEP is a government appointee in a state-owned company *and* is not a significant beneficial owner in that entity)
- money service businesses
- gambling and casino entities
- entities issuing bearer shares
- complex structures of four or more layers of ownership.

Determining the difference between EDD and NDD

If a retail/consumer relationship does not need to be classified as EDD, then you must determine whether it *should* be EDD or whether it *can*, in fact, be NDD. In this framework we take a modified approach and the relevant factors for making that decision are as follows:

- Product type – i.e. whether it is a liability product such as a deposit product (typically indicative of higher risk) or an asset product, such as a loan product (typically – though not always, as we shall see – indicative of lower risk).
- Geography – whether the relationship will entail the opening of a non-resident account from a high-risk country.
- The amount of the opening deposit – deposits above a certain threshold would indicate higher levels of risk, below that threshold would indicate lower levels of risk.

Figure 4.11 suggests a practical framework in which such criteria could be made to work. It contains a series of questions relating to the key criteria, the answers to which determine whether or not a prospective relationship is classified as either EDD or NDD. Answers indicative of lower-risk levels point the decision towards NDD, and vice versa for EDD.

So as long as the customer is not a PEP or linked to a PEP (something which triggers automatic EDD status) then if the proposed product is an asset (loan) product, the classification can be NDD.

In the case of liability (deposit) products, if the customer is from a high-risk country, opening a non-resident account, then again the status will be EDD. Even if the account is a domestic account or a non-resident account from a medium or low-risk country, then the account will still be assessed as EDD if the amount of the initial deposit exceeds $100,000.

If the customer is opening a domestic account, or is based in a medium or low-risk country and opening a non-resident account from there, *and* the amount of the initial deposit is less than $100,000, then the account may be rated as NDD. Remember that an SDD rating is not permissible for individuals.

Example retail banking risk assessment framework **Figure 4.11**

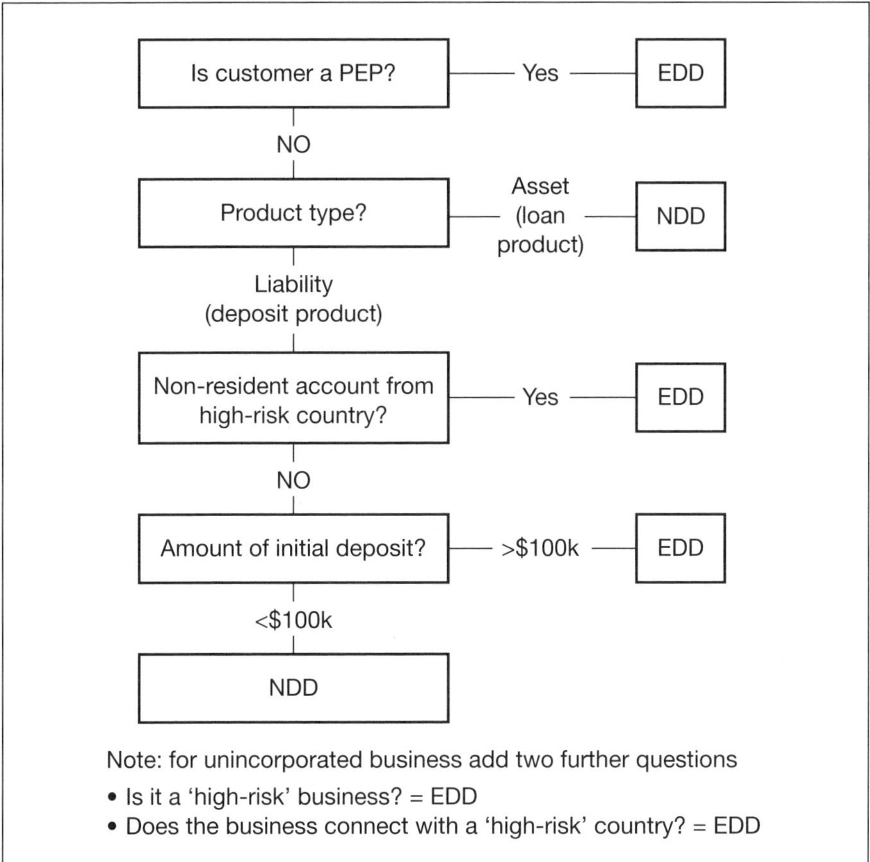

Under this example framework there are two further risk assessment considerations for unincorporated businesses (such as, for example, where a private individual or individuals are opening an account for a trading business that they run). If the business type is high risk (according to the business type risk tool) or if it is connected with a high-risk country (according to the country risk tool) then it must be rated as EDD.

Let's now put this example framework into practice with some case studies.

Case 1 – Sophie Marceau

Sophie Marceau has been posted to your country and wishes to open current and savings accounts with your bank. She presents herself in person at the main branch. She is a French national and will be resident in your country. The initial deposits on her account will be $20,000 or equivalent. She is a senior diplomat at the French Embassy in your country and is noted on your institution's alert list as such.

What risk classification would be appropriate and what CDD information and verification requirements would apply?

The answer in this case is EDD. This is because the prospective customer's PEP status triggers automatic EDD status under the example risk framework. As such, the CDD information required according to any CDD documentation list would probably be along the following lines:

- full name
- current residential address
- date of birth
- nationality
- identity document number
- nature and details of her employment
- the purpose and reason for her wishing to open the relationship
- the source of funds
- the anticipated level and type of activity on the account
- corroboration of her source of wealth.

In terms of verification, her identity would need to be verified either through an official document such as her passport, national identity card or driver's licence, with certified copies retained on the file.

Case 2 – Mr and Mrs John Vangora

Mr John Vangora wishes to open a joint current account with your bank. He is an electrician and his wife, Maria, works in a shop as a supervisor. They are local residents who plan to deposit $11,000 initially as well as taking out a home improvement loan for $7,000 to be repaid over five years.

What risk classification would be appropriate and what CDD information and verification requirements would apply?

The answer in this case is NDD. None of the triggers for mandatory EDD status are present (they are neither PEPs nor operating any high-risk businesses, they are not non-residents from high-risk countries and the proposed amount of their deposit is well below the $100,000 threshold). Nothing else about the case indicates higher levels of risk so an NDD classification is both correct and appropriate.

In terms of CDD information and verification, the requirements according to the CDD documentation tool would be as for the applicant in the previous case, except without the requirement to investigate and corroborate their sources of wealth. An important point to note is that since the account would be a joint account, identification and verification would need to take place for both Mr and Mrs Vangora. Any document verifying their address would need to be addressed to both of them, or separate documents would be required for each.

Case 3 – John Fantwe

John Fantwe is a financial consultant resident in Abuja, Nigeria. He travels to your country on a frequent basis for business purposes and wishes to open both a current account and to obtain credit card facilities. He indicates that because he anticipates having heavy expenditure requirements in the few months following the opening of his account, he will fund it initially with $180,000 coming from his bank in Nigeria.

What risk classification would be appropriate and what CDD information and verification requirements would apply?

The answer in this case is EDD. Applying the customer profile against both the policy requirements for mandatory EDD status and the flowchart in Figure 4.11, you can see that two features necessitate EDD status. First, the fact that Mr Fantwe is a resident of a high-risk jurisdiction (Nigeria) opening a non-resident account, and secondly, the amount of the initial deposit, which exceeds the $100,000 threshold stated in the flowchart.

The CDD information and verification requirements, therefore, would be as for the first case involving the PEP, Sophie Marceau. It would be important to determine exactly what type of financial consultant Mr Fantwe was and, in particular, whether any of his clients were PEPs or other high-risk individuals in his own country. Financial consultants and other types of agents and financial representatives acting as facilitators and middle-men for the movement and placement of funds obtained through corruption and state theft, for example, is a known route for money laundering and you would therefore have to be pretty certain about every aspect of Mr Fantwe's business before the account could be opened, even with its EDD status. This level of research would not be easy, but if you were unable to obtain satisfactory answers you could not open the account. In this regard you would deploy the source of wealth questionnaire tool shown earlier in this chapter.

CONSTRUCTING A CDD FRAMEWORK FOR PRIVATE BANKING

For the reasons discussed in the previous chapter, private banking and wealth management business entails money laundering risks which are higher than those for regular consumer and retail banking. Accordingly, use of a standard retail/consumer risk assessment framework will often be inappropriate. The framework for private banking needs to be more detailed and to contemplate a greater range of account activity.

Example private bank risk assessment framework

Prohibited relationships

- Shell banks, unlicensed banks and unregulated money service businesses
- Companies issuing bearer shares
- Wealth derived from prohibited business
- Subject to international sanctions or on a list of prohibited individuals/entities
- Convictions for specific criminal charges and/or activities inconsistent with your institution's policies and values
- Anonymous or numbered accounts
- Direct access to any concentration accounts (basically an account that commingles funds from multiple different beneficial owners).

For all other relationships

In this example framework you again see a prohibited client list leading to automatic account refusal and a list of features leading to automatic EDD status. However, in comparison to the retail/consumer framework, the simple asset product vs liability product combined with initial deposit amount methodology is replaced with a product risk methodology based on cash transactions and cross-border wire transfers, combined with a country risk vs customer business type risk matrix similar to that used in the corporate risk assessment framework.

In particular, this framework does not envisage automatic NDD status for loan accounts, but rather looks at the volume of activity on accounts (in and out) via either cash or overseas wire transfer payments.

In addition, there is an expanded list of prohibited relationships which now includes both 'convictions for specific criminal charges and/or activities inconsistent with our policies and values' and direct access to concentration accounts. This is an appropriate expansion, given what we know about the types of personalities who often use private banking services and the notorious misuse of some private banking secrecy products (such as concentration accounts) in reported cases.

As before, we can try out this example framework with some examples.

Case 1 – Wolfgang Hamann

Wolfgang Hamann is a German expatriate living in your country. His significant wealth derives from his family's business in the retail sale of pharmaceutical and medical products mainly in the EU, but also in China. Hamann International GMBH has been publicly quoted on the Frankfurt Stock Exchange since 1998 but Mr Hamann is still a significant shareholder

Example risk assessment framework for private banking/wealth management **Figure 4.12**

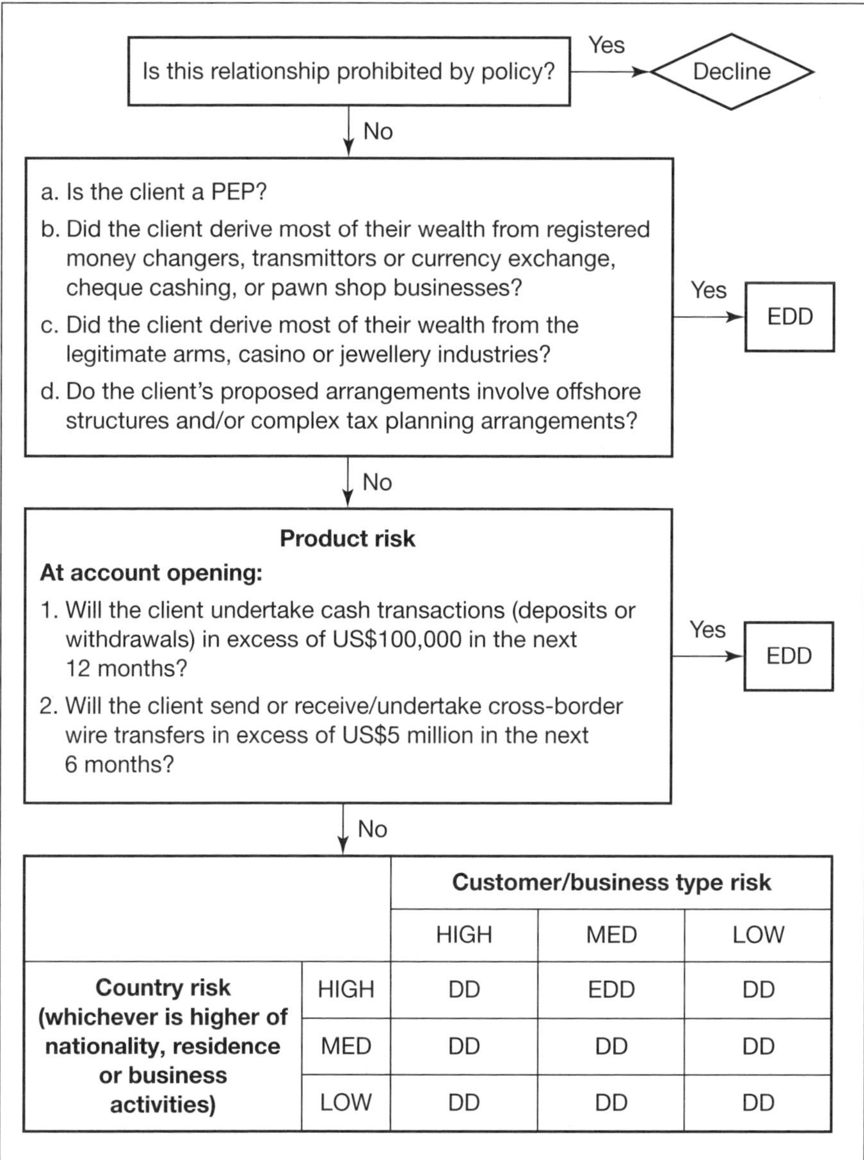

		Customer/business type risk		
		HIGH	MED	LOW
Country risk (whichever is higher of nationality, residence or business activities)	HIGH	DD	EDD	DD
	MED	DD	DD	DD
	LOW	DD	DD	DD

in the company and sits on its advisory board. He is interested in deploying some of his capital towards high-risk investments and to that end he is going to make $3.75 million available through an investment account, with instructions to focus on China. Internet searches reveal no allegations of criminality or nefarious activities.

What risk classification would be appropriate and what CDD information and verification requirements would apply?

The answer in this case is NDD. Running it through the example risk assessment framework above, none of the criteria for automatic prohibition are present. Hamann is not a PEP, nor is his wealth derived from automatic EDD businesses (in fact the retail sale of pharmaceutical and medical products is a medium-risk business according to the business type risk tool shown earlier). His wealth is not derived from the arms, casino or jewellery industries and we are not told of any offshore structures or complex tax planning arrangements. In terms of product risk, there are to be no cash deposits or withdrawals, or overseas wire transfers (whether into or out from the account) in excess of the EDD threshold limits stated in the framework.

Looking, finally, at the country risk vs customer/business type risk matrix, you have a country risk rating of medium (remember, the higher of country of residence, nationality or business will prevail, and China is stated in the country risk tool to be medium risk) and the business type risk is medium risk. That comes out at NDD in the matrix. There appear to be no other significant factors at play and therefore an NDD rating would appear to be appropriate.

In terms of information and verification, a CDD documentation tool for personal accounts would dictate information and verification requirments along the following lines:

Information

- Full name
- Current residential address
- Date of birth
- Nationality

Figure 4.13 **Application of risk calculator tool to Wolfgang Hamann**

		Customer/business type risk		
		HIGH	MED	LOW
Country risk (whichever is higher of nationality, residence or investment activities)	HIGH	EDD	EDD	NDD
	MED	EDD	NDD	NDD
	LOW	NDD	NDD	NDD

- National identification number/tax identification number
- Nature and details of business/occupation
- Source of funds for account opening
- Purpose and reasons for establishing the relationship
- The anticipated account activity.

Verification

- Passport viewed and copy taken
- Supporting document such as a utility bill showing the address
- Evidence of his connection with Hamann International GMBH (e.g. Company annual report).

Case 2 – Yuri Dimitrov

Yuri Dimitrov is the Russian owner of a former state-owned oil company V-Oil. Prior to his acquisition of V-Oil in 1992, Dimitrov's business interests lay in the hotel and leisure industry (specialising in casino resorts), with successful resorts on the Black Sea coast. He was already a multimillionaire at that point, but this was as nothing compared to the wealth generated after the privatisation of V-Oil and his acquisition of a controlling stake in it. He wishes to open dollar and euro accounts with your bank at its branch in Switzerland with an initial transfer of $10 million. He has no private residence in your country and has approached your private bank on the basis of a personal recommendation from one of his business partners.

What risk classification would be appropriate and what CDD information and verification requirements would apply?

At the level of the central nervous system this case is so obviously EDD as to perhaps make further analysis unnecessary ('gut reaction' is, after all, important). Nevertheless, we are in the business of analysing risk, not merely responding to personal instincts, so let us apply the example framework to the case and establish on what grounds this is an EDD situation.

Putting the facts through the flowchart, you can see immediately that since a substantial portion of Mr Dimitrov's wealth has come from the casino business, then for that reason alone the account would have to be classified as EDD. Even if it were not, the existence of dollar and euro cross-border wire transfer activity in excess of $5 million within a six-month period would necessitate an EDD risk classification. Even if that were not so, then an application of the country risk vs customer/business type risk matrix of 'high risk' and 'high risk', respectively, would yield an EDD classification.

On these types of cases, however, with these types of potential clients, one also has to look carefully at the reputational risks involved. In particular, the first question in the policy framework relates to whether or not the prospective client is of a prohibited client type. One of the prohibited client types is a person with a conviction for criminal offences and/or a person who is engaged in activities inconsistent with organisational policies and values. We know that the business environment in his country, Russia, during the early 1990s was extremely volatile, with business practices (particularly those associated with the privatisation of state-owned industries) that were aggressive, controversial and possibly illegal. We don't know from the facts as stated whether or not any of this applies to Mr Dimitrov, but we would definitely need to find out. Accordingly, this is one of those instances where the real question for many organisations would not be what risk classification to give to the potential client, but rather whether or not the client should be accepted for a business relationship at all (see Chapter 5 for more information on this).

If you do decide to take Mr Dimitrov on as a client, then the CDD information and verification requirements would be extensive. You would require not only all the NDD information listed in the previous case, but also much more extensive background checks as well as detailed source of wealth information.

5

Reputational Risk

Where you see the **WWW** *icon in this chapter, this indicates a preview link to the author's website and to a training film which is relevant to the AML CFT issue being discussed.*
Go to ***www.antimoneylaunderingvideos.com***

MANAGING REPUTATIONAL RISK

As we noted at the beginning of the book, money laundering and terrorist financing risks to organisations aren't just confined to the possibility that your organisation is actually used by criminals and terrorists to launder money and finance terrorist acts. There is a significant risk to the reputation of your organisation if you are found to have fallen short of the standards which are required of you, and this takes the form of financial penalties, public censure by regulatory authorities and of course negative media coverage.

The UK's Financial Services Authority defines reputational risk as:

> **'the risk that the firm may be exposed to negative publicity about its business practices or internal controls, which could have an impact on the liquidity or capital of the firm or cause a change in its credit rating.'**

The US Federal Reserve defines it thus:

> **'reputational risk is the potential loss that negative publicity regarding an institution's business practices, whether true or not, will cause a decline in the customer base, costly litigation or revenue reductions (financial loss).'**

Clearly, then, reputational risk involves a potentially uncomfortable meeting point between what you do as an organisation on the one hand, and how people judge what you have done on the other. The way you run your business, the actions you take, the risks you assume, the policies you implement (or don't implement, as the case may be), and the values which you espouse (or say you espouse) must pass the test of third party opinion, be it shareholders, customers, governments and regulators, politicians, NGOs and pressure groups, your fellow industry players and counterparties, the media, members of the public and – let's not forget this – anyone in possession of a blog, a Facebook page or a Twitter account. In a world of globalised markets, volatile share prices and instant communication, what people think about you and what they are saying about you matters as much as almost anything else you can think of. And when it comes to your dealings with (suspected) criminals, money launderers, terrorists and proliferators of weapons of mass destruction, it's not hard to see how the sensitivities can become extreme.

One of the things the organisation you work for is almost certainly trying to do is to demonstrate to the world that it is an organisation of integrity, that it is an organisation which they can trust. Failing regulatory tests and engaging in associations with those of a dark reputation are not ways to achieve such an objective.

It's crucial to note here an important distinction, however, which can sometimes be lost in the scramble to reduce reputational risk. Integrity and reputation are *not* the same thing. With professional management of an issue, it's possible to have an excellent reputation whilst actually being an organisation or a person of very little integrity. This is significant in two respects. First, if your organisation is caught out managing its reputation in this way – enjoying the financial benefits of selective lapses whilst milking its overall compliance for all it is worth – then the consequences are likely to be much worse. Secondly, and equally importantly, it must be remembered that customers, too, are aware of the benefits of reputation management and will often employ sophisticated techniques to bamboozle relationship managers and risk functions into thinking that they are a certain type of person when in fact they are the very opposite.

Ideally, therefore, in order to manage reputational risk effectively your organisation requires not only effective policies and controls combined with a genuine determination to apply them at all times (even when there are negative financial consequences to doing so), but also the capability to detect reputation management in applicants for business, and to respond appropriately through effective due diligence.

WHEN BANKS GO WRONG: CASES OF PUNISHMENTS AND PENALTIES

To demonstrate the wide range of areas in which financial institutions have been criticised and sanctioned for failing to meet recognised AML standards, below are brief examples of some major instances in recent years.

Bank of Ireland (BOI)

Example

These events at the Bank of Ireland in the UK occurred between 1998 and 2002, by which time there was already a heavy emphasis on AML standards in OECD countries. The regulatory requirements enforced in the UK at the time required that banks should operate 'such procedures of internal control and communication as may be appropriate for the purposes of forestalling and preventing money laundering', and that they should adopt 'reasonable care in countering financial crime'. They also stressed that special care was necessary for high-risk products and cash, and that a complete audit trail of beneficial ownership was essential. During the period in question the BOI operated a 'drafts outstanding account' in which a customer was allowed to deposit cash in exchange for BOI bank drafts (instruments drawn on the bank itself without reference to any underlining customer account), made payable to the BOI itself, which could then be deposited at other BOI branches in exchange for cash.

In fining BOI £375,000, the regulator, the Financial Services Authority (FSA) noted that by issuing drafts to itself, BOI broke its own internal controls in relation to the issuing of drafts and that the use of drafts was outside the customers' normal business activity. The FSA also noted that cash did not actually pass through the customers' accounts and was not, therefore, auditable. It found that staff understanding was incomplete and untested and extended only as far as the account opening process and the need for identification. For four years neither line management, peer review, nor audit identified the suspicious transactions despite 'cash for drafts' being identified as a potentially suspicious transaction type since 1994, in the bank's own policy manual.

Source: Information drawn from http://www.fsa.gov.uk/pubs/final/boi_3laug04.pdf

---

Example

Royal Bank of Scotland (RBS); Bank of Scotland (BOS)

These events occurred one after the other in 2002 and 2004 and both related to failings by the institutions concerned to retain proper records, particularly identification records.

In both cases the key regulatory requirement was that banks 'must take reasonable steps to find out who their clients are by obtaining sufficient evidence of the identity of any client' and 'to retain copies of identity evidence and records of where that evidence is kept'. Record-keeping standards also required maintaining account opening records for five years following the closure of the account and transaction records for five years following the transaction. In the case of RBS, the regulator's (FSA) inspection revealed that in 89 of 181 accounts sampled, there were insufficient identity documents, including a failure to retain copies of any details at all on some files. In the case of BOS, the FSA found a failure rate of 55 per cent across sampled accounts, with a particular concern being on the bank's apparent inability to identify at which point of the document process the deficiencies had occurred.

It is notable that both banks reported the deficiencies to the regulator having discovered them themselves, yet this was not sufficient to escape censure and punishment. It is also worth noting that the costs of remediation in both banks, amounting to millions of pounds, have vastly outweighed the predicted costs of implementing and enforcing proper procedures in the first place.

Source: Information drawn from http://www.fsa.gov.uk/pubs/final/rbs_12dec02.pdf and http://www.fsa.gov.uk/pubs/final/bos_12jan04.pdf

Raiffeisen Bank

Example

Raiffeisen Bank's (RZB) London branch operated in a regulatory environment which required that banks 'must set up and operate arrangements including the appointment of a Compliance Officer, to ensure that it is able to comply and does comply with the rules'. Those rules were wide ranging, covering the areas described already, and others. The regulator (FSA) visited RZB's London branch in September 2002 and discovered that the bank's anti-money laundering procedures had not been updated since June 1999. This was despite the fact that there had been major regulatory changes in the interim period, particularly dealing with recommended identification procedures. The regulator warned the bank that an inspection would take place later in that year, and that particular areas of concern were higher-risk areas such as agents, overseas corporations and trusts, non-European Union financial institutions and customers from Non-cooperative Countries and Territories (NCCT), third-party payments and non-face-to-face customers. In terms of identification records there was a failure rate of more than 50 per cent on sampled accounts. The inspections revealed the problems which RZB had had in retaining an effective Compliance Officer. A Compliance Officer had resigned in October 2001; a new one had resigned in July of 2002 and a third one, appointed in August 2002, had then not revised the bank's procedures in time for the inspection.

Source: http://www.fsa.gov.uk/pubs/final/r20_5april04.pdf

Abbey National

Example

Now part of the Banco Santander Group, Abbey National was one of Britain's largest mortgage lenders. The regulations in force required banks to take reasonable steps 'to ensure that any internal report of potentially suspicious activity was considered by the Compliance Officer' and, further, that if the Compliance Officer suspected money laundering, then they should report that promptly to the Financial Intelligence Unit (FIU). The regulations also require 'reasonable care in countering financial crime'. Abbey National had introduced a 'self-certification' process for Know Your Customer (KYC) measures in November of 2000. This included a capability for branches to self-certify their retention of identification records. In March 2003 an internal audit revealed failure rates on samples of 32 per cent in the identification documentation of new customers. The regulator (FSA) found that Abbey's failings were indicative of 'wider systems and controls failings across the group over a prolonged period of time'. Furthermore, there were serious shortcomings in the effectiveness of suspicious activity reporting. Some 58 per cent of reports were sent to the FIU more than 30 days after the internal reports had been filed with the compliance department. Of those, 37.6 per cent were sent up to 90 days after the initial report, and 8.4 per cent were actually sent up to 120 days after the internal report, with a further 12 per cent being sent more than 120 days after the initial internal report had been filed. This example proves the clear importance of having systems and procedures in place which facilitated the speedy processing and reporting of suspicious activity.

Source: http://www.fsa.gov.uk/pubs/final/abbey-nat_9dec03.pdf

Example

ABN AMRO

ABN AMRO fell foul of the US AML regulatory system, which required that banks must have a programme 'reasonably designed to assure and monitor compliance'. ABN's North American clearing centre in New York dealt with 30,000 fund transfers a day and had clients that were deemed to be high risk including hundreds of shell banks (a shell bank, it may be recalled, is a 'virtual' bank with no physical presence in its country of incorporation and which is not part of a larger banking group). Upon inspection, FINCEN (the US's Financial Intelligence Unit) found that violations of the Bank Secrecy Act 'were serious, long standing and systemic'. Only one person was in charge of monitoring this activity. There had been sporadic manual monitoring to start with and when suspicious activity reporting was automated, many reports were produced which, however, were never acted upon. There was inadequate due diligence on bank customers from higher-risk jurisdictions or in connection with higher-risk transactions, despite the fact that there had been numerous regulatory warnings about such customers and transactions. A poor record of suspicious transaction reporting, a non-existent training programme and no proper system of internal controls compounded the problems. ABN was fined $30 million along with other fines.

Source: http://www.nytimes.com/2005/12/20/business/worldbusiness/20bank.html and http://www.fincen.gov.news_room/nr/html/20051219.html

Note: a training film dealing with this case and the one below can be previewed at http://www.antimoneylaunderingvideos.com/player/punishments.htm.

Example

Lloyds TSB

In 2009 the UK-based bank, Lloyds TSB, was fined in the US after admitting to falsifying information on hundreds of millions of dollars' worth of international wire transfers – the electronic messages through which payments are made between counterparties in different countries. The wire transfers in question involved companies in countries that were the subject of sanctions by the US government. US investigators were probing links between the Iranian government and two Manhattan-based companies when they stumbled on a trail of Iranian money entering the city via Lloyds. The UK branch of an Iranian bank would send an electronic payment message to Lloyds via the SWIFT system. However, knowing that the suspicion of the US authorities would be alerted if the payment message made reference to Iran or to an Iranian company as the source of the funds, Lloyds staff would then re-key the data in the SWIFT message, leaving out any reference to Iran, before sending it on to the US. This process was known as 'stripping'. It didn't come about through the misdemeanours of a few rogue staff. Rather, it happened under standing operating instructions.

The US authorities have electronic filters to detect wire transfers from sanctioned countries, but the lack of identification details meant that the Lloyds transfers could get through, especially since they came from a reputable UK bank. Taken with other transactions involving another sanctioned country, Sudan, when confronted by the US authorities Lloyds admitted to over $350 million of illegal transactions between 2001 and 2004. The transfers in question were made to buy goods and services from US companies and from companies in other countries that wanted payment in dollars. The Manhattan District Attorney's Office said that they feared that some of the funds 'may have been used to purchase raw materials for long range missiles'. Lloyds was hit with a fine of $350 million – at the time the biggest penalty ever against a single financial institution for breaches of sanctions legislation. The bank also had to conduct an audit of a wide range of other transactions over the period in question to determine their legitimacy.

Source: http://www.treasury.gov/resource-center/sanctions/OFAC-Enforcement/Documents/lloyds_agreement.pdf

Note: a training film dealing with this case and the one above can be previewed at http://www.antimoneylaunderingvideos.com/player/punishments.htm.

WWW

Citibank Salinas: a seminal case study

Most of the above examples didn't involve actual proven money laundering but were instead breaches of applicable laws and international standards. The case below *did* involve actual money laundering. It was one of a series of cases affecting the same institution, Citibank, which put severe pressure on its reputation and arguably contributed to the changes that have taken place in the private banking sector in relation to AML issues since then. It counts as a seminal case and for that reason in 2007. I wrote the detailed article, below, for Lesson's Learned's house magazine.

Example

Citibank

With increased scrutiny and with seemingly ever greater due diligence expectations being placed on the world's banks and investment institutions, now seems like an appropriate time to revisit one of the classic archive cases – Citi-Salinas – and ask yourself some searching questions; namely, *'What has my institution learned from this?';'How can I be sure that our policies are being followed?';* and, always the most sombre, *'Could it happen to us?'*

It is more than 15 years since Raul met Amy and started opening the various Salinas accounts with Citibank in New York, Switzerland and elsewhere.

Below, we recount the facts of the case as revealed by the 1999 US Senate hearings, before turning to the lessons learned.

A PEP comes calling

Raul Salinas was the brother of the former President of Mexico, Carlos Salinas. For five years during the late 1980s he was Director of Planning for Conasupo, a Mexican state run agency regulating certain agricultural markets, with an annual salary of up to $190,000. From 1990 until mid-1992, he was a consultant at a government anti-poverty agency called Sedesol.

In January 1992, Carlos Hank Rohn, a prominent Mexican businessman and long-time client of Citibank's private bank, telephoned his private banker, Amy Elliott, and asked her to meet with him and Raul Salinas that same day. Elliott was Citi's most senior private banker in New York handling Mexican clients. At the meeting in New York, which was also attended by an even more senior private banker, Reynaldo Figueiredo, Carlos Hank provided the bankers with a strong personal reference for allowing Salinas to open an account. In May 1992, Elliott flew to Mexico and duly obtained Salinas' signature on account opening documentation. She proposed accepting him as a client without investigating his employment background, financial background or assets, and waiving all references other than the one provided by Mr Hank. The head of the Western hemisphere division of the private bank, Edward Montero, approved the opening of the account. Such was the secrecy involved that the private bank's country head in Mexico, Albert Misan, was not consulted and apparently did not even learn of the existence of the account until 1993. In June 1992 Elliott wrote in a monthly business report that the Salinas accounts had *'potential in the $15 to 20 million range'*.

Account set-up

After accepting him as a client the private bank opened multiple accounts for Mr Salinas and his family. The New York office opened five accounts and the private bank's trust company in Switzerland talked to him about opening additional accounts in the name of a shell corporation (a nameplate company existing as a purely legal entity, not as an operational one). A Confidas employee wrote in June 1992:

> 'The client requires a high level of confidentiality in view of his family's political background ... This relationship will be operated along the lines of Amy's "other" relationship; i.e., she will only be aware of the "confidential accounts" and will not even be aware of the names of the underlying companies ... Please note for the record that the client is extremely sensitive about the use of his name and does not want it circulated within the bank. In view of this client's background, I think we will need a detailed reference from Amy, with Rukavina's [Hubertus Rukavina – the head of the private bank and a Confidas board director] sign-off for our files ...'

The 'detailed reference' was never obtained and neither was Rukavina's sign-off, yet Citibank in the Cayman Islands activated a Cayman Islands shell corporation called Trocca Ltd to serve as the owner of record for private bank accounts benefiting Mr Salinas and his family. Cititrust used three additional shell or 'nominee' companies to function as Trocca's board of directors, Madeline Investments SA, Donat Investments SA and Hitchcock Investments SA, and a further three nominee companies to serve as Trocca's officers and principal shareholders, Brennan Ltd, Buchanan Ltd and Tyler Ltd. Cititrust controlled all six companies which were routinely used to serve as directors and officers of shell companies owned by private bank clients. Approximately one year later Cititrust also established a trust, identified only by a number (PT-5242), to serve as the owner of Trocca. The result of this elaborate structure was that Mr Salinas' name did not appear anywhere on Trocca's incorporation papers. Separate documentation establishing his ownership of Trocca was maintained by Cititrust in the Cayman Islands, under secrecy laws restricting its disclosure. Even Amy Elliott was not aware of the name of the shell corporation and Mr Salinas was not referred to by name, but by the acronym 'CC-2', or 'Confidential Client No. 2 (CC-1 being Carlos Hank Rohn).

After Trocca was established the private bank opened investment accounts in London and Switzerland in the name of Trocca and later, in 1994, a special name account was opened for Mr Salinas and his wife in Switzerland under the name of 'Bonaparte'.

Movement of funds

After his accounts were first opened, Mr Salinas made an initial deposit of $2 million via the account of Carlos Hank, who told the bank that these were monies provided by Salinas in respect of a business transaction which never proceeded. The funds were divided between the Salinas accounts in New York and the Trocca accounts in London and Switzerland. But it was in May 1993 that the arrangements under which the bulk of the Salinas funds were to be moved were set up. Elliott met with Salinas and his mistress (later to become his fiancée), Paulina Castañon, at his home in Mexico, where he explained that he wished to move funds out of Mexico to avoid the volatility which traditionally accompanied Mexican elections. In order to provide maximum confidentiality on this undertaking, it was also agreed that Ms Castañon, using an alias 'Patricia Rios' (Rios being her middle name) would deposit cashiers' cheques with Citibank's Mexico City branch, from where the funds would be wired through to a Citibank account in New York, for onward transmission to the London and Switzerland accounts. Although senior management in Mexico denied knowledge of the arrangements, Elliott herself cooperated fully, even setting up a meeting between herself, Castañon/Rios and a service officer at the Mexico City branch to explain the arrangements and ensure that the cheques would be accepted.

Cashiers' cheques were a form of instrument, similar to a bank draft, which were drawn on the banks themselves and which did not, therefore, reveal the beneficial owner of the funds in question, and the New York account to which the funds were then to be wired (marked for Amy Elliott's attention) was a 'concentration account' – an account which commingled the funds of various clients with other funds belonging to Citibank itself, without revealing who owned what. Given that neither Salinas nor Castañon/Rios held any accounts with Citibank in Mexico City (which must therefore have received the funds into its own nostro accounts), and given that the Salinas accounts in London and Switzerland were trust company or code name accounts, these arrangements had the effect of disguising completely the beneficial ownership of whatever volume of funds would eventually pass through them (see p. 173).

These funds turned out to be substantial, and in any event way above the initial '$15–20 million range', referred to by Elliott in her June 1992 business report. The sums involved were very large and were deposited within very short periods. For example, in May and June 1993, in a period of less than three weeks, seven cashiers' cheques were presented to the Mexico City branch totalling $40 million, and over a two-week period in January 1994 four cashiers' cheques totalling $19 million were deposited. By the end of June 1994 the total funds in the Salinas accounts originating from Mexican cashiers' cheques amounted to $67 million. A further $20 million was

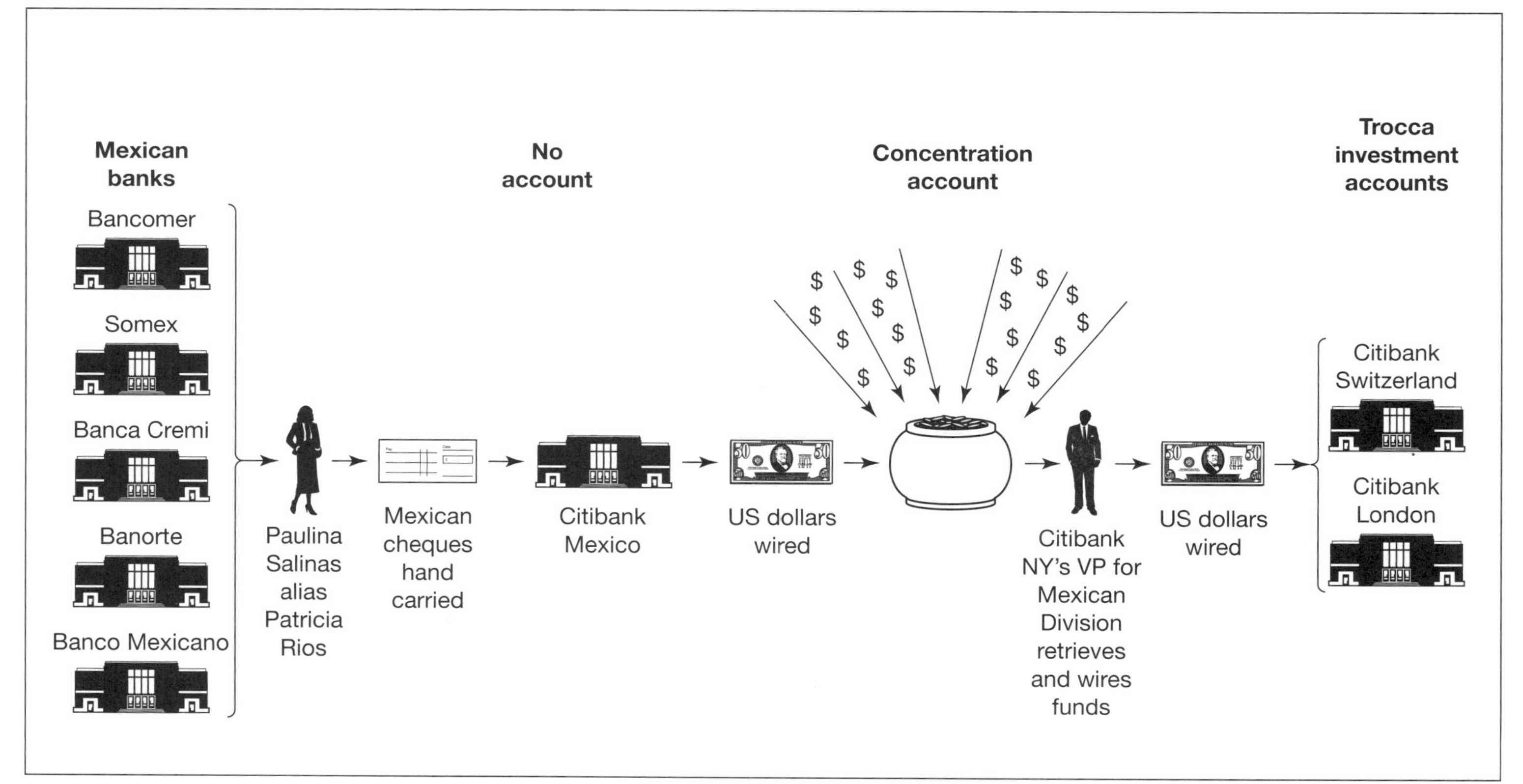

Source: http://www.gao.gov/archive/1999/os99001.pdf

transferred using other methods, leading to a grand total in excess of $87 million. In June 1993, Elliott emailed a colleague in Switzerland:

> 'This account is turning into an exciting and profitable one for us all. Many thanks for making me look good!'

The Salinas arrests and the private bank's reaction to them

In early February 1995, the Mexican press started to report that Salinas was under suspicion of murdering his former brother-in-law, Luis Massieu, a leading Mexican politician. Questioned by a presumably concerned Elliott, Salinas claimed that the charges were politically motivated and untrue. Then, on 28 February 1995, he was arrested and imprisoned in Mexico on suspicion of murder. (After a lengthy trial, a conviction followed, which was upheld on appeal in 1999.) Nine months later, on 15 November 1995, Salinas' wife was arrested in Switzerland and the following day the Swiss authorities froze more than $130 million sitting in Salinas controlled accounts with various banks – including Citibank. The rumours were that the Swiss authorities were investigating allegations that Salinas had been involved in laundering the proceeds of illegal narcotics and, sure enough, three years later in October 1998, proceedings in Switzerland were commenced on that basis.

The private bank's reactions to this reputational disaster unfolding before it have since become well documented, as has Amy Elliott's role as the classic relationship manager 'caught in the middle' of a corporate environment that claimed that anti-money laundering (AML) and client due diligence (CDD) policies were important, but which also, at that time, apparently did not enforce them consistently enough. They are revealed in detail within the pages of the report on the hearings of the Senate Committee on Investigations on private banking and money laundering in November 1999, and show the following.

- *Initial reactions*: in March 1995, soon after Salinas had been arrested for murder, tape transcripts of conversations between the bank's New York, London and Swiss offices reveal that the initial instincts of the bankers, far from making life more easy for the law enforcement investigations which were bound to follow, were rather to make it in practice more difficult for them. For example, the then head of the private bank, Hubertas Rukavina, mooted sending the funds held in the London accounts over to Switzerland so as to make their discovery more difficult – an option which was considered but rejected, apparently, however, primarily on the grounds that the transfer would be obvious in London's books. The same transcripts also reveal that the bankers discussed calling in loans which had been made to Trocca against its deposits, so as to ensure that the bank was not out of pocket in the event that the Trocca funds were frozen.
- *Absence of due diligence records*: it became clear during the hearings that despite the existence of clear policies requiring that information on clients' backgrounds and sources of wealth be collected within the bank's

CAMS (Client Account Management System), in fact no entries had been made at all regarding Salinas. There had been a complete blank throughout the three-year period of the relationship.

- *Backdating of due diligence records*: it then became clear that what records there were had only been completed *ex post facto* by Elliott in early March 1995 following Salinas' arrest, apparently at the behest of private bank senior management in London who wanted to feel 'more comfortable' about the source of wealth on the account, upon which in fact there was very little knowledge. Furthermore, faced in November 1995 with a request for information from the Swiss authorities following the arrest of Salinas' wife in Switzerland, the bank's legal department (who by now had operational control of the accounts) had effected further, after-the-event changes to the CAMS entries. They incorporated reference to a belief that Salinas had sold a construction company – something which Elliott had not included in her own initial attempts at completing the CAMS profile back in March 1995. None of the information had been verified to the extent required by bank policy.
- *Absence of effective enforcement of due diligence policies*: the senate hearings record how: 'during this same period, 1992 until 1995, top leadership in the Western Hemisphere division had sent numerous strongly worded memoranda urging, and ultimately ordering, its private bankers to complete and update information on their client account profiles' and how 'Several internal audits had specifically identified incomplete client profiles as a problem.'
- Yet apparently nothing effective had been done to ensure that these instructions were followed. None of the senior managers who waived additional personal references for Salinas beyond the Hank reference, enquired as to what other background checks were being made on Salinas and Elliott herself clearly believed that senior management – right up to the very top of the organisation – was both aware of and approved of the Salinas accounts, regardless of whether or not due diligence information was available. The account had earned $2 million in fees and interest for the bank and tapes of conversations made on the day after Salinas' arrest recorded Elliott saying: 'Everybody was on board on this … I mean this goes in the very, very top of the corporation, this was known, okay? ... We are little pawns in this whole thing, okay?'
- *Restricted reporting to the authorities*: the exact reporting obligations of any bank in the situation in which Citibank found itself, in terms of timing and content, will always be a matter of a legal interpretation dependent on a number of factors. But the senate documents make the point that when the bank filed a criminal referral form with US law enforcement officials on 17 November 1995 – the day after the freezing of the Swiss accounts – the report only referred to the New York accounts, which held only $200,000, and not to the London or Swiss accounts which held over $50 million.

- *Failure to identify discrepancies between actual and expected account activity*: Elliott had stated in her earliest business report that the account had potential in the '$15–20 million range', yet when the funds actually passing through the Salinas accounts topped $87 million – more than four times what was apparently expected – this did not trigger alarm bells or generate any action to validate the source of this apparently unanticipated stream of wealth.

The case concludes

Having started with a bang, the Salinas case concluded more quietly. The US District Attorney's Office initiated an investigation into whether money laundering charges should be filed against Citibank or any of its employees, but decided against it – presumably because there was no evidence that anyone in Citibank had suspected wrongdoing and therefore participated willingly in any scheme. It is always difficult being judged by new standards and it is possible to argue that, as the banking industry emerged from the world of 'anything goes' into the new era of regulation and public scrutiny, that this was the position which Citibank effectively found itself in. Its Chief Executive, John Reed, who apart from his appearance before the Senate Committee was also forced to endure the indignity of a day in the company of the Justice Department being interviewed about the affair, wrote to the Citibank board:

> 'Much of our practice that used to make good sense is now a liability. We live in a world where we have to worry about "how someone made his/her money", which did not used to be an issue. Much that we had done to keep private banking private becomes "wrong" in the current environment ...'

Amy Elliott, too, in some ways found herself betwixt two worlds, and paid a very public price for it. After describing the positive perceptions of the Salinas family which she had built up over the years, and the habits of Latin American elites in moving sometimes vast sums overseas in order to escape market volatility caused by political turmoil, she stated in her written testimony before the Committee:

> 'It is easy to ignore the context I have described and instead to focus on isolated details in this matter and make them seem questionable. The world in which I operated as a relationship manager in the early 1990s was different from the private banking environment today. Procedures, technologies and safeguards are very different today at Citibank ... I only ask you, with all due respect, to keep in mind the broader picture I have described as you frame your enquiry to me.'

Source: http://www.gao.gov/archive/1999/os9900/.pdf

Lessons learned

The world was surely different back then, and if you're a financial crime professional, re-reading the case makes you realise just how far things have come since the early to mid-nineties; Wolfsberg, the Patriot Act, EU III, the risk-based approach have all come into being. And yet despite the passage of time, some of the issues this case raises are timeless.

- If you have a state-of-the-art compliance policy, what good is it if it isn't followed at the 'coal face'?
- If mixed messages are being sent out with firm AML policies on the one hand but a failure to deal with non-compliance on the other, where does that leave the relationship managers – the 'poor bloody infantry' who have to deliver both compliance and revenue?
- If the corporate culture is perceived by staff as prizing revenue above all else, then where does that leave the organisation as a whole in terms of its reputational exposure when things go wrong?

Shortfalls identified included:

- no proper identification of the customer
- no effective KYC on the customer relationship
- adequate documentary links between client identity and ownership of assets were not maintained
- information on sources of wealth were not obtained
- the substantial discrepancy between expected versus actual funds volume was not spotted …
- and as a result, suspicious activity was not reported
- there was a delay in making a suspicious activity report for six months
- account documentation was doctored after the event to make it look as if proper KYC had been done
- staff were not supervised properly to ensure the KYC policy was being implemented
- senior management ignored multiple audit warnings.

Source: Parkman, T. (2007) The Salinas Case 'AML/CFT and Due Diligence Training for Global Markets', published in Lesson's Learned's house e-magazine.

Note: the training film *Too Good to be True* dealing with many of these issues can be previewed at http://www.antimoneylaunderingvideos.com/player/tgtbt.htm. **WWW**

The Riggs Bank/Augusto Pinochet real case

A second 'real' case which retains its relevance today actually saw one of the oldest names in US banking brought low and eventually disappear under the weight of regulatory disapproval and public censure. As the events of the Arab Spring continue to reverberate at the time of writing, the Riggs Bank/Augusto Pinochet case demonstrates just how badly things can go wrong when you miscalculate the effect of a banking relationship with a high-profile and controversial political figure such as a head of state.

Example

Riggs Bank

Riggs Bank was a Washington DC-based prestige bank which had built up its reputation over 150 years. It had served 20 US presidents including Abraham Lincoln and had supplied gold for the Alaska purchase in 1867. A major line of business for Riggs was the operation of accounts for foreign embassies in the US capital. Often this extended into private banking for diplomats, their family members and sometimes other officials from the country in question.

Under the US Bank Secrecy Act, banks at that time, and indeed now, were required to maintain an extensive compliance programme which included requirements that they perform due diligence against their customers, that they identified suspicious transactions involving funds of potentially illegal origin and that they report suspicious transactions to the authorities. Riggs' own Bank Secrecy Act compliance programme policies and procedures stated that:

> 'Riggs Bank will conduct business only with individuals, companies, trusts (beneficial owners) and grantors/power holders of such trusts that we know to be of good reputation and, through proper and thorough due diligence, we know to have accumulated their wealth through legitimate and honorable means.'

Augusto Pinochet Ugarte was a boy from a middle-class Chilean background who rose to become a general in the Chilean army and who seized power from the elected president Salvadore Allende in a bloody coup in 1972. Several years of violent repression followed with some reports putting the number of deaths under Pinochet's regime as high as 3,200, with tens of thousands imprisoned and tortured. During his rule, until his resignation in 1989, he was also accused of having connections with drug trafficking and illegal arms sales, and of corruptly accruing $28 million. But Pinochet still wasn't a 'bad guy' that everyone could agree on. Millions of Chileans and many in the West supported him because they believed he had saved the country from Communism and directed it firmly and safely to the path of economic growth and prosperity.

It was against this background that in 1994 a senior delegation of Riggs Bank executives visited Chile to solicit General Pinochet's business. His first personal account with Riggs was opened shortly thereafter, an account which saw balances ranging up to $1.2 million over the next few years. The Riggs Bank approach came despite the fact that General Pinochet was already known internationally as a controversial figure and despite this, in all that followed, no evidence was ever found of any KYC documentation on his account created or maintained by Riggs Bank. Some 18 months after the account was opened, Pinochet was indicted in Spain for crimes against humanity.

Between 1994 and 2002 Riggs opened three more personal accounts for Pinochet, these being a money market account which held balances up to $550,000, a checking account and a 'NOW' account, which contained balances of up to $1.1 million. Riggs also established corporate accounts with complex structures for the Chilean ex-president. These included offshore shell corporations (i.e. corporations with no real physical presence, employees or staff) for the receipt of certificates of deposit which benefited General Pinochet and his family. The companies, Ashburton Limited and Althorp Investment Co Limited, all had nominee shareholders (a function which was performed by Riggs Bank (Bahamas) and directors and officers from the accounting firm which was managing the affairs of Riggs Bank in the Bahamas). So Pinochet's name didn't appear anywhere on the incorporation papers. At times, these corporate accounts held balances up to $4.5 million.

Much of this activity was occurring despite the fact that in 1998 the Spanish courts had issued international warrants for General Pinochet's arrest and had issued attachment orders against his accounts throughout the world. In the UK, the Pinochet had been arrested pursuant to the Spanish warrant and was subject to an extradition hearing. Yet no suspicious activity reports were filed by Riggs, which continued to operate the Pinochet accounts without the knowledge of the US authorities. In May 2001, a senior executive at Riggs, Stephen Pfeiffer, forwarded a memo to two senior Riggs Bank officials, containing extensive information on Pinochet's alleged crimes and the litigation surrounding him.

In the spring of 2002, during a routine examination, the Office of the Comptroller of the Currency (OCC) discovered evidence of the Pinochet accounts at Riggs. Initially the Bank resisted cooperating with the investigation, but in the end it did cooperate and finally, in the summer of 2002, the Pinochet accounts were closed. Federal regulators fined and required various contributions from Riggs Bank to a total sum of $53 million and World-Check has estimated that $130 million was wiped from Riggs' share value as a result of this and other money laundering scandals. In July 2004 Riggs Bank was sold to the PNC Financial Services Group Inc. and the famous 150 year-old name became extinct.

In its reports on the Pinochet accounts and other accounts where Riggs Bank fell short, the US Senate Permanent Sub-Committee on Investigations stated that 'Riggs has disregarded its Anti-Money Laundering (AML) obligations, maintained a dysfunctional AML program despite frequent warnings from OCC regulators, and allowed or, at times, actively facilitated suspicious financial activity.'

Lessons learned

How should we assess the significance of the Riggs Bank/Pinochet case and what lessons can be learned from it? Clearly it was very significant because it was one of a number of cases which pointed out the very real reputational risks that exist in doing business with controversial political figures. A key lesson learned from the case is the importance of undertaking a comprehensive risk assessment before a relationship has commenced, which covers not just the sources of wealth and the origin of the funds expected to come into the account, but also the wider reputational issues surrounding allegations against the potential client – both current and historic. If Riggs Bank *did* do this, then clearly they got it badly wrong. Secondly, it is important that with such individuals, such assessments – and the due diligence which goes with them – should not be a 'one-off' event, but should take place on a constant and regular basis, such that new evidence concerning the client is taken into account and processed and so that there can be an ongoing assessment about the suitability of a particular client for a continued business relationship. In this regard, the Riggs Bank/Pinochet case also demonstrates the importance of not allowing relationship managers who may have developed a very close personal relationship with a client, or who may be influenced by their own political views, to override the organisation's wider sensors regarding the continued suitability of a particular account. Finally, failures in suspicion reporting and in the level of KYC and due diligence on an account will always be punished heavily by regulators, and this case was no exception.

Source: Based on facts from www.access.gpo.gov/congress/senate/pdf/109hrg/20278.pdf

MANAGING REPUTATIONAL RISK: THE EXPERIENCE OF THE MDBS

Forging a workable policy for managing reputational risk

Multilateral Development Banks (MDBs) and International Financial Institutions (IFIs) have devoted a lot of attention in recent years to developing their management of reputational risk. They face a difficult task. On the one hand, they are mandated to invest and lend in countries which badly need them, such as less developed economies in the former Communist world, parts of Asia, Africa and Latin America. After all, there is no point in such institutions existing if they are not going to make funds available to help improve people's lives. On the other hand, the very places where the funds are most needed are, almost by definition, high risk. They often have high levels of corruption and crime. Their institutions are either new and less rooted than their equivalents in the developed world or have actually been compromised by corruption and crime for many years. 'Integrity' and 'transparency' are viewed by many as luxuries in societies where the real way to get on has been to play fast and loose with whatever rules exist and to get as far as you can as quickly as you can.

How, then, should such institutions deal with applications for financing from, say, a private sector entrepreneur whose business plan seems to offer good returns and great benefits (potentially) to the economic development of the country, but whose past is often shrouded in mystery? This is a crucial question when the past activities of the people concerned may come back and bite the ankles of the institution in a very public way. Just as importantly, regardless of the negative publicity, if they lend to or invest in 'the wrong person' then the project itself is unlikely to be successful. Are the MDBs then part of the solution or part of the problem?

Integrity due diligence

Commercial banks may not possess the same social and economic development obligations of the MDBs and IFIs. But particularly since the 2008 financial crisis, the social impact of their operations has never been under such close scrutiny. You can argue about the value or otherwise of allegedly 'socially useless' proprietary trading and arbitrage activities, but the provision of financial services to wicked despots and dodgy businessmen and politicians is universally unpopular and today's banks need some kind of framework within which to analyse a range of integrity-related reputational risks. These risks extend beyond money laundering and terrorist financing into corruption, tax evasion and other forms of criminality, political exposure, corporate governance, regulatory investigations and lawsuits, and the general personal and corporate reputations of the people and companies involved.

The advantages of having such a framework are clear. Whilst each case is unique and must be looked at on its merits, passing each through a common framework of assessment and analysis introduces consistency into what might otherwise be a very subjective process. It forces people to ask difficult questions and provides a common way of both finding the answers and assessing the impact of the answers, all looked at through the prism of the organisation's reputation: 'doing the right thing' and (just as important) being seen to be doing the right thing.

In order to gain some perspective on this, we will look now at the type of framework being followed increasingly by a number of the MDBs/IFIs.

What is described here is a generalised version of what are in fact a number of different processes which are specific to each institution. Nevertheless the broad principles tend to be the same.

The process is known as the Integrity Due Diligence (IDD) process. Its key components are:

- an integrity red flags checklist – a list of questions designed to elicit relevant information (see pp. 188–90)
- due diligence research tools – ways of obtaining that information (see p. 190)
- IDD assessment guidelines – policy guidance on interpreting the information and making decisions.

In essence the process is as follows.

The IDD process: initial stage

After the project has been proposed in concept form (usually as a result of a proposal by an applicant), a detailed investigation is undertaken by the banking team responsible for the transaction using the red flags checklist and the due diligence research tools. Documents and other evidence are filed and the outcome of the investigation is subject to an initial, conceptual 'in principle' assessment, using the IDD assessment guidelines, to determine whether it passes a 'funnel test' of policy principles. This stage of the process is depicted in Figure 5.1.

The four filters shown in Figure 5.1 are drawn from the IDD assessment guidelines and stipulate the circumstances which, all else being equal, will effectively prevent the deal from going any further. They are embodied in the following principles:

1. The transaction cannot proceed if beneficial ownership is unclear

This is a base-level requirement – if you don't know who the ultimate beneficial owner of a business, structure or asset is, then how can you be sure that it is not owned by a criminal, a terrorist or a political figure? Corporate structures must be investigated back up the chain until all significant beneficial owners have been identified. If this cannot be done then the project cannot proceed, period. Sometimes complex structures will be in place which will make discovering beneficial ownership difficult, particularly in environments where record keeping and the availability of public information may be poor. Sometimes (in fact, quite often) beneficial ownership will not even appear on any written record, but will simply be a matter of fact or, more often, of rumour. Whatever, if the project is worth it (see later) then persistence must be deployed and beneficial ownership established. Sometimes complex structures deployed to disguise beneficial ownership may be an indicator of criminal activity (e.g. tax evasion). But equally, they

Figure 5.1

IDD process – initial stage

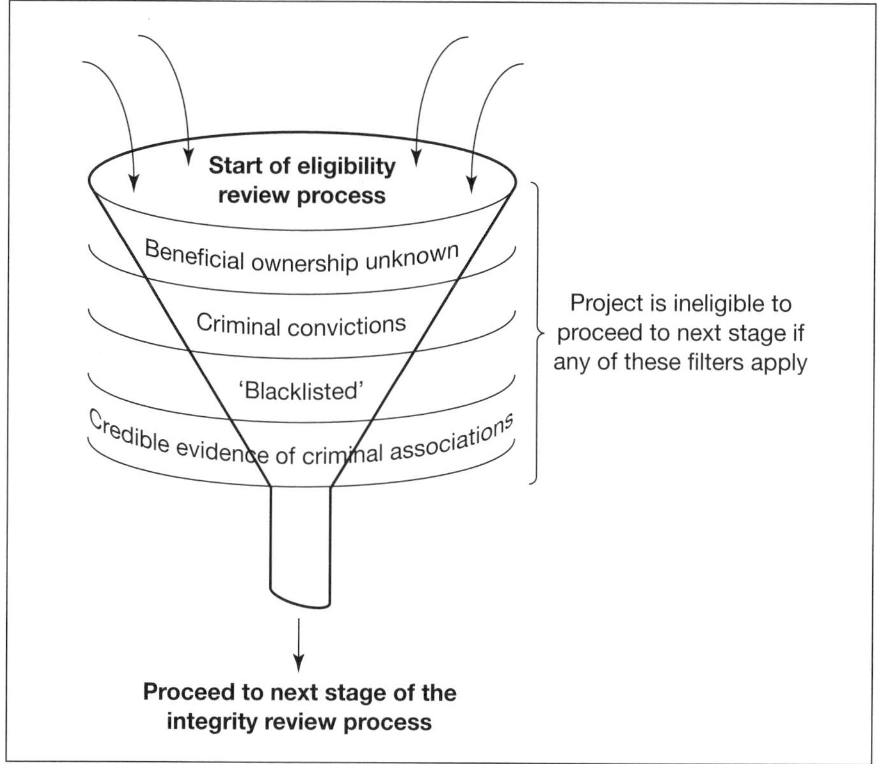

may simply reflect a business reality in the country in question in which business owners must attempt to disguise the full extent of their wealth in order to avoid demands for payments by corrupt officials. So the presence of a complex structure in itself will not necessarily prevent the transaction from proceeding, but lack of knowledge of beneficial ownership will.

2. No transaction can proceed with parties who have been convicted of, or who are currently under investigation for, serious criminal offences

Serious criminal offences basically mean the predicate offences included in the FATF list of crimes which can give rise to money laundering and constitute, therefore, for example people trafficking and sexual exploitation, racketeering, corruption and bribery, fraud, tax evasion, counterfeiting, murder and kidnapping, robbery and theft, smuggling, extortion, forgery, piracy, insider trading and market manipulation as well as participation in drug trafficking, money laundering, terrorism and terrorist financing offences. In many countries the presence of a conviction or an ongoing investigation is not necessarily indicative of either guilt or a serious case to answer, as the case may be. Likewise, the absence of a conviction or an ongoing investigation is not necessarily indicative of innocence and/or no case to answer. Issues such as the nature of the crime, how long ago it occurred and whether or not it was politically or commercially motivated will be relevant. But, generally, the presence of a conviction or an investigation will prevent the transaction from proceeding.

3. A transaction cannot proceed if a party is currently on a recognised blacklist

This is self-evident and lists checked would include those of the United Nations, the US Department of Treasury and the Office of Foreign Assets Control, the FBI, the Securities and Exchange Commission, the Financial Services Authority and those of major central banks and other MDBs/IFIs.

4. The transaction cannot proceed where there is credible evidence of existing links to organised crime and criminal activities

In some instances there will be allegations and rumours that a particular individual or group of individuals are or have been associated with organised crime. Here, the issue of 'credibility' is important; the most credible evidence will be that which is corroborated by multiple, independent, impartial sources, as opposed to an allegation made by a single individual who is, say, involved in a commercial or political dispute with the person in question. The criminal activities referred to are the same as those discussed in item 2, above.

Tax affairs are becoming an increasingly important consideration. Involvement of complex structures and Offshore Financial Centres (OFC) may offend tax evasion laws and, as we have seen, tax evasion is now included in the list of predicate offences issued by the FATF. It is also the subject of an increasingly active and determined international effort, orchestrated through the OECD Forum, to reduce it and to punish tax evaders. Therefore, any complex tax structure must be understood so as to ensure that it does not offend against relevant tax laws in the jurisdictions concerned and any OFC involved must be one which has been deemed compliant with the OECD Tax Forum's international standards on tax information exchange.

If the proposed transaction passes this funnel test, and if it is attractive in other terms (see below) then conceptual clearance is given and more detailed investigations conducted during the secondary stage of the IDD process, depicted in Figure 5.2.

The IDD process: secondary stage

Completion of the red flags checklist at first instance will usually have revealed a number of important issues requiring further investigation. At this stage, assuming all available public sources of information have been accessed using the due diligence resources available (see below), if the transaction is worthwhile in terms of the organisation's mandate then specialist

Figure 5.2

IDD process – secondary stage

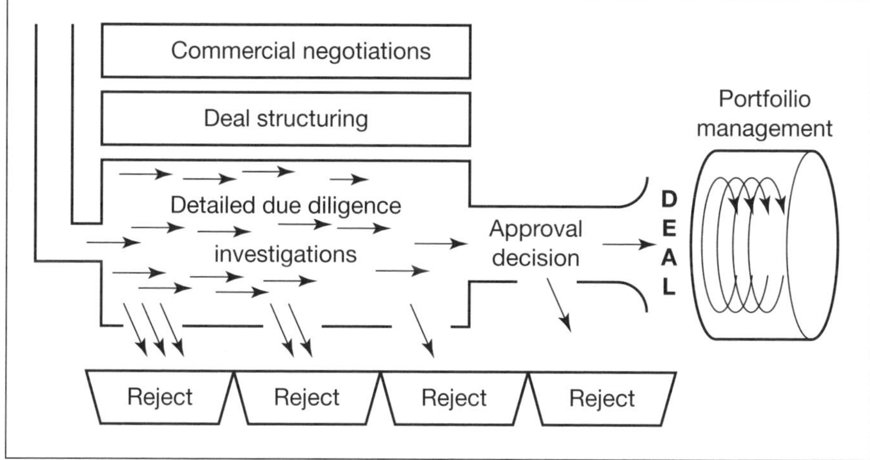

investigations consultants may be instructed to investigate specific areas of concern revealed in the initial research. Here, the assumption is that they will have access to non-public sources of information, although clearly the use and methods of obtaining such information must remain legal. If such investigations harden any of the evidence of the existence of items 1, 2 and 4 above, then a decision is made to drop the project. More often than not, however, despite the added perspective which such investigations usually give, there are no clear answers and a decision has to be made on the basis of the risks versus the mandate.

In this regard reference is then made to the following types of interpretation and assessment principles.

5. Relationships with PEPs and other high-risk clients require enhanced due diligence

The involvement of a PEP does not necessarily prevent the transaction from proceeding, but for reasons examined earlier, it creates notable levels of risk which need to be managed. All PEPs are not equal, and generally the involvement in a business transaction of, say, a head of state, president, prime minister or a senior cabinet minister, as well as governors of large regions and mayors of major cities is considered too risky and will prevent the transaction from proceeding.

For those PEPs in lower positions, MDB and IFI organisations will generally refrain from transactions if there is an apparent conflict of interest created by a PEP's interest in the business transaction on the one hand, and their public duties on the other: for example where a minister of transport owns shares in a bus or train company. Compliance with local law is important, as many public sector service rules will prohibit participation by a public servant in a commercial enterprise.

The types of enhanced due diligence investigations regarding source of wealth described earlier on must be undertaken. If a transaction involving a PEP is to proceed, it must also be subject to enhanced ongoing monitoring (to check that the assessment of risks has not changed in the light of new information). The transaction structure should also be constructed with a view to minimising risks. For example, if permitted by local law, the irrevocable transference of share and ownership rights into the control of an independent third party and documented pre-recusals of the PEP from decisions benefiting or potentially benefiting or being perceived to benefit the financed entity. The same rules apply to close family members and associates of PEPs.

Although the due diligence resources must be used in order to determine whether or not someone is a PEP, generally this is less of a problem than the bigger issue which is establishing whether or not someone may actually be *fronting* for a PEP. Such situations are common; there is a rumour or an allegation that the disclosed owner of a business structure is not in fact the true beneficial owner, but is fronting for Junior Minister X or Senior Civil Servant Y. In such circumstances, unless the available evidence supports the argument fairly robustly that the rumour is unfounded, then the operation of principle 1 (see p. 182) will generally prevent the transaction from proceeding.

6. Mitigating factors can be taken into account when assessing integrity risks

If a particular transaction is attractive from the perspective of the MDB's or IFI's mandate, and if it is not blocked by the operation of principles 1–4, but if there are still concerns about some of the issues which have been discovered during the due diligence process, then mitigating factors can be taken into account when deciding whether or not to proceed. Typical mitigating factors include:

- *Time* – if a significant period of time has elapsed since the last serious allegation.
- *Willingness to change* – cynics may scoff, but there is a view (borne out in part by history) that some business people who have pursued illegal activities previously, do reach a point where they intend to leave it behind them and move on to an exclusively legal future, unclouded by their illegal past. (The US 'robber barons' of the late nineteenth century are the classic examples often cited.) If there genuinely appears to be little chance of repetition of illegal activities in the future – say because the amount of a person's reputation and capital invested to date makes the costs too high – then, all else being equal, it becomes possible to take a calculated risk on the individual, subject to the next bullet point.
- *Ability to mitigate risks* – if the applicant is willing, there is often a series of concrete actions which can be taken to mitigate some of the integrity concerns which may have been raised in the red flags checklist. For

example, complex ownership structures can be simplified and made more transparent; international accounting standards can be adopted; independent directors can be appointed to the board of a company; a wide range of warranties and covenants can be included within legal documentation requiring the disclosure of wrongful acts and cooperation with investigations by the lender – all linked to events of default which, in turn, are linked to personal guarantees which place personal rather than corporate wealth at stake; and certain companies, individuals (such as agents) and proposed transactional elements or agents and other individuals can be removed from the deal if they are considered too risky.

If integrity concerns can be mitigated using such methods, then this can result in a move towards a decision in favour of the transaction proceeding.

The remaining four principles are effectively operational ones that concern how the inside process must be undertaken.

7. There must be full disclosure of all risks from as early a stage as possible

8. Transactions must be covenanted and documented in a manner which reflects their risk

See 6 above.

9. Integrity risks must be reviewed throughout the life cycle of a project

Information changes over time and risks need to be reassessed and action needs to be taken accordingly. These requirements form an integral part of the portfolio management process.

10. Where a project is potentially controversial, a clear explanation of the organisation's rationale for undertaking it should be available

Sometimes, even after the application of sophisticated procedures and thinking, decisions will be made on a hair's breadth one way or the other. No organisation can be expected to get such decisions 'right' 100 per cent of the time. On those occasions when the organisation gets it 'wrong' – and when it is accordingly subject to public criticism – it pays to be able to state very clearly what steps the organisation took to try to get it right, and the grounds on which the decision to lend or invest were made.

The reputational decision which has to be made in each case is summed up in Figure 5.3.

In this forcefield analysis, serious integrity concerns, unproven rumours and allegations, the risks of the organisation's reputation from getting it wrong and the mission risk (objectives not achieved, money not repaid, etc.) are weighed against mitigating factors such as time, recent behaviour, a willingness to undertake reforms, to adopt sound management practices and to accept and embrace mitigation measures.

Figure 5.3

Forcefield analysis of key factors in IDD decisions

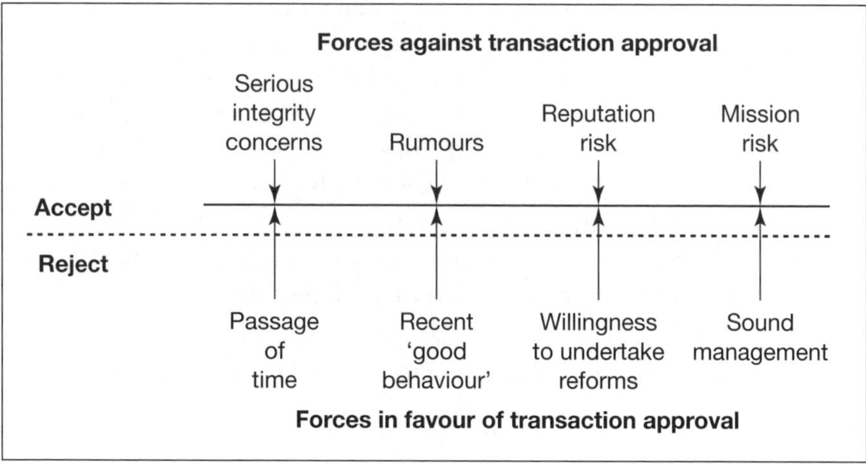

Each case will be different, but these principles can bring consistency to the analysis. Ultimately, commercial banks operate within their own defined parameters of corporate social responsibility and in order to preserve and enhance their reputations it is against those parameters that they must make their assessments and their judgements.

THE INTEGRITY 'RED FLAGS' CHECKLIST AND THE DUE DILIGENCE INVESTIGATION TOOLS

What types of questions should be asked and hopefully answered during the initial stage of the IDD process? What tools and resources can be used to obtain such information?

Table 5.1 shows, in checklist format, the areas to be covered and questions to be asked.

Table 5.1

Example 'red flags' checklist

Project background
A. Is the company private or public? Are there any risk implications? B. What is the industry of operations of the company? Are there any risk implications? C. What is the country of operation of the company? Are there any risk implications?
Category 1: Criminality, criminal associations and convictions
1. Have the proposed senior management or co-owners of the company ever been convicted of a criminal offence?

2. Have they been or are they under investigation by law enforcement agencies?
3. Have they ever used criminal means (e.g. blackmail, intimidation)?
4. Have they ever been involved or associated with criminals?
5. Have they ever been involved or associated with money laundering?

Category 2: Bribery and corruption

6. Have they ever been involved in the misuse or misappropriation of public property?
7. Have they ever been involved in bribing public officials to influence public decisions or processes?
8. Has there been any involvement in business sectors frequently characterised by corrupt practice?
9. Are there any unexplained pools of cash or near cash investments in the company's or senior managers'/co-owners' finances?
10. Have there been any inappropriate or above-market economics, fees or local costs in the company's activities?
11. Have there been any instances of transfer pricing, bid-rigging or financial misrepresentation?
12. Are there any unknown or suspicious sources of wealth?
13. Do any of the senior managers/co-owners display an ostentatious lifestyle which appears to be inappropriate to their financial situation?
14. Are they reluctant to discuss integrity or corruption issues?

Category 3: Political exposure

15. Do any of the senior managers/co-owners have major political affiliations or have they made political financial donations?
16. Are any politicians or government officials involved with the company, e.g. as directors or beneficial owners?
17. Are any of the owners/senior management from 'political families' within the country concerned?
18. Are any of the owners or senior managers known members and supporters of extremist political or religious groups?

Category 4: Beneficial ownership and corporate governance

19. Have the senior managers/co-owners of the company ever committed fraud or misappropriation of assets against shareholders?
20. Are there any undisclosed or unusual beneficial ownership or carried interests?
21. Have there been any sudden or unexplained withdrawals of large and/or western companies from transactions?
22. Have there been any sudden or unexplained changes of shareholders, auditors, accountants, lawyers or other professional advisers?
23. Are there any unnecessarily complex ownership structures?
24. Has there been any tax evasion by the company or the senior managers/co-owners?
25. Are there any 'suspicious' (seemingly unnecessary) offshore companies within the corporate structure?
26. Has there been any non-market compensation of key participants, such as the company itself, the senior management/co-owners or other shareholders?
27. Have there been any other examples of poor corporate governance?

Category 5: Regulatory investigations, fines and lawsuits
28. Have there been any large or serious lawsuits, fines or regulatory or public findings which have impacted negatively on the reputation of the company or the senior managers/co-owners? 29. Are there currently any outstanding large or serious lawsuits or regulatory or public investigations which remain unresolved?
Category 6: Personal and corporate reputation (including blacklisting and press/media reports)
30. Do any of the senior managers/co-owners appear on any UN List of persons suspected of involvement in terrorist activities or any other watchlists referred to by the Bank (e.g. US Dept of Treasury, OFAC, SEC, FBI, EU, FSA (UK), HKMA (HK))? 31. Have there been any media references to illegal or disreputable activities or actions or any actual evidence of the same?

The past decade or so has seen a significant increase in the capability of organisations to access, and therefore to analyse, publicly available information through the internet and via various business information products that provide a useful service in information collection and analysis. But traditional methods still count – or should count – for a lot. In all cases, the information needs to be gathered meticulously and either copied and placed on file together with the data research, or recorded as a contemporaneous note. Table 5.2 lists a range of due diligence tools.

Table 5.2 **Due diligence tools**

- Searches of newspaper and business publications and websites
- Searches of society and sports magazines (e.g. sailing, polo, philanthropy) and websites, where relevant
- Informal discussions with industry, sector and country contacts
- Checks with foreign banks and other foreign companies who may be able to give an informed opinion
- Searches of relevant public information and private subscription search engines and websites, such as Google and World-Check
- Searches of public registries and record offices (to the extent that these are deemed sufficiently helpful and reliable) in the country or countries concerned, such as companies' registries and court and judicial offices
- Structured discussions with the applicants themselves
- Investigations by specialist firms of consultants

PRACTICAL APPLICATION

How might this overall framework apply in a real case? What would the file look like in terms of relevant information and how would the IDD assessment guidelines operate in practice?

We attempt to bring this to life in the form of a fictitious case. First read the project summary to get an initial outline of the proposed project and then access the types of information which you would obtain on such a case were you handling it for real and using the research tools referred to above. Finally, there is an assessment of the project according to the assessment guidelines discussed.

Case: Zubin Deslan and the Belvin Keffl Group

Project summary

- Belvin Keffl (BK) is a former state-owned farming company in the EU candidate country of Moldavia.
- BK diversified after the fall of communism into areas such as food, transport, chemicals, retail and construction.
- It was privatised in 1991 and became owned by the Deslan Group of companies, whose majority shareholder, chairman and chief executive is Zubin Deslan.
- The proposal is for loan financing for the general upgrading and expansion of Belvin Keffl's truck production facilities in the major cities of Krestinberg and Bantt, which used to produce the old 'Paka' state trucks and buses.
- The amount of the proposed investment – €20 million – is to be spent on factory and plant rebuilding using capital equipment purchased from member countries – notably from the Finnish engineering giant, Sarbel Engineering.
- The project has been brokered through the auspices of Peter Valburg, a former Sarbel employee now based in Moldavia and used as an independent consultant throughout the region.

Commercial viability of the project

Commercial viability is good. The market for trucks is likely to remain strong as this robust emerging country continues to grow and the government is a major customer with a constant need for fleet upgrading and renewal. As an oil exporter Moldavia is likely to benefit from high oil prices and this will benefit the economy as a whole. Market research indicates that executives in Moldavian companies are quite patriotic and are prepared to back a national champion if it meets reliability requirements, particularly in the snows of winter, which is where the use of Finnish expertise and *matériel* will become most useful. Costs are predicted to grow by 6 per cent a year, whilst revenues are estimated to grow by 25 per cent year on year as the business development plan unfolds. There are considered to be potential regional export possibilities, too.

Compliance with environmental policies and strategies

Like many engineering production facilities within the former Eastern Block, BK has suffered from chronic underinvestment, dangerous, outdated facilities, health and safety issues for employees, and high pollution levels, with associated contamination of air, rivers and countryside around the plants. An attractive feature of this project will be bringing the plants up to the latest international standards in these respects.

Moldavian overview

Moldavia has 20 million people, set to grow to 30 million by 2050 with oil and mineral resources. Moldavia is a vast, untapped country which is likely to grow in stature and become a major regional player. It is modernising rapidly and the view is that it is a good country for business, with the current government, formed by the Moldavian National Progress Party (MNPP), apparently committed to the implementation of a full set of market reforms with a view to securing EU membership by 2025. Despite a plethora of government backed initiatives, corruption, however, is still viewed by many foreigners as endemic in everything from the award of business contracts, to the making of regulatory decisions, to the securing of preferment and promotion in both the private and public sectors. Many Moldavians appear to take a relaxed view, nevertheless, at least about 'soft' practices such as the giving and receiving of expensive gifts, the payment of small favours to lowly officials in return for expediting bureaucratic processes and the involvement of family members in both business contracts and positions of employment. Practices which they refer to as '*chaznar traltir*' (literally, 'greasing the axle') and which they believe to be globally widespread.

There is a crime problem in Moldavia. It is improving but organised crime undoubtedly exists and the use of intimidation, violence and even murder to resolve political and business disputes, whilst much less common than it was during the 1990s, still occurs from time to time.

Deslan Group overview

The group is substantial in national terms and has shown a strong business performance over a sustained period. There has been undisturbed profit growth year on year since 1993 and an aggressive acquisitions strategy has seen core businesses grow rapidly, particularly following the hard-fought acquisition of AIA Group in 1994. Construction and transport still contributes more than 50 per cent to profits, helped no doubt by continued good relationships with the public sector. The strategy is to continue to grow these businesses strongly, leveraging their excellent market positions, as well as the renewed focus on the trucks business.

The group is organised through a series of divisional structures, with operating companies owned by a series of holding companies, which in turn belong to the main holding company, Deslan Holdings, which is believed to be 80 per cent owned by Zubin Deslan and various family members, all of whom operate through nominees (i.e. legal entities such as companies and trusts which hold on behalf of a beneficial owner). Corporate administration appears sound, with all books up to date, meetings held and minuted, all returns filed within time and no fines or other censure or criticism from the Moldavian Corporate Authority (MCA).

Financially the group appears strong and although it undoubtedly has the funds to finance the proposed project itself, this would mean that it could do virtually nothing else – a situation that makes no sense at all given the multiple opportunities the group is presented with.

Zubin Deslan

Born in 1961. Deslan is the son of a university professor and a teacher and has five siblings. He is quiet and non-demonstrative – not your average Moldavian businessman, who tends to be a 'larger than life', street trader, *bon viveur* type. He got a first class honours in Biochemistry from Krestinberg University, followed by two years' national service in the air force, 1983–85. His career in the Ministry of Agriculture culminated in a position as a director general of Belvin Keffl in 1989.

Deslan bought Belvin Keffl from the Moldavian government in 1991 (aged 30) apparently using finance raised from contacts he made on a short-term summer management programme at Stanford Business School in the late 1980s and grew the business from then into the conglomerate which it is today. He has successfully raised funds from FFIs in the past, including from Goldman Sachs and UBS. His acquisition of AIA Group in 1994 was bitterly contested and controversial at the time, as victory effectively handed Deslan control of the food and agricultural sectors in Moldavia, as well as giving him a substantial slice of the chemicals and construction sectors. Both Deslan personally and Deslan Group, were financial contributors to the ruling MNPP who won last year's elections on a wide-ranging (and popular) programme of reform and liberalisation based on getting people to consign the country's poverty-stricken communist past to the history books, and unite around a bright and prosperous future. The MNPP is bitterly opposed by the other main political party, the Moldavian People's Power Party (MPPP), which claims that modernisation has been a disaster for the poorest, and advocates a more state-led approach to the economy to protect wages and living standards.

Information 1 – obtained from a public registry

COMPANIES REGISTRY OF MOLDAVIA

CERTIFICATE: DESLAN HOLDINGS PUBLIC COMPANY
Breakdown by owner category of numbers of shares held

A. Other listed private sector companies – 0
B. Private individuals – 0
C. Publicly owned bodies – 0
D. Nominee companies – 5,625,766

Information 2 – obtained from the website of Transparency International

Relevant sections from Transparency International's Anti-corruption Index, contained in its latest annual report (1 = least corrupt):

123.Moldavia

124.Bulgaria

125.Ukraine

126.India

127.Pakistan

128.Indonesia

Information 3 – obtained from a conference call with the country manager, who obtained it orally from an attorney friend

Note 20/8/12

Telephone conference call with our local manager, who has been speaking to a local investigator and has uncovered the following information:

- Deslan investigated twice, both times no charge
- 1) In 1996 re privatisation of BK in 1991. Alleged bribery of State official, Henrik Bolsan, responsible for sale, but NOTHING PROVEN.
- 2) In 1999 re allegations that BK/DG acquired AIA Group illegally in 1994 via secret agreement with CEO Georges Vandreau who pushed through sale at undervalue in exchange for a $12m payment to an offshore bank account. NOT PROVEN.
- Investors in AIA lost €€€ millions on sale after collapse of investment scheme promoted by Vandreau. V based in London 10 years – old man and died of cancer just before election last year.
- No further investigations. Police files on both cases above now closed. Reason given – NO EVIDENCE.

Information 4 – obtained from a local newspaper by the country manager

Handwritten note faxed over by local manager

Deslan and Deslan Group are donors to the MNPP and he does a lot of this kind of thing with them, as indeed do many Moldavian businessmen. But I thought you should be aware of it. Regards, JL
17/8/12

Information 5 – obtained from an international newspaper

FINANCIAL NEWS

But Moldavia may yet come to terms with its tumultuous past and, in particular, construct a permanent settlement betweent the state and the private sector concerning the corrupt and self-serving ways in which state assets were sold off after the demise of communism.

PAY YOUR TAXES

The recent statement by Finance minister Egbert Aldoa is a case in point. In a wide-ranging interview for CNN Business, he indicated that the Moldavian Government would no longer be looking to prosecute cases of alleged acquisition at undervalue from the 90s, as long as those suspected behave as good corporate citizens and pay their taxes here and now in the 21st century.

One person who will welcome such statements is undoubtedly Zubin Deslan, creator and CEO of the eponymous Deslan Group, a sprawling Moldavian conglomerate which is into everything from food and agriculture to mines, construction, chemicals and trucks. The previous government tried unsuccessfully to bring corruption charges against him and Agriculture Secretary Henrik Boslan in 1996 in relation to Deslan's acquisition of the state-owned Belvin Keffl Group (a decision signed off by Boslan) but these failed due to lack of evidence and Aldoa's ruling MNPP has shown little appetite to resurrect the case, especially since Boslan himself succumbed to terminal cancer last year and Deslan is both an eloquent and generous supporter of the ruling MNPP party.

RIGHT TRACK

Those close to the Moldavian political and business elite now believe that if the country can cement this settlement and continue with the economic reform programme, then the future would be bright, heralding prosperity and, whisper it softly, even power.

"Moldavia has some of the largest oil reserves in the region", says Patrick Climbe, Head of the Economic Research Institute in Krestinberg. "It has minerals, a sizeable population that is set to be larger than Canada's by 2050, and is well placed politically to act as a bridge between Russia and the West."

But others are more sceptical and point to rampant corruption, a simmering historical enmity with neighbouring Moldachia, and an opposition party which is far from weak and which is itching to return to power and settle some old scores. "Moldavia is only ever one election away from a return to state economics and a catastrophic war with Moldachia" says Prof. Marian Divlas of the Chair of international studies at Krestinberg University. "That's what I tell anyone who starts getting too starry-eyed about the future."

Information 6 – obtained by country manager from local business people

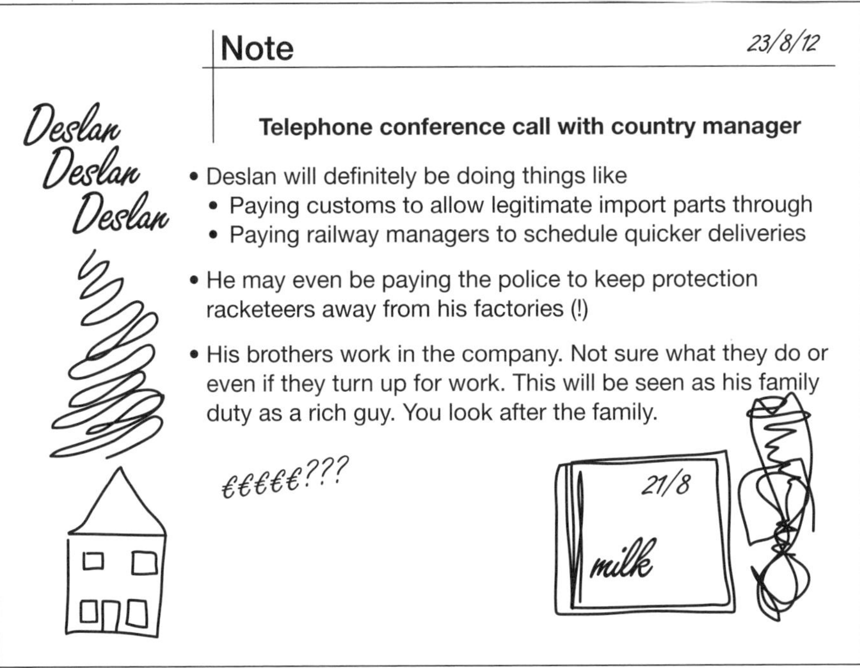

Note
23/8/12
Deslan
Deslan
Deslan
Telephone conference call with country manager
• Deslan will definitely be doing things like
• Paying customs to allow legitimate import parts through
• Paying railway managers to schedule quicker deliveries
• He may even be paying the police to keep protection racketeers away from his factories (!)
• His brothers work in the company. Not sure what they do or even if they turn up for work. This will be seen as his family duty as a rich guy. You look after the family.
€€€€€???
21/8
milk

Information 7 – obtained from the legal department via local lawyers after analysis of the company's constituent documents

Confidential Memorandum

LEGAL; PRIVILEDGED AND CONFIDENTIAL

The Bank's lawyers in Krestinberg, Messrs Panaca Dale, have provided the following assessment of the corporate governance levels of both BK and Deslan Group. Please note that this is the initial assessment and is subject to any further information provided by the company.

"The legal framework and company charter provide for basic shareholders' rights such as the registration of shares in share registers, the right to transfer shares, to participate in general shareholder meetings and to elect and dismiss board members. However, there are no sufficient mechanisms to ensure protection of such rights or redress in cases of violation. Minority shareholders are not necessarily granted equitable treatment (e.g. the voting rights of different classes of shares are not well defined, insider dealing is not properly regulated etc). Stakeholders' rights are not necessarily recognised. There are certain disclosure requirements of material information on the company, which however do not allow shareholders to get a thorough understanding of the financial situation of the company, with such information being provided on an infrequent basis. There is little transparency to third parties, which are given limited access to company financial information or its ownership structure. The company board is required to have some degree of accountability to shareholders, although the enforcement mechanisms of such requirement are overall ineffective."

I would add two more things

The actual shareholdings of Deslan and his family appear to be through nominee companies, meaning less transparency all round.

In this regard I am led to believe that Mr. Deslan himself is prepared (even keen, some say) to follow any suggestions we may make regarding the creation of greater transparency (real and perceived).

I think an early meeting is in order.

Sincerely,

Kate Bryan

Senior Legal Advisor

Information 8 – obtained from the local public registry

22 Krestinberg Square
Krestinberg 20098
Republic of Moldavia

Fax Transmission

To: Project Team
From: Jan Larsson, Representative Moldavia
Re: Belvin Keffl
Date: 20 August 2012

MESSAGE
As requested I have conducted a search of the newly completed Moldavian National Criminal Archive, which reveals NIL convictions for either Deslan, his known family members or any of his senior management.

Best regards,

J. LARSSON
Representative, Moldavia

Information 9 – obtained from an industry contact

Transcript of telephone conversation with Alan Greenton, a business acquaintance and former US banker with a good knowledge of Moldavia

YOU: What can you tell me about Peter Valburg?

GREENTON: Peter Valburg? Oh I know Valburg quite well. There are a few of these guys knocking around in Krestinberg and Valtana [capital of neighbouring Moldachia] and, well, what can I say? They're very well connected, they know a lot of people and many would say – and they themselves would say – that they provide a valuable service to people wanting to do business in Moldavia for the first time. They make the introductions, they negotiate the labyrinth of regulations, they know about starting an operation, investment rules, local taxes etc. etc. Cynics, of course, would say that they're just there to make the FPS (facilitation payments) and, where necessary, the bribes, and to provide the necessary tax deductible invoices to western companies … And of course, they're working it both ways. As westerners, they can hop on a plane back to Copenhagen or London or New York or wherever and sell the best deals to the highest bidder …

YOU: So he's corrupt.

GREENTON: Well, what's corrupt these days? Is he walking into the prime minister's office with suitcases full of cash? No, of course he's not. But if a local manufacturer with some easy government contracts needs western capital equipment and a guy like Valburg sets up the deal with, say, the British company which was willing to make the largest 'thank you' payment, and they get some western bank to finance the whole thing, well is that corrupt? You tell me …

Information 10 – obtained from a Google search against 'Sarbel'

Sarbel bribes reached around the world

Evidence from key witness details millions of euros paid in bribes to officials in Nigeria, Russia and Libya

Sarbel, the engineering group at the centre of the biggest bribery scandal in Finnish corporate history, paid millions of euros in bribes to cabinet ministers and dozens of other officials in Nigeria, Russia and Libya.

The payments were made as the company sought to win lucrative contracts for engineering and transport equipment, according to court documents revealed in *The Wall Street Journal* today.

A ruling by a Helsinki court last month names four former Nigerian telecommunications ministers as well as other officials in Nigeria, Libya and Russia as recipients of 77 bribes totalling about €12 million (£8.6 million). Sarbel accepted responsibility for the misconduct and agreed to pay a €201 million fine decreed by the court.

The court focused on bribes between 2001 and 2004 connected to Kiki Rakkinen, a Sarbel employee who was a manager in a sales unit.

Mr Rakkinen has been charged with embezzlement and is co-operating with prosecutors.

According to separate court documents, Mr Rakkinen has told prosecutors that he knows about bribes beyond Nigeria, Russia and Libya, that were made with the knowledge of senior managers.

His evidence could lead to other criminal investigations and additional fines in other countries where Sarbel is active, including the US. Mr Rakkinen alleges he has knowledge of corruption involving Sarbel managers in more than a dozen countries, including Brazil, Cameroon, Egypt, Greece, Poland and Spain.

If Sarbel is found to have acted corruptly in certain other countries, including the US, it will also face bans on public-sector contracts.

Last week, Sarbel said that it had largely finished its internal investigations and had found €1.3 billion in suspicious payments for tax purposes and that the scandal had cost it €1.3 billion–€1.4 billion so far. The CEO, Per Anders, has resigned and the company has undergone a board shake-up and a complete reorganisation of its compliance function.

Case analysis

Using the integrity risk management framework described earlier, an analysis of the above due diligence information would reveal the following core issues:

- *Initial finance* for the purchase of Belvin Keffl – how was this raised, who from and what were the terms? Was the initial source of wealth therefore legitimate? *Further investigations would be necessary.*
- *Beneficial ownership* of the Deslan Group and Belvin Keffl. Are Deslan and family really the owners? Could they be fronting for others (e.g. political friends)? The nominee structure has the effect of hiding ownership. What about the 20 per cent that is not in Deslan's hands: who does that belong to? *Further investigations would be necessary. Failure to obtain comfort on beneficial ownership would offend against principle 1 and prevent the deal going ahead.*
- *Bribery allegations on (1) the Belvin Keffl purchase and (2) the acquisition of AIA Group.* The absence of criminal trials and convictions is not necessarily evidence of innocence in a country like Moldavia. Also, both men who allegedly took bribes from Deslan have recently died, albeit from apparently natural causes (cancer). *Further investigations would be necessary, but probably not much more could be found out about this.*
- *Political connections.* Deslan is very close to the ruling party and is a financial donor. This exposes business relationships between them to allegations of corruption and conflicts of interest, particularly since Belvin Keffl enjoys the benefit of government truck contracts. It is also possible that Deslan would become a target of the main opposition party if it achieved power, and could then reopen investigations against him.
- *Poor business practices and poor corporate governance.* Corporate governance is poor, with no independent oversight of the board and inadequate financial information, which is a credit and a fraud issue as much as an integrity and corruption issue. Apart from the major bribery allegations referred to above, the information reveals with some certainty that Deslan and his companies engage in a variety of practices ranging from the making of facilitation and other unorthodox payments to police and officials through to the awards of contracts and jobs on the basis of family and friendships rather than on merit. *Many countries now make no distinction between bribes and facilitation payments. If the allegations are believed to be true, and the activities are ongoing, with no prospect of cessation then this would offend against principle 4, notwithstanding the absence of a conviction, and would prevent the deal going ahead.*

- *Sarbel Engineering and Peter Valburg.* A proposed beneficiary of the financing, Sarbel, has recently been subject to a media storm in relation to proven bribery and corruption allegations across its global operations. Nevertheless, Sarbel is also one of the largest corporations in Europe, has removed its chairman and CEO and has embarked on a substantial anti-corruption programme to 'defumigate' the company and bring it into line with required international standards. It does not help, however, that Sarbel has been introduced to this business by Peter Valburg, who one source claims is possibly engaged in brokering payments for business, kick-backs and the negotiation of contracts at non-market rates. *Peter Valburg would have to be removed from the transaction.*

In mitigation of all of the above, the acquisitions of Belvin Keffl and the AIA Group took place a long time ago. Deslan appears willing to adopt better corporate practices and it is possible that he has 'moved on' from the worst excesses of his early career. He is not blacklisted and there are no allegations that he has ever been involved with organised crime or money laundering. If the beneficial ownership issue could be resolved and some real comfort gained that he had ceased making facilitation payments to minor officials, then given the absence of any convictions for serious crime, that would mean that he would actually be capable of passing the 'funnel tests' currently operated by the MDBs. In addition, following further investigations (almost certainly using external specialist investigations firms) it would be for the lender to weigh up the uncertainties against the benefits, in light of the mitigating factors referred to, plus any relevant covenants, undertakings, representations and warranties which could be incorporated within the deal documentation, such as:

- a corporate restructuring to flatten the ownership structure and make beneficial ownership more clear and transparent
- a corporate governance overhaul to provide protection for minority shareholders and improve access to company information; also the adoption of international accounting standards and the appointment of independent directors to the board
- undertakings by owner and management not to engage in corrupt and illegal practices (as defined) – linked to events of default and personal guarantees connecting default to personal wealth
- undertakings by owner and management to report immediately instances of actual or suspected fraud or corruption
- representations denying the historical allegations of bribery and disclosing the source of the initial wealth used for the purchase of Belvin Keffl – again linked to events of default and calls on personal guarantees should these subsequently be proven to be untrue.

6

Suspicion Recognition

Where you see the **WWW** *icon in this chapter, this indicates a preview link to the author's website and to a training film which is relevant to the AML CFT issue being discussed.*
Go to ***www.antimoneylaunderingvideos.com***

BACKGROUND AND GENERAL PRINCIPLES

A critical requirement for financial institutions and others charged with responsibilities for the detection and prevention of money laundering and terrorist financing is that they report instances where they have become suspicious that their facilities and/or services may be being used for criminal purposes (see Chapter 2). This requirement begs the twin questions of what it means to be 'suspicious' and under what circumstances a person should be *deemed* 'suspicious'. Or, putting the issue another way, when does it become *un*reasonable for a person *not* to be suspicious?

It is possible to view 'suspicion' as lying somewhere in the territory between *speculation* and *belief*, on a spectrum of awareness with *ignorance* at one end and *knowledge* at the other (see Figure 6.1).

Figure 6.1 **The 'suspicion spectrum'**

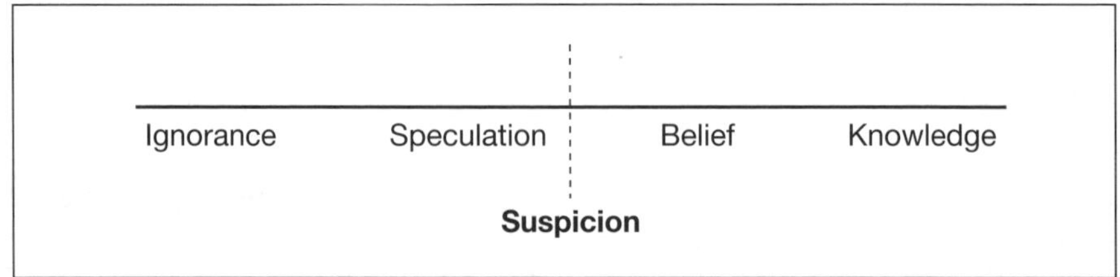

An English judge, interpreting national legislation, has described it thus:

> **'A degree of satisfaction, not necessarily amounting to belief but at least extending beyond speculation, as to whether an event has occurred or not';**

and

> **'Although the creation of a suspicion requires a lesser factual basis than the creation of belief, it must nonetheless be built upon some foundation'.**

Source: www.jmlsg.org.uk/industry-guidance/article/further-amendments-to-2007-guidance-20-december-2011

At certain points, therefore, it becomes unreasonable either to suspect or not to suspect somebody of something.

So, at what point is it reasonable to become suspicious?

Example

'S' was a getaway driver on a burglary whose defence in court was that he hadn't known that he was taking part in a burglary – he thought he was simply driving some friends to and from a business meeting that they were attending at a private residence.

In convicting him of aiding and abetting, the jury rejected this on the grounds that his accomplices had put stockings over their heads and armed themselves with batons, jemmies, holdalls and a variety of other tools prior to exiting the car he was driving …

Applying the above reasoning to a terrorist financing case, clearly it is unreasonable to suspect a person of being a terrorist or a financier of terrorism simply because they are from an ethnic group which has terrorists operating within it. Likewise it is unreasonable *not* to suspect a person of money laundering if they were receiving millions of dollars through their account each month, when their annual salary was $30,000 and there was no credible reason for the activity on the account.

Is the test for suspicion under law 'subjective' or 'objective'?

Example

Alicia is a relationship manager in the AlnaBank corporate division. Her customer, Amwell Trading, has an office in Columbia from which it remits frequent large sums of unknown origin to its UK account, which are then wired straight through to the account of another company at a bank in an offshore location, purportedly in respect of debts owed to that company by Amwell. She files no suspicious activity report because she is not suspicious. Suddenly, the company's accounts are frozen under a court order as being criminal proceeds from Amwell's suspected drugs operation and Alicia is interviewed by the police. She agrees to submit to a lie detector test, in which she is asked, 'Did you at any time suspect that Amwell might be engaged in criminal activity?' She answers, 'No' and passes the test. But colleagues, advised of the facts, state that they would have filed a report had they been managing the account.

In fact, having originally been subjective, the test for bank staff reporting suspicions is now generally an objective one. In other words, it does not matter that you yourself (like Alicia, above) were genuinely *not* suspicious about a client's activities. If reasonable people in your position, knowing what you knew, *would* have been suspicious, then you will have fallen short of the required standard of vigilance if you yourself do not suspect.

The typologies

In the remainder of this chapter, a wide variety of different money laundering and terrorist financing typologies and methodologies are described and depicted. The methods shown are by no means exhaustive, but they do constitute a wide ranging collection from multiple sources.

The Financial Action Task Force (FATF) regularly publishes reports of the latest methodologies or 'typologies' being used by money launderers around the world. In each case the method is described, followed by an analysis of its key features, its attractiveness from the launderer's perspective and a summary of the warning signs or 'red flags' that might alert staff to potential money laundering or terrorist financing.

FATF has published a number of these reports on general typological trends. In addition it has been very active in recent years in researching areas of specific risk and has published further reports targeting such risks. During 2010 and 2011, for example, FATF has reported on the following specific areas:

- 'Combating proliferation financing' (February 2010)
- 'Money laundering vulnerabilities of free trade zones' (March 2010)
- 'Money laundering using trusts and company service providers' (October 2010)
- 'Money laundering using new payment methods' (October 2010)
- 'Money laundering risks arising from trafficking in human beings and smuggling of migrants' (July 2011)
- 'Organized maritime piracy and related kidnapping for ransom' (July 2011)
- 'Laundering the proceeds of corruption' (July 2011).

Developing skills in recognising typologies

Knowing the signs of potential money laundering and terrorist financing is arguably the single most important capability which staff within financial organisations should have. Accordingly, through training and awareness programmes, Compliance Officers must ensure that staff know what they are looking for in a suspicious transaction.

In our company, Lessons Learned Ltd, we have developed a number of tried and tested training techniques which we use with client organisations to raise awareness and understanding of different typologies and how to recognise them. We have provided examples of three of these techniques below in our descriptions of different typologies. The training techniques in question are:

- three-part slide presentations
- account analysis practice exercises
- 'accumulation of evidence' case studies.

All these can be complemented with online videos to add interest and engage staff with the issues.

Three-part slide presentations

Discussions focus on a specific typology and are based around three presentation slides. The first of these provides an animated explanation of the typology and how it works. The second slide lists key facts about the typology. The third and final slide lists 'red flags' to look out for as possible signs of the typology in action. The three slides can be used either for a straightforward presenter-led explanation of the typology, or they can be linked to discussion questions such as, for example, 'How does typology X work?', 'What is attractive about it from a money laundering perspective?' and 'What red flags or indicators might make you suspicious that this typology is being used?'

Account analysis practice exercises

Participants are given printouts showing sequential transactions on an account. They work in groups to identify and explain potentially suspicious features in the transaction patterns shown.

'Accumulation of evidence' case studies

Participants are given some initial information about a client and their relationship with a financial institution. They are given further bits of information one at a time which, eventually, should start to raise concerns, points of doubt and possible suspicions regarding the client's activity within the relationship. The use of such case studies can demonstrate how the nature of relationships can change over time, with initially innocuous relationships becoming unusual and potentially suspicious as new behaviours emerge.

Soft copy pdfs of these different types of suspicion recognition exercises along with trainer's notes can be requested by purchasers of this book by emailing info@lessonslearned.co.uk. **WWW**

MONEY LAUNDERING TYPOLOGIES

Alternative remittance services

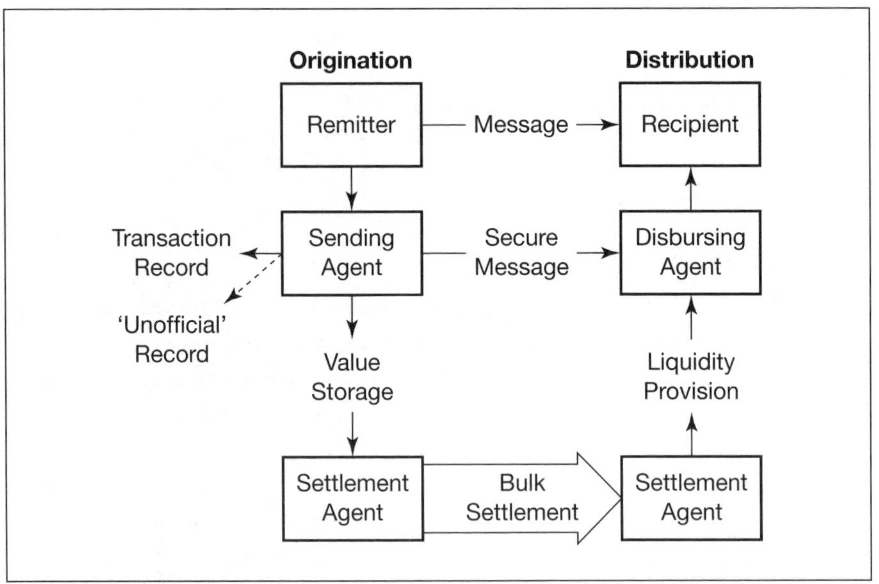

Source: © Lessons Learned Ltd 2012

How they work and potential for misuse

1 The remitter instructs the sending agent to make a remittance and deposits its funds with it, often in cash.

2 The remitter may send its own message to the recipient independently of the sending agent, to alert it to the fact that money is on its way.

3 The sending agent contacts the disbursing agent with instructions to issue funds to the recipient, which the disbursing agent duly does.

4 The sending agent makes a record of the transaction, and the remitter's funds sit in storage, accruing value and ready to complete the settlement via a settlement agent (if one is used).

5 The sending agent either issues funds directly or via a settlement agent to the destination country, where the money is held in storage and available for use.

6 On receipt of the settlement funds the disbursing agent is reimbursed for the funds issued and the transaction is complete.

7 Problems arise when the settlement amounts are transmitted as a bulk transfer, in which case it is relatively easy for laundered funds to be hidden in with the legitimate ones.

8 Unscrupulous ARS operators may also keep a separate 'unofficial' record of these covert transactions, this unofficial record being maintained separately from records of legitimate transactions.

Key facts

Alternative Remittance Service (ARS) is a term which can describe any system for transferring money outside of normal banking channels. There are many perfectly legitimate ARS operators as well as a few rogues. There are often ties between certain systems and particular geographic regions, and such systems are often described using a variety of specific terms including *hawala*, *hundi* and *fie-chien.*

It is clear that the vast majority of people who use ARS operators are perfectly ordinary and law-abiding with no criminal intentions whatsoever. There are a number of legitimate reasons for such people to want to send money via an ARS operator rather than through normal banking channels, for example:

- *Reasons of accessibility*: many people are denied access to normal banking facilities because of where they are based geographically, or because of their personal creditworthiness; these people have no choice but to use ARS operators to send money.
- *Cultural familiarity*: in certain parts of the world (e.g. many parts of the Middle East and Asia) systems such as *hawala*, *hundi* and *fie-chien* are culturally perfectly normal and may well be chosen in *preference* to the normal banking system.
- *Personal contacts*: extended families spread across the world may often use informal agreements to exchange money on behalf of friends and associates who require money to reach a particular person perhaps more quickly than the banking system can arrange; there is nothing illegal in what these people's contacts do for them, they are just being pragmatic and helpful.
- *Speed*: as explained above the banking system is not always fast enough, and informal arrangements via networks of associates can offer a quicker service where one is needed.
- *Anonymity/secrecy*: clearly remittances that bypass the normal banking systems can be carried out in relative anonymity and secrecy, and it goes without saying that this is why money launderers find the ARS systems attractive.

Money launderers' perspective

The attraction for money launderers is, as stated above, the opportunity for concealment that ARS can sometimes offer. ARS operators are generally unregulated and not subject to scrutiny by the authorities. The operators themselves often use codes in their records rather than specific individuals' names, and this also aids concealment.

Possible red flags

FATF has identified a number of possible suspicion indicators which might indicate that an ARS operator's business is being used for money laundering. Indicators include:

- remittances in excess of the norm for the customer's known economic background
- unusual escalation in levels of remittance for an individual
- personal remittances sent to destinations that do not have an apparent family or business link
- remittances made outside migrant remittance corridors
- reluctance of customer to give explanation for remittance
- personal funds sent at a time not associated with salary payments
- requests for a large transfer but settling for smaller amounts – potential structuring.

Note: A training film dealing with ARS operators can be previewed at http://www.antimoneylaunderingvideos.com/player/ars.htm

WWW

Auctions

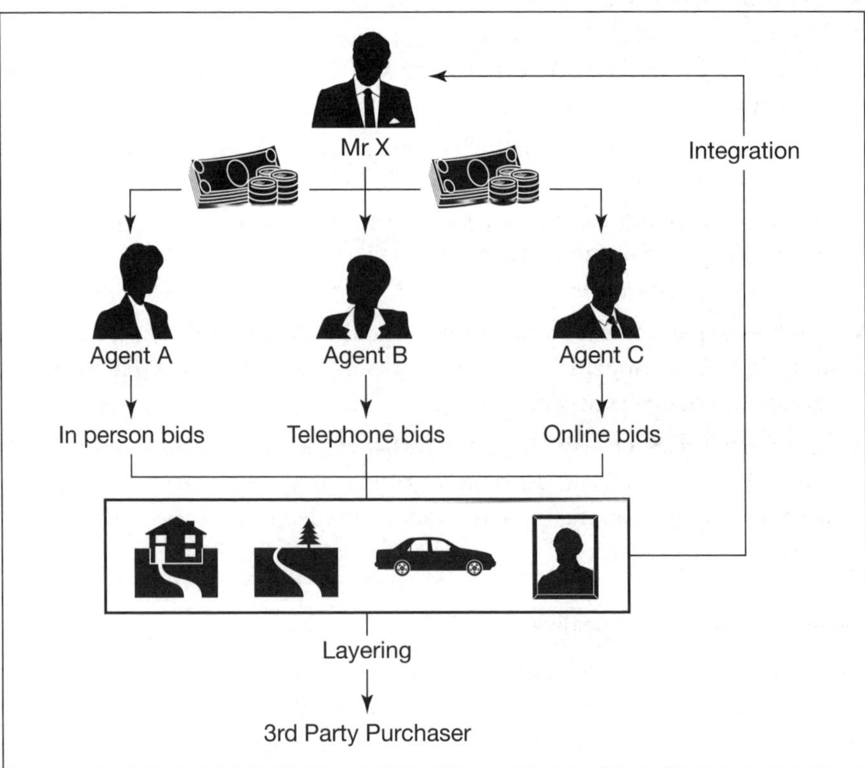

Source: © Lessons Learned Ltd 2012

Money laundering via auctions

1 The launderer distributes the cash proceeds of crime to a network of agents. Agents either retain the proceeds in cash form or bank the cash in own name bank accounts.
2 Agents go to auction and bid via whatever means is necessary, i.e. in person or over the telephone via another third party at physical auctions or electronically for online auctions.
3 Agents bid successfully for a range of high-value assets (e.g. real estate, cars, fine art). Identification presented is that of the agent or an alias, and the paperwork is completed in the agent's or alias's name.
4 Property acquired from auctions may be sold on to uninvolved third parties and the proceeds reinvested elsewhere (layering), or returned to the original source for his or her personal enjoyment (integration).

Key facts

Auctions can be used in a variety of ways. Cash purchases can be used to place criminal cash into the system, but auctions might also be used as a vehicle for buying a lot of different high-value items and then trading them on almost immediately in exchange for clean money which can then be reinvested elsewhere.

It goes without saying that the kinds of auctions that money launderers are most likely to be interested in are the ones where high-value items such as fine art, cars, antiques or real estate (both property and land) are being offered for sale. However, auctions of lower-value goods (e.g. second-hand car auctions) can also provide a ready marketplace in which criminal gangs are able to offload stolen property in exchange for hard cash, or change criminal cash into saleable assets.

The increasing availability of online auction sites offers the added attraction in that as a relatively new phenomenon they are not as yet subject to rigorous regulation. Online auctioning also enables participants to trade in relative anonymity, and to trade virtually anything with virtually anyone without too much scrutiny.

Money launderers' perspective

The attraction of auctions from the money launderers' point of view is the option to carry out the majority of transactions without ever having to be physically present or in direct contact with the other participants.

The auction environment is one in which it is quite normal for paying participants to act via intermediaries or agents, and so the non-presence of a purchaser does not draw attention.

Another advantage of the auction environment from the launderers' point of view is that many of the transactions are 'one-offs' and not the kind of relationship transactions involved in many kinds of other financial business.

Possible red flags

Transaction features and behaviours that might give cause for concern include the following:

- unwillingness or inability on the part of purchasers or their agents to give identification or other details
- cash settlements where cash would not normally be used as the method of settlement, particularly where the amounts involved are very large
- unusual purchasing patterns that do not appear to fit with what is known about the purchaser or their agent (e.g. purchase of a large number of high-performance cars when the purchaser does not appear to be in the car business or to have any other reason for making such a purchase, other than to use up large amounts of money)
- successful high-value bidders who are unwilling or unable to identify themselves
- third party intermediaries who are unwilling or unable to identify their clients
- cash settlement of high-value purchases, where use of cash would be unusual
- large-scale purchase of multiple items which cannot be explained and does not match the apparent business of the purchaser (e.g. car dealership, property developer).

WWW

Note: A training film dealing with laundering via auctioneers can be previewed at http://www.antimoneylaunderingvideos.com/player/auctioneers.htm

Black market peso exchange

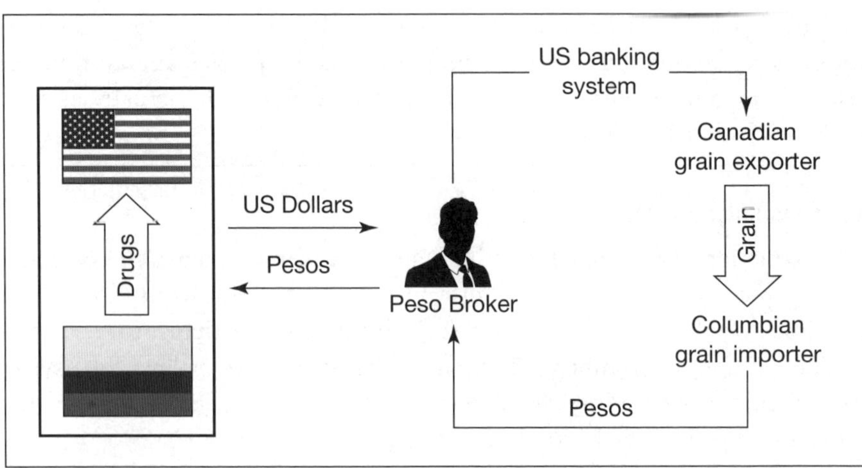

Source: © Lessons Learned Ltd 2012

How it works

This example is based on a real case.

1. A Colombian drug cartel imports and sells drugs in the US for US dollars cash.
2. The cartel then sells the US dollars to a peso broker for Colombian pesos, which are banked by the cartel in Colombia.
3. The peso broker pays the US dollars into US bank accounts he controls using 'smurfs'.
4. He then uses the funds to pay a Canadian company to ship grain to Colombia (on behalf of a Colombian import company).
5. The Colombian grain importer sells the grain in Colombia for pesos and repays the broker in pesos, thus replenishing the broker's supply of Colombian currency.
6. The cartel has no involvement beyond the initial shipping and sale of drugs and the sale of the criminal proceeds to the peso broker. The rest of the activity is carried out independently of the cartel.

Key facts

The term 'black market peso exchange' has its origins in the 1980s when the Colombian drug cartels dominated the illegal drugs trade in the US. Black market peso exchange was the system developed by these cartels to repatriate profits from drug sales in the US. The system has been adopted by criminal organisations in other parts of the world and the term 'black market peso exchange' is now applied more generally to the same system of money laundering, wherever it is used.

The system requires the collusion of an importer. It is made attractive to importers by providing them with the currency they need at a better rate of exchange than would normally be provided by local banks.

Money launderers' perspective

From the money launderers' point of view the system has a number of attractions. For one thing, the favourable exchange rate means that launderers may not have difficulty in finding an unscrupulous importer willing to collude with them. Also, the way in which this collusion works means that the launderers can do away with techniques such as over-invoicing or under-shipping in order for the colluding party to make a profit, since the profit can be made legitimately when the goods are sold on at their final destination. Since fraudulent tactics such as over-invoicing are not required, the goods and their value can be presented to customs exactly as they are and, since no other crime has been committed, there is a greatly reduced risk that the authorities' attention will be alerted.

Another great advantage for the launderers is that, once the initial risky enterprise of importing and selling drugs has been completed and the cash proceeds offloaded via a peso broker, the connection between the money and the criminal activity that produced it is virtually broken. The cartel has no involvement beyond its initial dealings with the peso broker, and so the risk of exposure is greatly reduced.

Possible red flags

These are:

- any 'money brokering' business that deals in cash exchanges of currencies commonly associated with this type of exchange system
- frequent cash deposits just below the local cash transaction reporting threshold (where one exists)
- a regular financial relationship with an import/export business where such a relationship does not fit what is known about the customer
- revenue streams do not make sense, given what is known about the entities involved and their normal business activities.

WWW Note: a training film dealing with the black market peso exchange can be previewed at http://www.antimoneylaunderingvideos.com/player/black_peso.htm

'Blood' diamonds

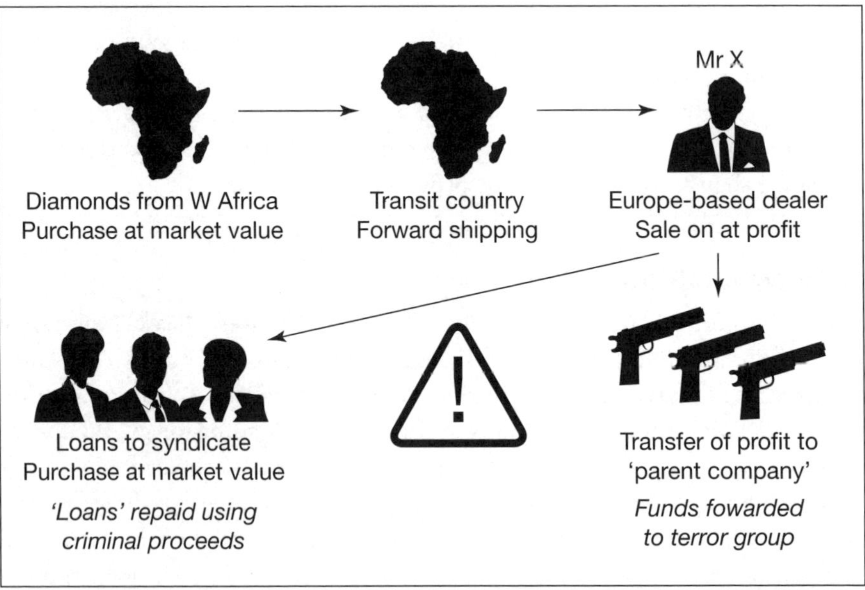

Source: © Lessons Learned Ltd 2012

Use of 'blood diamonds' in relation to criminal funds

This example is based on a real case.

1. 'Blood diamonds' were purchased at the local market value in Western Africa and shipped through another country, arriving eventually with a Europe-based diamond dealer, for sale on to other customers at a profit.
2. Amongst the various customers purchasing these diamonds were members of another diamond dealing family who were also involved in a number of criminal activities including illegal diamond trafficking. They raised loans which were used to purchase diamonds from the dealer. The terms of these loans were such that they were able to repay them quickly, using criminal funds. In other words, the legitimate loan funds were exchanged for diamonds and then replaced with criminal funds.
3. The diamonds could then be sold on legitimately at a profit.
4. Whilst using the sale of diamonds to help these criminals to launder their funds, the dealer was also using the profits from other sales to help fund terrorism.
5. Profits from sales were transferred on to an intermediary entity, before being passed finally to Al-Qaeda.

Key facts

Diamond production across the world is concentrated into a relatively small number of countries, including several countries in Western Africa where war and conflict have led to the breakdown of formal and legitimate controls in the diamond-producing regions. In the absence of such controls the 'warlords' and criminal gangs have taken their opportunity to move in and exploit diamond production for their own ends.

Many of the proceeds of diamond sales from these regions are used by the warlords to fund arms purchases and further conflict. It is this association between bloodshed and diamond production in the region which has given rise to the term 'blood diamonds'.

In recent years there have been increasing concerns that terror groups may also be using the market in 'blood diamonds' to fund their own activities.

Money launderers' perspective

Diamonds and other precious gems have long been used by money launderers as a means to convert criminal cash into a high-value, compact and easily tradable asset.

Their compactness and lack of weight and odour means that they can be easily concealed and are therefore easy to transport across borders.

Diamond production and diamond trading are both concentrated in a relatively small number of locations, and it is clearly in these locations or in transactions *involving* diamonds that particular vigilance for this money laundering typology is required.

As regards 'blood diamonds' the obvious high-risk jurisdictions are the diamond producing countries of Western Africa. High value, cross-border transactions involving these countries carry at least some risk of a link with the trade in 'blood' diamonds.

Possible red flags

Transactions that might give cause for concern and should certainly give rise to enhanced due diligence include the following:

- transactions that have originated in or passed through countries associated with the production of 'blood' diamonds
- any unusual transactions involving companies active in the diamond trade
- any cash transactions (deposits or withdrawals) that can be linked to the trade in diamonds
- any transaction that can be linked to the trade in diamonds and which does not fit with the known business of the individual or entity in question
- significant unexplained deposits from companies active in the diamond trade
- large-scale, cross-border, funds transfers involving countries known to be a source of 'blood diamonds'
- cross-border funds transfers involving nationals/residents of diamond producing areas of Western Africa
- unexplained large international funds transfers to known diamond traders, followed by immediate withdrawal in cash
- very 'regular' levels of funds and cash flow in diamond trading businesses (fluctuations would be more normal)
- any transaction with the diamond trade that cannot be explained by an individual's or company's known business.

WWW

Note: A training film dealing with blood diamonds can be previewed at http://www.antimoneylaunderingvideos.com/player/diamonds.htm

Casinos

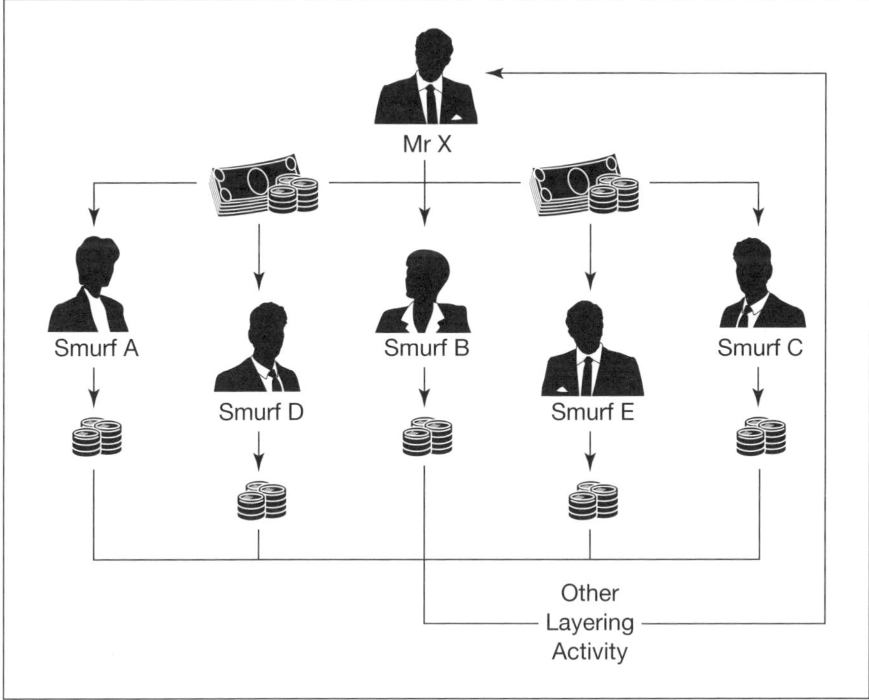

Source: © Lessons Learned Ltd 2012

Casinos as a vehicle for the placement of criminal funds

1 The launderer distributes the cash proceeds of crime in relatively small amounts to a large number of 'smurfs'.

2 Each smurf exchanges cash for chips at a casino.

3 Smurfs play some of the chips but then credit the remainder to an account in their own name or some other third-party account.

4 The banked money is then reinvested elsewhere as part of the layering process before finally being returned to the criminal for his or her enjoyment.

Key facts

Casinos are primarily of use for placement activity, since they provide an environment in which cash circulates freely and in fairly large quantities. It is not, therefore, too difficult for the criminals to introduce the cash proceeds of their illegal activities into this circulation.

The placement activity occurs in the exchange of cash for gambling chips. This exchange generally takes place in a physical casino rather than an online casino environment.

However, online gambling websites offer patrons the opportunity to set up accounts where they can deposit funds and have them available for play. The same accounts can also be used by money launderers as temporary places to store money and keep it circulating gently via a bit of online gambling, before it is moved wholesale to be reinvested elsewhere.

Money launderers' perspective

From the money launderers' point of view the casino environment is uniquely suitable for placement purposes because of the large amounts of cash which are moving around and the rapid speed at which all this cash can change hands.

It is also possible from the launderers' point of view to establish a fairly large network of willing collaborators ('smurfs') who are only too happy to help process the money in exchange for some gambling 'pocket money'.

Possible red flags

Things to look out for include the following:

- patrons who are unable or unwilling to provide identification when purchasing chips or cashing chips in
- patrons whose chip purchases consistently do not match their gambling, i.e. purchases in very large quantities of which the patron then only plays a very small proportion, before cashing them all in again
- patrons whose appearance and apparent status appear inconsistent with the values of their chip purchases (may indicate that they are making the purchase on behalf of a wealthier third party)
- instructions to forward the cash-in value of leftover chips to someone other than the patron (may also indicate that they are acting as an intermediary for an unknown third party).

WWW

Note: A training film dealing with laundering through casinos can be previewed at http://www.antimoneylaunderingvideos.com/player/casinos.htm

Correspondent banking

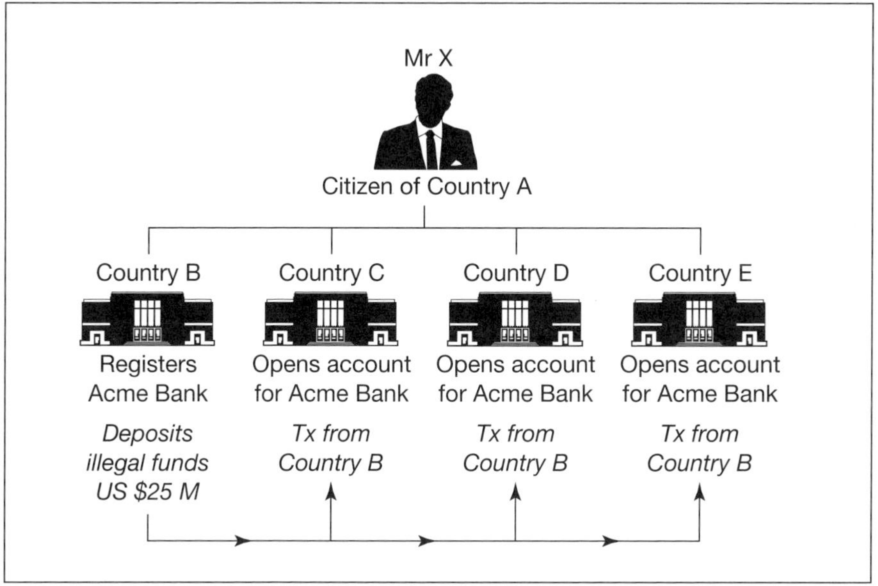

Source: © Lessons Learned Ltd 2012

Use of correspondent bank accounts for money laundering

This example derives from a real case. Mr X was a citizen of Country A. He registered a bank in Country B ('Acme Bank'). Acme Bank was a shell bank, had no real physical presence, no staff and no remit ever to provide services to anyone other than Mr X; in fact its sole purpose was to act as a vehicle for Mr X's criminally obtained money. Mr X deposited $25 million of his money before moving on to Country C.

In countries C, D and E Mr X went to various banking institutions and, acting as a representative for Acme Bank, established correspondent banking accounts in the bank's name. He then used the correspondent banking services of the host banks to transfer funds to Countries C, D and E from Acme Bank's accounts in Country B.

Using this network of correspondent banking accounts Mr X was able to move money across jurisdictions, from where it was used for the purchase of high-value and highly tradable goods.

Key facts Correspondent banking relationships are effectively agreements for one bank to provide services for another in jurisdictions where the first bank does not have a physical presence. It is a customer–supplier relationship in which the 'respondent' bank is the customer and the 'correspondent' bank the one that provides the services. The relationship permits the respondent bank to move money via the correspondent bank's own accounts and thus to offer its customers a range of services in countries where it does not normally operate. There are inherent risks in the relationship, because in many of these transactions the correspondent bank does not have direct contact with the customer entity and has to rely on the efficacy of the respondent bank's customer identification and due diligence effort.

Money launderers' perspective

Weak or inadequate customer identification and due diligence procedures on the part of the respondent bank, combined with the indirectness of the relationship between the customer entity and the correspondent bank, provide increased opportunities for concealment and this of course is attractive to money launderers. The fact that the money is transferred via the respondent bank's accounts and not via personally named accounts further enables this concealment.

Money launderers might also seek to create their own 'banks' and use these to establish their own correspondent banking relationships. The banks registered by the money launderers may be 'shell banks' that exist in name only or 'pocket banks' controlled by a single individual or group. The deposits they hold are the criminal funds that the criminals are seeking to launder. These shell or pocket bank identities are then used to establish correspondent banking relationships with legitimate banks around the world. The relationship enables the money launderers to move their criminal funds from the shell banks' accounts, via the legitimate banks' own accounts, to new destinations in other countries and other banks.

Possible red flags

There are two specific problems to look out for:

1. potential flaws or weaknesses in a respondent bank's own AML standards and procedures
2. use of shell bank structures to establish correspondent banking relationships for the sole purpose of laundering money.

With regard to potential problems in the AML and due diligence carried out by the respondent bank, 'red flag' issues include:

- a lack of background knowledge about the bank's customers
- absence of originator or beneficiary information for transfers passing through the bank
- slackness with regard to the entities to whom the bank provides its own correspondent banking services.

With regard to the possible use of shell bank structures in relation to correspondent banking, 'red flag' issues include any problems in identifying the owners of the bank or its location, or in obtaining evidence of its normal operating activities.

It is also possible that a legitimate bank may unknowingly use its own correspondent banking relationship to transfer via the correspondent bank's accounts criminal funds that it has failed to identify. Tell-tale signs that a bank's relationship with another bank might be being used in this way include:

- numerous requests for large volume wire transfers
- unusually frequent and repetitive transactions
- transfers whose destination do not conform with the respondent bank's normal business activities
- the respondent bank's ownership structure cannot be verified
- the respondent bank has no real physical presence
- the respondent bank is unable to provide background detail regarding entities for whom it has requested services
- the respondent bank is unable to provide originator details for transfers for which it is an intermediate bank
- the respondent bank provides correspondent banking services for shell banks
- the respondent bank permits third parties direct access to its accounts for 'payable through' transactions
- when the direction of transfer does not appear to fit with normal or expected business activity.

Note: A training film dealing with laundering via correspondent banks can be previewed at http://www.antimoneylaunderingvideos.com/player/correspondent.htm

WWW

Credit cards

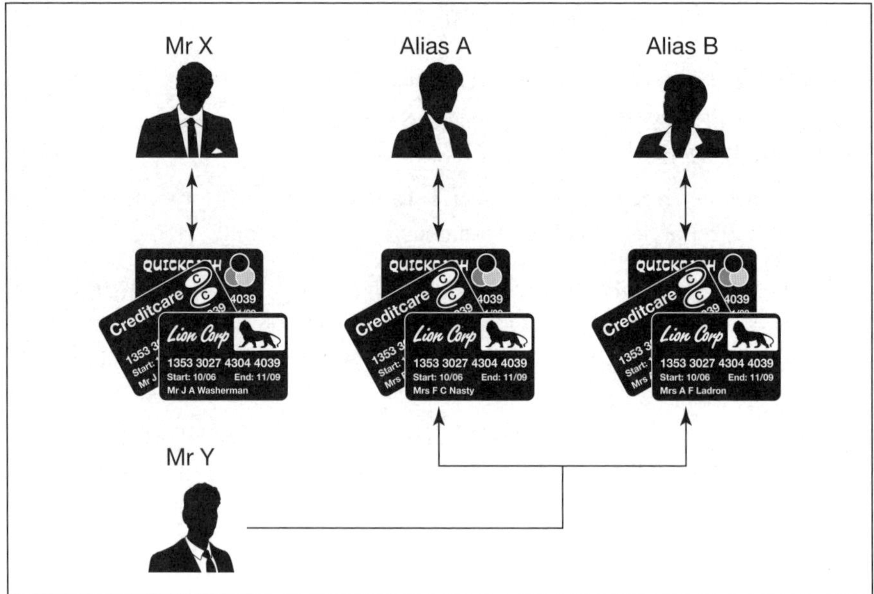

Source: © Lessons Learned Ltd 2012

Use of credit cards for money laundering

This example derives from a real case.

1 A single individual (Mr X) fraudulently obtains a number of credit cards from different institutions, using a variety of different names and aliases. In some cases he holds several different cards with the same institution.

2 Using the same method of aliases he establishes further credit card accounts overseas.

3 He then uses the credit cards to make some fairly ordinary purchases (e.g. restaurant meals) and some very expensive purchases (e.g. cars, paintings, expensive jewellery).

4 He uses criminal funds to pay off the credit card debts incurred. Some of the payments are made by cheque from accounts in the name of the given card holder. Some are made by an apparently unconnected third party, Mr Y.

5 The valuable assets purchased in this way are subsequently sold on to other uninvolved parties and the proceeds of the sales are invested elsewhere.

6 The ordinary card purchases are simply used as a guise to give the impression of 'normal' daily usage of the cards.

Key facts

Credit cards are widely used in most of the world's economies and generate billions of transactions worldwide each year. No one really knows the extent to which they are used for money laundering purposes, but there is a consensus view that they are not likely to be used at the placement stage (where criminal cash is first introduced into the financial system), and are much more likely to have a role in layering and integration activities.

Money laundering using credit cards will also tend to go hand-in-hand with other credit-card related crimes, for example, theft, where an innocent third party's identity is taken from a stolen credit card and used to establish new card accounts, and credit card fraud, where such falsely obtained cards are used to purchase goods fraudulently.

Credit cards are in such prevalence and are so widely used that *all* financial institutions across the world are potentially affected by credit card crimes.

Money launderers' perspective

One of the great benefits of credit cards for legitimate card holders is the ability, via ATM machines, to be able to access money from just about any financial institution, anywhere in the world. This benefit is clearly also advantageous to money launderers, since it gives them a means by which they can, very quickly and simply, move quite large amounts of money across international borders, without ever having to come face-to-face with a member of staff from the institution in question.

The remoteness of many credit card transactions (transactions over the telephone, over the internet, etc.) also assists money launderers in concealing their identities.

Finally, credit cards can be used to buy just about anything, with the credit card account being paid off regularly. This helps money launderers in converting their criminal funds into legitimate and saleable assets that can be sold on as part of the layering process.

Possible red flags

Transactions that might give cause for concern include the following:

- A sudden change in the transaction patterns on a credit card account, or transactions that do not fit with the known business of the named card holder (this may indicate that the card has been stolen, or that the card account has been accessed and is being used by an unauthorised third party).
- Multiple cards in different names linked to a single residential address and/or third party settlor (this may indicate that multiple identities and different aliases are being used by a single individual).

- Third party settlement of credit card accounts (this might indicate the use of aliases as described above; or it may indicate that the card holder is in fact using the card to make purchases/launder money on behalf of an unknown third party).
- Unusually large cash settlement of credit card accounts (people *do* sometimes settle their accounts in cash, but rarely for large amounts; very large cash settlements might however be used as a means to start clearing criminal cash through the financial system).
- Unusually large and frequent cash withdrawals from off-shore credit card accounts (this use of credit cards may indicate an attempt to 'layer' criminal money by moving it between jurisdictions).

WWW

Note: A training film dealing with laundering via credit cards can be previewed at http://www.antimoneylaunderingvideos.com/player/cards.htm

The terrorists involved in the 9/11 attacks used credit cards via the ATM system to withdraw money from offshore credit card accounts. Funds were paid into these accounts by third parties overseas. The terrorists drew on the funds to pay for their day-to-day living expenses, and the costs incurred in setting up their terror attacks.

Insurance

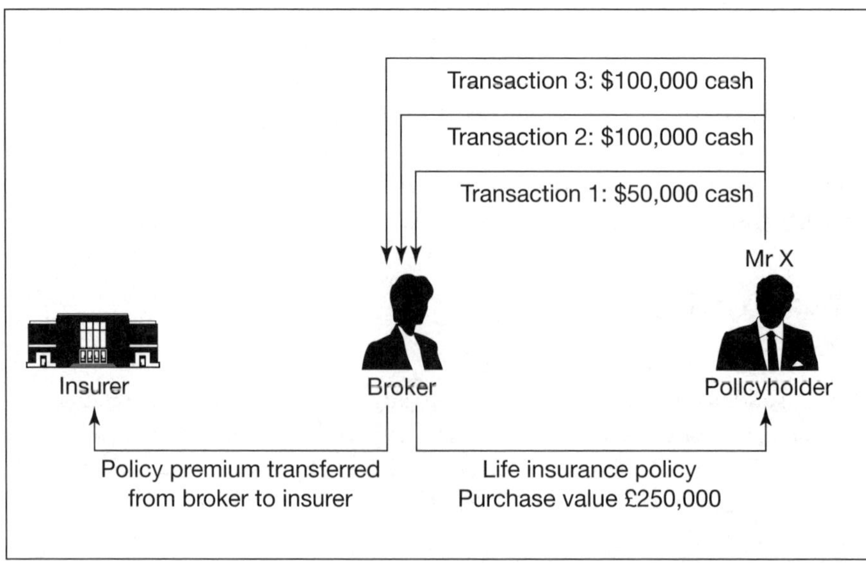

Source: © Lessons Learned Ltd 2012

Use of insurance policies for money laundering

This example is derived from a real case.

1 The customer purchased a life insurance policy from a broker, for £250,000.
2 The £250,000 purchase price was paid in three cash lump transactions of £50,000, £100,000 and £100,000. The broker accepted these cash payments and banked them, apparently without question.
3 The broker then paid the policy premium to an insurance company, who then activated the policy on behalf of the customer.
4 The insurance company had no reason to know that the policy had been paid for by the policyholder via three suspiciously large cash transactions. They trusted the broker to have carried out adequate due diligence.

The intermediary relationship shown in this example and the heavy reliance of insurance providers on the integrity and competence of the brokers who broke their business is typical of many insurance transactions and is one of the insurance industry's greatest vulnerabilities.

Key facts

Historically, until relatively recently, the insurance industry was inconsistently regulated and training was generally not provided. As a result, again until recently, awareness of anti-money laundering is not always at such a high level as in some other financial service sectors. The industry is also one that is particularly vulnerable because of the nature of the products it sells and the way in which those products are sold.

The products themselves are insurance policies – life, general, etc. The beneficiaries of these policies are sometimes someone different from the named policyholder. The benefit of policies can also, quite normally, be transferred from one beneficiary to another (e.g. when the primary beneficiary of a life policy dies the benefit passes to the next named beneficiary, and so on). The fact that the beneficiaries to a policy can be so readily changed makes it easier for launderers to transfer the benefit of policies, and this makes them attractive as instruments for money laundering where they have a surrender value.

The method of sale is also helpful from the money laundering point of view, because the heavy reliance on intermediaries and agents means that launderers may never need to present personally to the company that insures them. All they need to do is find themselves an unscrupulous or unsuspecting and careless agent who is prepared to transact business without asking too many questions.

Money launderers tend to exploit insurance products using a number of basic techniques:

- placing criminal cash in the financial system by using the cash to purchase the product
- overpaying premiums and then claiming back the overpayment from the insurer
- taking out fixed term policies which are then cancelled or redeemed (the launderer pays a penalty, but the money returned is now 'clean')
- paying a heavy insurance premium and then redeeming the money indirectly, via a number of false insurance claims paid by the insurer.

Money launderers' perspective

From the money launderers' point of view the common use of intermediaries and brokers in the industry greatly assists them in concealing the identities of the named policyholders and/or beneficiaries to policies. Whilst the insurance companies themselves might insist on rigorous due diligence they have to trust the brokers to do what is required, and if the broker does not do this the company is at risk of being used for money laundering.

Furthermore, the insurance companies that provide the policies will obviously pay the proceeds of those policies into their own bank accounts. The account holding bank is very unlikely to question the origin of the funds paid in, since the funds are paid in under the insurer's name and the bank will assume that the funds are from a legitimate source.

Another benefit from the launderers' point of view is that insurance products can *generate* money as well as laundering it. False claims on an insurance policy give additional (criminal) revenues and income earning policies accrue value, so the launderers earn legitimate-appearing income from their insurance investments at the same time as they are using these products to launder the proceeds of crime.

Finally, the relative ease with which products can be transferred between beneficiaries is obviously advantageous in that it can be used to disguise the legal and beneficial ownership of any funds that the policy may pay out.

Possible red flags

Transaction features and behaviours that could give cause for concern in relation to insurance products include the following:

- pre-signed policy application forms
- purchase of products which do not make economic sense or do not fit the policyholder's apparent business needs
- payment for products via unrelated third parties
- payment for products using large amounts of cash
- unusual overpayments of premiums followed by a request to return overpaid amounts

- early redemption of policies which cannot be satisfactorily explained
- change of beneficiaries which cannot be satisfactorily explained
- unusual and frequent claims on policies, especially when payout is made to an unconnected third party.

Note: A training film dealing with laundering via credit cards can be previewed at http://www.antimoneylaunderingvideos.com/player/insurance.htm

WWW

Mortgages

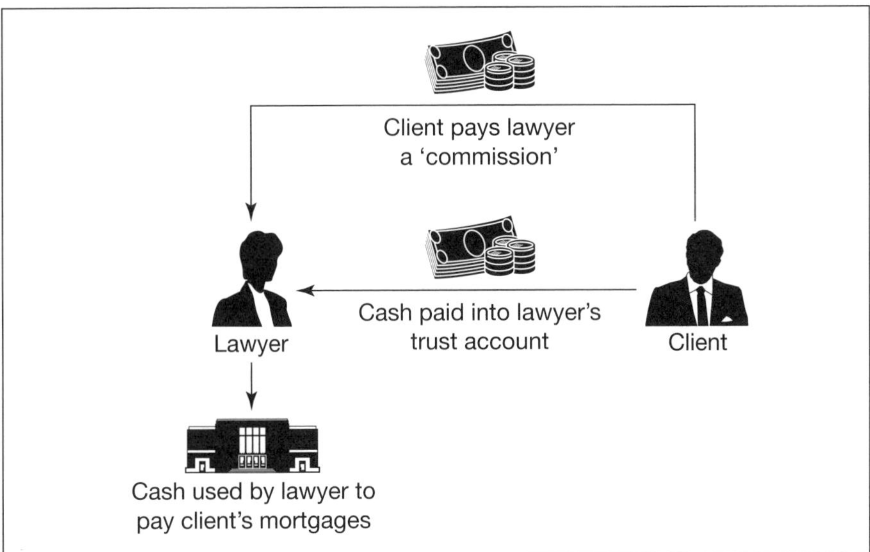

Source: © Lessons Learned Ltd 2012

Mortgages as a vehicle for money laundering

This example is based on a real case.

1 A lawyer was instructed by his client, a drug trafficker, to deposit cash into the lawyer's trust account and then make routine payments to mortgages on properties beneficially owned by the drug trafficker.

2 The lawyer received commissions from the sale of these properties and for his services in brokering the mortgages.

Key facts

Any type of loan provides money launderers with an opportunity to acquire clean funds via the legitimate means of a loan application, and then to replace these funds in the form of loan repayments with dirty funds from their criminal activities. A mortgage is just another type of loan that can be used in exactly this way by launderers.

However, mortgages have an added attraction in that they can be raised for very substantial amounts of money (assuming the mortgagor is able to demonstrate their ability to repay), and so they are particularly useful for the wholesale clearance of large amounts of criminal funds.

All types of mortgage are vulnerable. Launderers might use the vehicle of a property management company to purchase and develop property as part of a real business enterprise. The developed property can be sold on at a profit or rented out via letting agents. The real estate in question might be domestic *or* commercial, it does not really matter; the main thing from the money launderers' point of view is that the property is valuable and that they can raise a large mortgage on it.

The mortgage is operated as expected for a period of time, with the agreed payment instalments being made regularly and on time. Then suddenly large overpayments are made, using large amounts of criminal money wired in from accounts elsewhere, or even sometimes paid over in cash. The mortgage is fully paid off well within the agreed loan term and using criminal funds. The property, now debt-free, constitutes a significant asset which the criminal can now sell on to another third party, often at a substantial profit.

Money launderers' perspective

Mortgages are an attractive form of loan because they are linked to real estate and real estate is often a good investment that gives a good return. In other words, the launderers can build a legitimately profitable business out of their property portfolio.

Also, if the launderers are operating mortgages for different properties via a property management company, then that same company structure might also be used as a vehicle for other types of trade-based money laundering, for example over- and under-invoicing practices involving contractors hired to do work on the properties.

Possible 'red flags'

Transactions and behaviours that should give cause for concern include the following:

- difficulties at application in securing identification and background details for the mortgagor
- payments from apparently unconnected third parties
- overpayments which are inconsistent with the known wealth and business of the mortgagor
- large cash payments used to reduce the amount of a mortgage
- early and unexplained repayment of a mortgage in full.

WWW Note: A training film dealing with laundering via mortgages can be previewed at http://www.antimoneylaunderingvideos.com/player/mortgages.htm

Trade finance

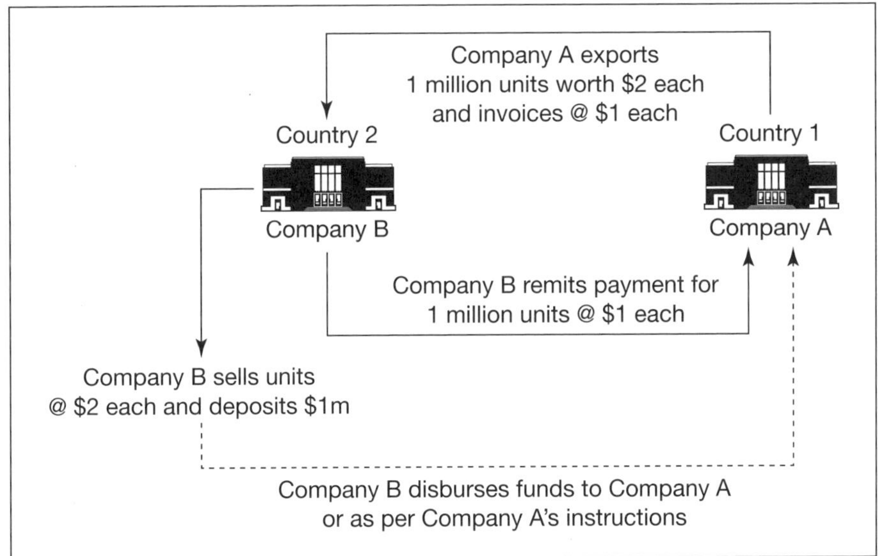
Company A exports
1 million units worth $2 each
and invoices @ $1 each
Country 2
Country 1
Company B
Company A
Company B remits payment for
1 million units @ $1 each
Company B sells units
@ $2 each and deposits $1m
Company B disburses funds to Company A
or as per Company A's instructions

Source: © Lessons Learned Ltd 2012

Trade-based money laundering via under-invoicing

1 Company A exports to Company B 1 million units of a product, each of which has a fair market value of $2.

2 Company A invoices Company B for only half the fair market value of the products supplied. Company B pays the invoice, wiring $1 million to Company A.

3 Company B then sells the products at their true market value of $2, making a $1 million profit.

4 The $1 million in profit is deposited by Company B and later disbursed according to Company A's instructions (with Company B being paid a 'consideration' in return for its services).

Key facts

Trade-based money laundering is a generic term used to describe a range of different laundering techniques using trade transactions.

The basic techniques are as follows:

- over- and under-invoicing: where there are discrepancies between the value invoiced and the value of the actual goods received
- multiple invoicing: where a product or service is supplied once but several invoices are generated (this has the same overall effect as over-invoicing)

- over- and under-shipment of goods: where there are discrepancies between the goods as described and the actual goods themselves (e.g., goods described as low-value high street clothing items but are actually high-value designer brands) – this has the same overall effect as over- and under-invoicing
- falsely described goods and services: for example, where a printing company submits an invoice for services which have never in fact been requested or provided and which are then 'paid for' using criminal proceeds.

With an increasingly global economy the opportunities for money launderers to exploit trade transactions for money laundering purposes (particularly in relation to import–export business) are also increasing.

Money launderers' perspective

From the money launderers' point of view the advantages of trade transactions are that they are so numerous. A single business can perform hundreds of transactions every day. It is relatively easy therefore to disguise a few spurious transactions in amongst all the legitimate ones. The complexity of international and foreign exchange financing arrangements can also help to obfuscate what is really going on. Illicit funds can also be commingled, concealed and transmitted alongside legitimate funds. This is particularly true where a genuine import-export business has been co-opted into the laundering arrangements.

Possible red flags

There are a number of suspicion indicators that should give cause for concern in relation to trade activities. A number of these indicators are listed below.

- the bill of lading description of goods does not match those on the invoice
- goods described do not match the actual goods shipped
- the invoiced value of the goods/services exceeds the fair market value
- the volume/type of goods/services is inconsistent with known size/ nature of the entity's regular business activities
- the business transaction does not make economic sense
- goods are shipped through one or more jurisdictions for no apparent economic reason
- repeatedly amended or frequently extended letters of credit
- cash settlement of transactions from apparently unconnected third parties
- supplier and customer relationships and transactions that do not fit with the known business of the corporate entity.

WWW

Note: a training film on money laundering through trade finance can be previewed at http://www.antimoneylaunderingvideos.com/player/blood_in_the_water.htm.

TERRORIST FINANCING TYPOLOGIES

Diversion of charitable funds

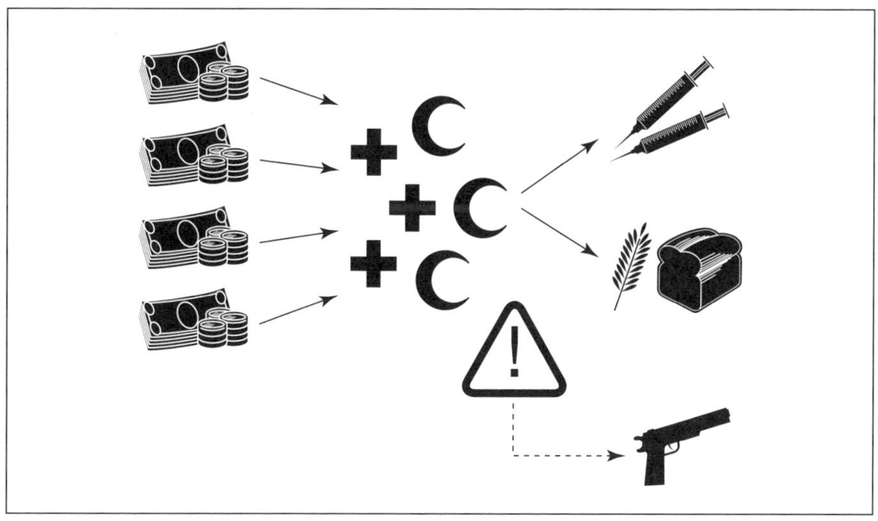

Source: © Lessons Learned Ltd 2012

How it works

The concept of the 'front company' will be familiar to anyone who deals with the prevention of money laundering through corporate structures. In the world of terrorist financing, charitable and humanitarian organisations are particularly at risk of being targeted by terrorist financiers and used by them as 'front' organisations to disguise the movement of terrorist funds.

1 At the start, everything is perfectly legal. The charity is a bona fide charity, doing exactly what it says it does. It receives legitimate donations from lots of different sources, often all over the world. The money received is deposited and pooled in the charity's bank accounts …

2 From there it is sent to fund relief projects and other charitable activities around the world. The money is sent to banking outlets in or near the organisation's projects, from where it is withdrawn, often in cash, which is used to pay for the charity's local needs.

3 These cash withdrawals are 'hijacked' by the terrorists at the point of withdrawal, i.e. the person who goes into the bank to receive the withdrawn money is an impostor acting for the terrorist group who simply poses as a worker for the charity, takes the money and vanishes, thereby channelling the money to the terrorists.

Key facts

Why should charitable and humanitarian organisations in particular be so vulnerable to exploitation by terrorist groups? The answer is simple: terrorists are frequently at their most active in the world's relief 'hot spots', which means that relief organisations and terrorists are often active in the same geographical areas. The charities and terrorists both need to move funds to the same places, and the terrorists simply use the charities to do it for them.

The fact that these areas often operate a cash economy and that the transferred funds are received in a cash form ready to use makes it that much easier for terrorist impostors to steal and divert the funds to their own causes.

Sometimes the money is 'hijacked' before it even reaches its destination via a 'plant' within the charity – a member of staff who is a sympathiser or whose cooperation has been obtained under duress, and whose authority is used to order transfers specifically for the benefit of terrorists.

Terrorist financiers' perspective

The fact that charities may operate in the same geographical areas as terrorist groups is clearly very convenient for the terrorists, since the charities' transactions to that area provide them with a ready-made means to move their money to where it can be used by local operatives.

By 'piggy-backing' on the charities' transactions they can shift their own terrorist funds as well as hi-jacking funds that were originally intended for the charities' legitimate activities. The fact that they can do all this under the cover of a third-party organisation clearly helps with the problem of disguising the true purpose of the funds and the identities of those involved.

Possible red flags

These include:

- incongruities between the known sources of a charity's funding and the value of funds deposited into its account or moved through it
- mismatches between the pattern and size of financial transactions and the stated purpose and activity of the charitable organisation
- discrepancies between the known regions where the organisation is active and the destination of transferred funds
- changes in signatories that coincide with changes in the volumes and destination patterns for overseas remittances
- sudden unexplained increases in the frequency of financial transactions and the sums paid in and out of accounts.

WWW

Note: A training film dealing with terrorist financing via charities can be previewed at http://www.antimoneylaunderingvideos.com/player/charities.htm

International business transactions

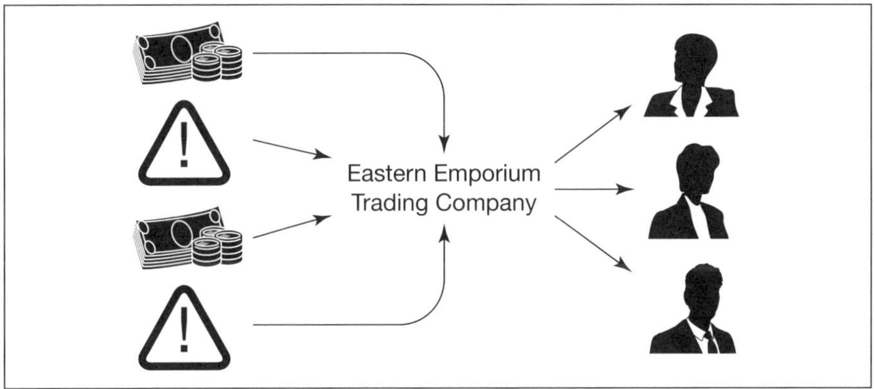

Source: © Lessons Learned Ltd 2012

Use of business accounts

This example is based on a real case.

1 A business in a high-risk country sources and exports ethnic crafts for sale overseas. Customer businesses pay legitimate amounts of money in payment of invoices received from the business, for goods that have been supplied and purchased legitimately. The payments are often made by electronic transfer, given that the customer businesses are based overseas.
2 Alongside these legitimate revenues from its customers the business receives wired terrorist funds. These funds are commingled with the legitimate revenues in the business's accounts.
3 Individuals with signatory authority for the business's accounts then withdraw funds via local bank branches in the terrorists' target country, to fund local terrorist activities.

Key facts

Businesses that have a connection – either through their ownership, their location or through their trading – with high-risk countries clearly constitute a higher-risk of involvement and may require enhanced due diligence.

Diaspora-owned businesses around the world are particularly vulnerable, since they can provide the terrorists with a ready-made network of business accounts and the assistance of the business owners of those accounts (whether willing or forced by threats of violence) can be particularly valuable.

Terrorist financiers' perspective

As indicated above, diaspora-owned businesses are potentially higher risk and may require enhanced due diligence, as the diaspora who own them (immigrants or refugees from their country of origin) may actively support the terrorists' causes in their homeland and may be quite willing to allow their businesses to be used. Alternatively there have also been cases where diaspora owners of businesses have been *forced* to cooperate with the terrorists under the threat of possible repercussions for their families, if they do not.

The network of businesses across the world – and in particular the use of import–export businesses – provides the terrorists with a network of legitimate international business via which electronic transactions may be carried out frequently, with terrorist financing transactions hidden within.

Possible red flags

These include:

- the use of a business account to channel funds to a small number of overseas recipients, without apparent reason.
- individuals and businesses in a country of specific concern who are connected by unusual or unexplained payments.
- an unusually high volume of wire transfer activity into and out of a business account
- large and unusual currency withdrawals from a business account
- a business owned by nationals of countries of specific concern which undergoes a sudden and unexplained change in profile.

WWW Note: A training film dealing with terrorist financing through international business transactions can be previewed at http://www.antimoneylaunderingvideos.com/player/business.htm

Places of worship

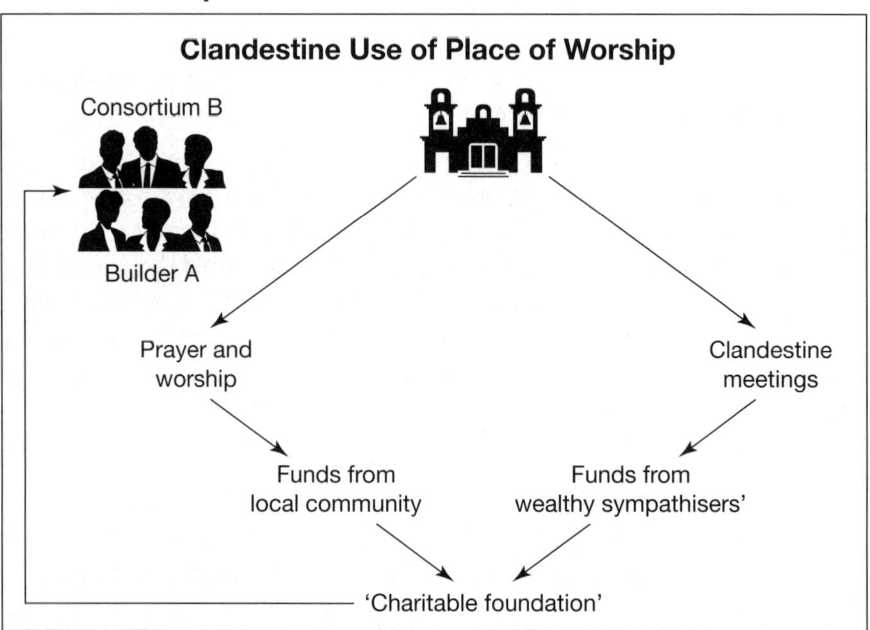

Source: © Lessons Learned Ltd 2012

Clandestine use of places of worship

This example is derived from a real case.

1 Builder A is the local owner of a local building company. He is also a member of a religious extremist group. He uses his company to purchase a property for renovation and sale.

2 The property is renovated and converted into a place of worship, ownership of which is then transferred from Builder A to Consortium B who are overtly a consortium of wealthy local businessmen but covertly religious extremists with links to terrorism.

3 The place of worship is opened for use. On the one hand it operates legitimately as a place for the local community to pray and worship. On the other hand it provides a convenient venue for local and visiting extremists to hold clandestine meetings.

4 Extremist meetings are used as an opportunity to raise funds from sympathisers. Legitimate donations from the local community are also collected in support of their place of worship.

5 Donations from both sources are paid into a 'charitable foundation' that determines how and where the funds will be spent.

6 The foundation is placed under the control of Consortium B, who channel funds from the foundation into terrorist causes of their choice.

Key facts

Not all terrorists are religiously motivated, and clearly it is primarily only those terror groups that have a religious fanatical agenda who are likely to make places of worship a centre for their activities.

Terrorist financiers' perspective

For religious extremist terror groups, such institutions are an obvious target as a centre for fund-raising since the people who use them for worship will be of the same religious persuasion and, even if not extreme in their views, are more likely to sympathise with some aspects of the extremists' cause and possibly to be persuaded towards supporting their ideas.

Possible red flags

These include:

- difficulties in establishing and identifying who owns and controls a centre for religious worship
- unexplained large volumes of 'donations' that are inconsistent with the size and wealth of the local faith community
- financial movements including forward transfers to third parties whose connection with the centre and its business are unknown or unexplained
- connections between the local faith community and countries known to be at a high risk from terrorism.

Overseas funds transfers

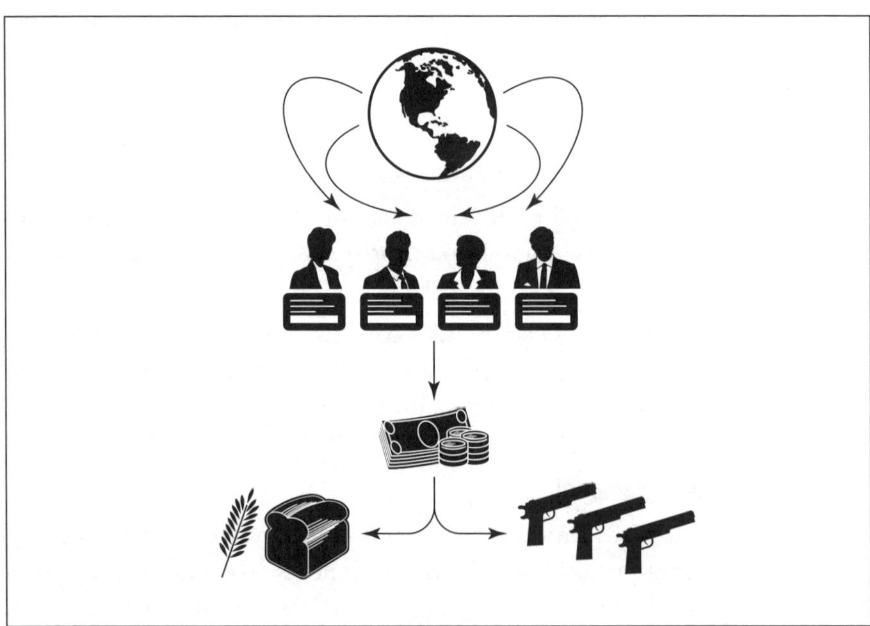

Source: © Lessons Learned Ltd 2012

How they can be used to fund terrorism

This example is based on what really happened behind 9/11.

1 Operatives used student visas or other official permissions to base themselves legitimately in the target country, where they opened bank accounts.

2 Funds were received into these accounts via electronic transfers from various overseas third-party accounts.

3 The operatives used ATM cards to make cash withdrawals.

4 They used the cash to fund their day-to-day living costs of food, rent, college fees, etc.

5 They also used the cash to fund purchases and activities in preparation for terror attacks within the host country.

Key facts

With modern technology (and in particular since 9/11) it is a universal requirement that careful records must be kept of the originator (and now the beneficiary) details for any electronic financial transactions. This is clearly a risk to terrorists as it increases the chances of detection. However, the sheer volume of electronic transactions that are carried out globally each day acts in the terrorists' favour and reduces the likelihood that their transactions will be detected. Transactions that are unremarkable in their features are unlikely to attract the attention of banking staff or even of a bank's automated monitoring systems, and provided the terrorists keep their transactions within the bounds of what appears normal, there is a chance that they will pass unnoticed.

It is also known that the third-party originators of these overseas transfers are usually unconnected with terrorism and so would not automatically arouse suspicion when identified. The terrorist group provides the funds, but the people providing the account facilities and named as the originators of the transfers are often family members or others who are able to provide a legitimate and plausible reason for their association with the operative to whom the funds are being sent.

Terrorist financiers' perspective

Given the heightened risk of detection, why would terrorists *use* electronic transfers? One reason is the speed and immediacy of the transaction; money can be relocated and then moved electronically again and again before the authorities have even *begun* to notice anything suspicious.

Another attraction from the terrorists' point of view is the fact that electronic payment is a perfectly legal way of moving money around – unlike cash smuggling which is clearly *illegal* and a more risky method.

Possible red flags

These include:

- volumes of cash flowing in and out of an account that do not match the known business and resources of the account holder
- unexplained large payments from overseas accounts with no apparent reason for such payments
- account holder's transaction patterns and expenditure patterns do not match what would be expected
- transfers move to, from or through territories that are known to have a high risk of terrorist activity.

Spurious NPO networks

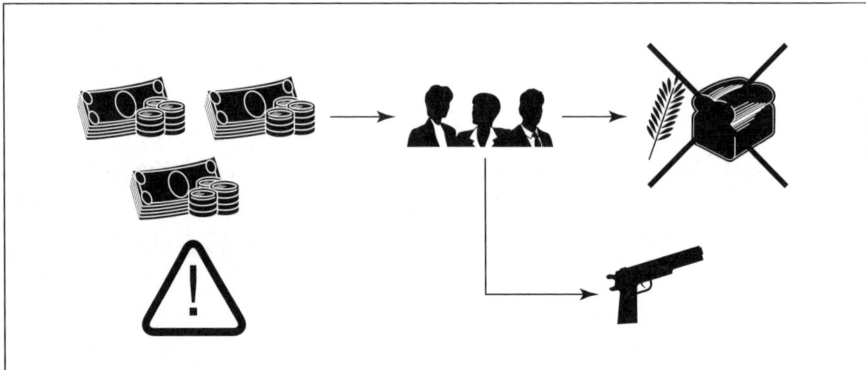

Source: © Lessons Learned Ltd 2012

Use of spurious NPOs

Charitable and humanitarian organisations provide a useful vehicle for terrorist financiers, because the operations of such organisations are often in much the same geographical area as the terrorists' own operations. Terrorist groups might infiltrate and use the banking facilities of *legitimate* charities or they might set up a few charities of their own. Here's how it works.

1. Donors pay money (often via websites) to organisations presenting themselves as not-for-profit organisations apparently engaged in 'good works' in the world's trouble spots.
2. The money is donated on the pretext that it will be used for charitable purposes.
3. But the shadowy, unseen owners and beneficiaries of these organisations are the terrorists.
4. The money is never destined for charitable works, and is diverted instead to fund terror activities.

Key facts

Spurious NPOs will operate in much the same way as shell banks, i.e. they are 'virtual' entities that have no real physical presence at any specific location. As such, most of their fund-raising will be carried out by virtual means (e.g. via the web).

The knowledge that such organisations exist does a great dis-service to legitimate, smaller and less well-known charities, since it makes people suspicious of these organisations' intentions and may make them less willing to donate funds, because of doubts about how those funds might ultimately be used.

These smaller NPOs will quite often target specific communities (e.g. immigrant populations), and the spurious NPOs run by terror groups may tend to do the same, appealing to those communities' concern for their compatriots in their home country. Donors will often be unaware that the cause they are supporting is a terrorist cause rather than a humanitarian one.

Terrorist financiers' perspective

From the terrorist financier's point of view, the NPO is simply a useful 'front' behind which to hide their real and sinister cause of raising funds for terrorism.

Possible red flags

These include:

- difficulties in identifying the ownership structure and true owners behind the organisation
- lack of any real physical presence (e.g. a business address, land line, identifiable staff members)
- mismatches between the pattern and size of financial transactions and the stated purpose and activity of the organisation.

ACCOUNT ANALYSIS EXAMPLES

Operations, cash management and back office staff, along with managers and supervisors called upon to review accounts which have been flagged up as potentially suspicious, will need to develop a familiarity with suspicious transaction patterns, as well the compliance officers themselves. Here is a selection of accounts displaying some FATF noted patterns of potential suspicion, with explanations after each one. Soft copy versions of the accounts themselves and the explanatory notes can be requested by purchasers of this book by emailing info@lessonslearned.co.uk.

WWW

Sample Account 1

Account Holder: Mr J M Johnson					
Date	Description	Details	Receipts	Payments	Balance
30-Jan-04	Eurobank Paris	TFR		$6,750.00	$176,186.12
07-Nov-04	Eurobank Warsaw	TFR	$7,560.00		$183,746.12
15-Nov-04	Counter Deposit	Cash	$9,461.21		$193,207.33
25-Nov-04	Counter Deposit	Cash	$14,874.08		$208,081.41
28-Nov-04	University of W. America	TFR		$48,682.67	$159,398.74
12-Dec-04	Agri-Bank Kiev	TFR	$7,506.54		$166,905.28
15-Dec-04	Cash Withdrawal	ATM		$405.00	$166,500.28
22-Dec-04	ML Investments London	TFR		$71,069.27	$95,431.01
04-Jan-05	Fortuna Bank Santiago	TFR	$7,796.09		$103,227.10
08-Jan-05	Counter Deposit	Cash	$18,099.56		$121,326.66
22-Jan-05	Counter Deposit	Cash	$10,315.59		$131,642.25
31-Jan-05	Counter Deposit	Cash	$3,253.45		$134,895.70
02-Feb-05	Bonds of London	TFR		$97,966.13	$36,929.57
06-Feb-05	University of W. America	TFR		$32,677.75	$4,251.83
07-Feb-05	Counter Withdrawal	Cash		$4,251.83	$0.00
07-Feb-05	A/C Closed				

There are a number of important questions that need to be asked about this account:

- Payments to and from bank accounts in other countries: who owns the other accounts involved? what is the purpose of these transactions? what legitimate business might Mr Johnson have in France, Poland, Ukraine and Chile where the other accounts are based?
- Payments to the University of W. America: does this university exist? why might Mr Johnson be making large, quarterly payments to this university – does one of his children study there?
- Payments to ML Investments and Bonds in London: who are these companies? who owns them? what legitimate business do they have with Mr Johnson?

If Mr Johnson's business with these overseas recipients of his funds cannot be adequately explained, then that would be an immediate cause for suspicion.

Other indicators that might give grounds for suspicion include the following:

- the account has lain dormant for nine months, and then in the space of three months has been used to receive and transmit several sums overseas, some modest and some quite large
- at the end of a three-month period of activity the majority of the remaining funds is suddenly transferred overseas, and the outstanding balance is withdrawn in cash, before closing the account
- a large amount of cash has been paid into the account over a three-month period; where does this cash come from, and does it make sense for Mr Johnson to have this quantity of cash?

Sample Account 2

Account Holder: Mr B Harris-Beckford					
Current Account					
Date	**Description**	**Details**	**Receipts**	**Payments**	**Balance**
01-Jan-05	A/C Opened		$0.00	$0.00	$0.00
24-Jan-05	Radney Automotive Systems	REM	$1,611.63	$0.00	$1,611.63
25-Jan-05	Withdrawal	ATM	$0.00	$675.00	$936.63
01-Feb-05	B Harris-Beckford Loan Account 10594832	TFR	$0.00	$537.17	$399.47
12-Feb-05	Cash Withdrawal	ATM	$0.00	$337.50	$61.97
24-Feb-05	Radney Automotive Systems	REM	$1,611.63	$0.00	$1,673.60
25-Feb-05	Cash Withdrawal	ATM	$0.00	$675.00	$998.60
01-Mar-05	B Harris-Beckford Loan Account 10594832	TFR	$0.00	$537.17	$461.43
17-Mar-05	Cash Withdrawal	ATM	$0.00	$337.50	$123.93
24-Mar-05	Radney Automotive Systems	REM	$1,611.63	$0.00	$1,735.56
25-Mar-05	Cash Withdrawal	ATM	$0.00	$675.00	$1,060.56
01-Apr-05	B Harris-Beckford Loan Account 10594832	TFR	$0.00	$537.17	$523.40
15-Apr-05	Cash Withdrawal	ATM	$0.00	$337.50	$185.90
24-Apr-05	Radney Automotive Systems	REM	$1,611.63	$0.00	$1,797.53
25-Apr-05	Cash Withdrawal	ATM	$0.00	$675.00	$1,122.53
01-May-05	B Harris-Beckford Loan Account 10594832	TFR	$0.00	$537.17	$585.36

16-May-05	Cash Withdrawal	ATM	$0.00	$405.00	$180.36
24-May-05	Radney Automotive Systems	REM	$1,611.63	$0.00	$1,791.99
25-May-05	Cash Withdrawal	ATM	$0.00	$810.00	$981.99
01-Jun-05	B Harris-Beckford Loan Account 10594832	TFR	$0.00	$537.17	$444.83

Loan Account

Date	Description	Details	Receipts	Payments	Balance
01-Jan-05	A/C Opened		$0.00	$23,490.00	-$23,490.00
31-Jan-05	Interest	DD	$0.00	$469.80	-$23,959.80
01-Feb-05	B Harris-Beckford Current Account 10644978	TFR	$537.17	$0.00	-$23,422.64
28-Feb-05	Interest	DD	$0.00	$468.45	-$23,891.09
01-Mar-05	B Harris-Beckford Current Account 10644978	TFR	$537.17	$0.00	-$23,353.92
31-Mar-05	Interest	DD	$0.00	$467.03	-$23,820.95
01-Apr-05	B Harris-Beckford Current Account 10644978	TFR	$537.17	$0.00	-$23,283.79
06-Apr-05	Loan Repayment	Cash	$1,822.50	$0.00	-$21,461.29
21-Apr-05	S Ericsson	TFR	$16,875.00	$0.00	-$4,586.29
30-Apr-05	Interest	DD	$0.00	$91.73	-$4,678.02
01-May-05	B Harris-Beckford Current Account 10644978	TFR	$537.17	$0.00	-$4,140.86
10-May-05	S Ericsson	TFR	$4,140.86	$0.00	$0.00

Mr Harris-Beckford appears to have a regular monthly salary of $1,611.63 and no other source of income, yet he is able to pay off a $23,490.00 loan within just a few months.

The source of the funds paid in settlement of the loan is a third party called 'S Ericsson' and not Mr Harris-Beckford himself. Who is this 'S Ericsson', and why would he or she be settling Mr Harris-Beckford's loan for him?

Sample Account 3

Account Holder: Ms T Abrams (Student)					
Date	Description	Details	Receipts	Payments	Balance
05-Aug-04	Balance C/F				$670.77
05-Aug-04	Mercator	Card Purchase		$106.65	$564.12
12-Aug-04	Counter Deposit	Cash	$7,220.82		$7,784.94
12-Aug-04	Cash Withdrawal	ATM		$3,000.00	$4,784.94
15-Aug-04	Counter Deposit	Cash	$8,264.16		$13,049.10
14-Aug-04	American Express Card Repayment	DD		$1,487.58	$11,561.52
16-Aug-04	Cash Withdrawal	ATM		$3,000.00	$8,561.52
21-Aug-04	Visa Card Repayment	DD		$1,680.69	$6,880.83
22-Aug-04	Counter Deposit	Cash	$15,957.79		$22,838.62
23-Aug-04	Adidas	Card Purchase		$109.41	$22,729.21
25-Aug-04	Mexx	Card Purchase		$172.29	$22,556.92
26-Aug-04	Jugoexport	Card Purchase		$91.74	$22,465.18
29-Aug-04	Mango	Card Purchase		$87.09	$22,378.09
02-Sep-04	Escada	Card Purchase		$660.00	$21,718.09
07-Sep-04	Counter Deposit	Cash	$7,738.38		$29,456.47
08-Sep-04	Cash Withdrawal	ATM		$3,000.00	$26,456.47
10-Sep-04	Mercator	Card Purchase		$362.94	$26,093.53
10-Sep-04	Cash Withdrawal	ATM		$3,000.00	$23,093.53
14-Sep-04	Cash Withdrawal	ATM		$3,000.00	$20,093.53
14-Sep-04	American Express Card Repayment	DD		$764.55	$19,328.98
21-Sep-04	Visa Card Repayment	DD		$1,187.82	$18,141.16
22-Sep-04	Cash Withdrawal	ATM		$3,000.00	$15,141.16

Ms Abrams is a student, and most students would have very limited financial resources. However, Ms Abrams is different:

- She appears to enjoy shopping (there are a number of card purchases at department stores).
- Her credit card balances by far exceed a typical average monthly income and yet she seems able to pay these off without any problem.

- She makes large cash withdrawals ($3,000 a time).
- She seems to be getting a lot of cash from somewhere ($31,442.77 in one month alone).

How can a student afford to fund what appears to be a fairly lavish lifestyle? And where does all her cash come from? Ms Abrams' expenditure clearly does not fit the typical pattern of most students. Should you be suspicious?

This is where a knowledge of the customer and their background is so important. If Ms Abrams is known to have a rich and tolerant father who regularly gives her money and pays her debts, then the activity on her account might make sense. But if Ms Abrams does *not* have an explainable and legitimate source for her money, then there are clear grounds to be suspicious.

Sample Account 4

Account Holder: 'La Giaconda Bellisima' Italian Restaurant					
Date	Description	Details	Receipts	Payments	Balance
Thu 08-Jul	Balance C/F				$19,139.62
Fri 09-Jul	Counter Withdrawal	Cash		$2,647.75	$16,491.87
Fri 09-Jul	Counter Deposit	Cash	$3,699.88		$20,191.75
Mon 12-Jul	Counter Deposit	Cash	$7,709.84		$27,901.59
Tue 13-Jul	Counter Deposit	Cash	$3,681.18		$31,582.77
Wed 14-Jul	Counter Deposit	Cash	$4,189.99		$35,772.76
Wed 14-Jul	Naturalis Food Wholesalers	TFR		$2,439.84	$33,332.92
Thu 15-Jul	Counter Deposit	Cash	$3,654.15		$36,987.07
Fri 16-Jul	Counter Deposit	Cash	$4,141.88		$41,128.95
Fri 16-Jul	Counter Withdrawal	Cash		$2,647.75	$38,481.20
Fri 16-Jul	Porticano Vintners & Importers	TFR		$9,238.31	$29,242.89
Mon 19-Jul	Counter Deposit	Cash	$11,228.16		$40,471.05
Tue 20-Jul	Counter Deposit	Cash	$3,983.44		$44,454.49
Wed 21-Jul	Naturalis Food Wholesalers	TFR		$2,296.53	$42,157.96
Wed 21-Jul	Counter Deposit	Cash	$3,730.65		$45,888.61
Thu 22-Jul	Counter Deposit	Cash	$3,822.45		$49,711.06
Fri 23-Jul	Counter Deposit	Cash	$3,992.45		$53,703.51
Fri 23-Jul	Counter Withdrawal	Cash		$2,647.75	$51,055.76
Mon 26-Jul	Catering Supplies	TFR		$2,051.56	$49,004.20
Mon 26-Jul	Counter Deposit	Cash	$15,229.62		$64,233.82
Tue 27-Jul	Counter Deposit	Cash	$3,815.31		$68,049.13
Tue 27-Jul	Naturalis Food Wholesalers	TFR		$2,417.06	$65,632.07

Wed 28-Jul	Counter Deposit	Cash	$3,643.78		$69,275.85
Thu 29-Jul	Counter Deposit	Cash	$3,984.46		$73,260.31
Fri 30-Jul	Counter Deposit	Cash	$4,138.99		$77,399.30
Fri 30-Jul	Counter Withdrawal	Cash		$2,647.75	$74,751.55
Fri 30-Jul	Porticano Vintners & Importers	TFR		$9,155.69	$65,595.86
Mon 02-Aug	Rubicon	TFR		$32,938.86	$32,657.00
Mon 02-Aug	Counter Deposit	Cash	$15,027.15		$47,684.15
Tue 03-Aug	Counter Deposit	Cash	$3,643.95		$51,328.10
Wed 04-Aug	Naturalis Food Wholesalers	TFR	$0.00	$2,416.21	$48,911.89
Wed 04-Aug	Counter Deposit	Cash	$4,000.44		$52,912.33
Thu 05-Aug	Counter Deposit	Cash	$3,772.81		$56,685.14
Fri 06-Aug	Rubicon	TFR		$50,297.22	$6,387.92
Fri 06-Aug	Counter Withdrawal	Cash		$2,647.75	$3,740.17
Fri 06-Aug	Counter Deposit	Cash	$4,000.95		$7,741.12
			115,091.53		

This account demonstrates the features of a 'front business', i.e. an apparently legitimate business that uses its normal cash activities as a 'cover' for laundering criminal cash.

The restaurant's daily cash takings average between $3,500 and $4,000. Takings for Friday and Saturday are banked together in a single deposit, every Monday. If the average daily takings are as described above, then the Monday deposits should be between $7,000 and $8,000. On Monday 12 July the restaurant deposits $7,709.84 into its account, which seems fine. However, on Monday 19 July the deposit has increased to $11,228.16. A week later, the deposit is even bigger ($15,229.62). A similar amount ($15,027.15) is deposited a week later.

The restaurant owners might argue that the increased deposits simply reflect the increasing success of their restaurant. But the daily takings throughout the rest of the week have not increased. Also, the restaurant makes regular payments to its suppliers (weekly payments to Naturalis, fortnightly payments to Porticano and monthly payments to Catering Supplies) and these do not appear to have increased to reflect any increasing throughput in restaurant trade. And although turnover has apparently doubled, the restaurant continues to pay the same in cash wages to staff ($2,647.75 per week). If the restaurant were taking more customers then you would expect to see a corresponding increase in the restaurant's expenditure, but the payments to suppliers and staff remain constant.

What all this indicates is that the restaurant is using the cover of its takings to deposit increasing amounts of criminal cash. On Mondays the restaurant deposits its taking from both Friday and Saturday, which means that the amounts involved are larger than on other days of the week. The restaurant is hoping that the bank will not notice that these large Monday deposits are getting even larger each week.

Then, all of a sudden, the restaurant appears to experience some sort of financial crisis. Almost all the restaurant's funds are suddenly transferred in two large transactions on 2 and 6 August, to a company called 'Rubicon'.

This gradual accumulation of criminal funds under cover of an operating business, followed by the sudden transfer of the funds to a third party, is typical 'fronting' behaviour.

Note: a training film dealing with a front company can be previewed at
WWW http://www.antimoneylaunderingvideos.com/player/red_flags_aml.htm.

Sample Account 5

Account Holder: Ms G Browning					
Date	**Description**	**Details**	**Receipts**	**Payments**	**Balance**
21-Aug-04	A/C Opened				€0.00
24-Aug-04	Eurobank Paris Acct #30248588	REM	€25,000.00		€25,000.00
	Eurobank Dusseldorf Acct #30484858	REM	€27,750.00		€52,750.00
	B V Duran	REM	€24,300.00		€77,050.00
	Counter Deposit	CASH	€14,957.00		€92,007.00
	J Rocca	REM	€23,550.00		€115,557.00
	Agri-Bank London Acct #39575739	REM	€25,000.00		€140,557.00
	Counter Deposit	CASH	€14,890.00		€155,447.00
	R Inman	REM	€23,750.00		€179,197.00
25-Aug-04	Eurobank London Acct #23043957	REM	€27,500.00		€206,697.00
	Eurobank Madrid Acct #305848749	REM	€22,550.00		€229,247.00
	B V Duran	REM	€25,460.00		€254,707.00
	K Priss	REM	€25,870.00		€280,577.00
	Counter Deposit	CASH	€14,950.00		€295,527.00
	Agri-Bank Roma Acct #39575739	REM	€23,750.00		€319,277.00
	K Priss	REM	€25,000.00		€344,277.00
29-Aug-04	R Toledo	REM	€25,550.00		€369,827.00
	Eurobank Paris Acct #30248588	REM	€27,500.00		€397,327.00

	J Rocca	REM	€24,750.00		€422,077.00
	Counter Deposit	CASH	€14,989.00		€437,066.00
	B V Duran	REM	€26,700.00		€463,766.00
	Agri-Bank London Acct #39575739	REM	€27,000.00		€490,766.00
	R Inman	REM	€24,500.00		€515,266.00
30-Aug-04	F W Professional Services	TFR		€375,000.00	€140,266.00
04-Sep-04	FW Professional Services	TFR		€125,000.00	€15,266.00

This account demonstrates several features consistent with it being used as a conduit for criminal funds and cash, which are then transferred on to other accounts for further laundering.

Ms Browning's account shows several receipts each day, from a variety of different sources. These receipts include a large number of transfers from other bank accounts, all between €20,000 and €30,000 in size. These are not insubstantial transfers. They were made via banks all over Europe, and by a large number of different originators. This is not a normal banking pattern for most people and would, in most cases, give immediate grounds for suspicion.

Ms Browning's account also shows a number of cash deposits at just under €15,000 indicating that she is possibly aware that cash transactions of more than €15,000 are likely to be subjected to intensified KYC. It is notable that the cash transactions shown here all fall below the €15,000 threshold, thereby avoiding the additional scrutiny that they might otherwise attract. This pattern of transactions is typical of 'smurfing' behaviour.

After several days during which money is deposited into the account, Ms Browning suddenly transfers most of the money out again. The money is transferred in two instalments to a single beneficiary, identified as 'F W Professional Services'.

This account profile should give rise to at least two key questions:

1 Who are the depositors of funds, and what business do they have with Ms Browning?
2 What kind of business is 'F W Professional Services', and who are the beneficial owners behind it?

Sample Account 6

Account Holder: The Enlightenment Trust - Raising Awareness of Poverty - Euro Account					
Date	Description	Details	Receipts	Payments	Balance
01-Feb	A/C Opened				€0.00
01-Feb	Opening Deposit	TFR	€1,800,000.00		€1,800,000.00
28-Apr	Interest		€9,000.00		€1,809,000.00
28-Apr	Petrolisum #2 Account	TFR	€525,000.00		€2,334,000.00
28-Jul	Interest		€11,670.00		€2,345,670.00
28-Oct	Interest		€11,728.35		€2,357,398.35
28-Jan	Interest		€11,786.99		€2,369,185.34
05-Feb	Santo Rico Investments	TFR		€2,369,185.34	€0.00
05-Feb	A/C Closed				

This account has been opened and has then laid virtually dormant for a whole year, accumulating interest on its deposits. At the end of the year, the total funds in the account are suddenly and inexplicably remitted to a third party called 'Santo Rico Investments'. The account is then closed.

This is just one of several transaction patterns that has been identified as potentially suspicious by the Financial Action Task Force:

- account is opened
- account lays dormant
- large transactions are effected
- account is closed or rendered inactive again.

Key questions to ask about this account might include the following:

- What is the source of the initial opening deposit?
- Who are the 'Enlightenment Trust' and what do they do?
- Does the amount of money involved fit the known business of the 'Enlightenment Trust'?
- Who are 'Santo Rico Investments' and what is their involvement with the 'Enlightenment Trust'?

Remember that people involved in the financing of terrorism have sometimes deliberately chosen account names to give the impression that the funds belong to an organisation with charitable status. Such accounts can receive or handle 'donations' from a wide number of 'donors' without appearing unusual or suspicious. It is important to 'know your customer' and to be as sure as you can be that their stated business purpose is legitimate, and not just a 'cover' for something more sinister.

Sample Account 7

Account Name: Janus Investments					
Date	Description	Details	Receipts	Payments	Balance
22-Jan-11	A/C Opened				$0.00
22-Jan-11	Opening Deposit	Cheque	$111,475.00		$111,475.00
26-Feb-11	Janus Holdings Boston	TFR		$55,400.00	$56,075.00
28-Feb-11	Janus Investments Dubai	TFR		$56,075.00	$0.00
28-Feb-11	A/C Closed				

Account Holding Branch: Boston MASS					
Account Name: Janus Holdings					
Date	Description	Details			Balance
01-Feb-11	A/C Opened				$0.00
01-Feb-11	Opening Deposit	Cheque	$110,057.50		$110,057.50
03-Feb-11	Counter Deposit	Cheque	$51,648.46		$161,705.96
26-Feb-11	Janus Investments Boston	TFR	$55,400.00		$217,105.96
01-Mar-11	Janus Investments Dubai	TFR	$50,000.00		$267,105.56
03-Mar-11	Counter Withdrawal	Cash		$9,500.00	$257,605.56

Account Holding Branch: Dubai					
Account Name: Janus Investments					
Date	Description	Details			Balance
22-Feb-11	A/C Opened				$0.00
25-Feb-11	Opening Deposit	Cheque	$51,070.00		$51,070.00
26-Feb-11	Counter Deposit	Cheque	$58,775.00		$109,845.00
28-Feb-11	Janus Investments Boston	TFR	$56,075.00		$165,920.00
01-Mar-11	Janus Holdings Boston	TFR		$50,000.00	$115,920.00
07-Mar-11	R J Janus	TFR		$51,770.00	$64,150.00

Account Holding Branch: London					
Account Name: R J Janus					
Date	Description	Details			Balance
05-Mar-11	A/C Opened				$0.00
05-Mar-11	Opening Deposit	Cheque	$110,812.50		$110,812.50
07-Mar-11	Janus Investments Dubai		$51,770.00		$162,582.50

Here we have four bank accounts, held at three different branches of Pecunia Bank. The account names ('Janus Investments' in Dubai, 'Janus Holdings' in Boston and 'R J Janus' in London) are different, but are all quite similar. It is possible, therefore, that the ownership of these accounts might be connected. The fact that money has been transferred between these accounts strengthens the perception that there may be a connection in their ownership.

Client ownership of multiple accounts in different branches of the same bank is one of several behaviours that has been identified as potentially suspicious by the Financial Action Task Force. Questions that might need to be asked about such accounts include the following:

- Does there appear to be a legitimate purpose for these multiple accounts, other than the moving around of funds?
- Is there any economic purpose to the transfers of money made between such multiple accounts?

The movements between the various accounts don't appear to make much sense at all. For example, why would 'Janus Investments' in Dubai need to receive $56,075.00 *from* 'Janus Investments' in Boston, only to transfer $50,000.00 back *to* 'Janus Holdings' in the Boston branch of Pecunia Bank the following day? Such transactions do not make sense, seem to serve no economic purpose and should give grounds for suspicion.

Sample Account 8

Account Holder: PRLC Legal & Financial Consultants					
Date	Description	Details	Receipts	Payments	Balance
01-Feb-11	Balance C/F				€118,445.32
08-Feb-11	Invoice #39476	REM	€6,782.45		€125,227.77
10-Feb-11	Invoice #39480	REM	€2,938.05		€128,165.82
15-Feb-11	Invoice #39481	REM	€1,394.54		€129,560.36
15-Feb-11	Kubik Camden & Partners	TFR		€1,293.45	€128,266.91
17-Feb-11	Invoice #39482	REM	€3,456.21		€131,723.12
22-Feb-11	Invoice #39483	REM	€3,342.53		€135,065.65
26-Feb-11	Salary account	TFR		€1,862.89	€133,202.76
26-Feb-11	Tubacon SA, Roma	TFR		€50,435.56	€82,767.20
27-Feb-11	Invoice #39484	Cash	€68,495.45		€151,262.65
01-Mar-11	Invoice #39485	REM	€3,094.54		€154,357.19
01-Mar-11	Nortran (Office Rental)	TFR		€3,405.00	€150,952.19
03-Mar-11	Invoice #39486	Cash	€54,606.35		€205,558.54
05-Mar-11	Invoice #39487	Cash	€74,523.54		€280,082.08

05-Mar-11	Invoice #39489	REM	€3,424.12		€283,506.20
09-Mar-11	Invoice #39488	Cash	€34,958.76		€318,464.96
11-Mar-11	Invoice #39478	REM	€8,795.34		€327,260.30
11-Mar-11	Invoice #39490	REM	€4,958.54		€332,218.84
11-Mar-11	Tubacon SA, Roma	TFR		€85,402.32	€246,816.52
18-Mar-11	Invoice #39479	REM	€4,938.45		€251,754.97
25-Mar-11	Invoice #39477	REM	€15,837.67		€267,592.64
26-Mar-11	Salary account	TFR		€1,862.89	€265,729.75
27-Mar-11	Invoice #39491	REM	€2,493.56		€268,223.31
27-Mar-11	Tubacon SA, Roma	TFR		€97,495.34	€170,727.97
28-Mar-11	Invoice #39492	Cash	€54,495.45		€225,223.42

This appears to be a legitimate consultancy business, but if you look at the pattern of transactions something is not quite right about the invoices that have been issued to and apparently paid by clients:

- Invoices up to and including Invoice #39483 were all paid by electronic transfer.
- The amounts invoiced up to and including Invoice #39483 are all below €16,000.
- Invoice #39484 is for a much larger amount (€68,495.45) and has been paid in cash.
- From this point forward, more than half the invoices issued are for these much larger amounts and, wherever these larger amounts occur, the invoice is invariably settled in cash.

This change in transaction behaviour appears to have no legitimate explanation. Has this business suddenly got itself involved in money laundering? The change in invoiced amounts and the shift towards cash settlements could be indicative of this. The FATF specifically identifies a shift towards cash transactions (where previously these did not happen) as an indicator of potential suspicion.

Sample Account 9

Account Holder: J Gregor					
Current Account					
Date	Description	Details	Receipts	Payments	Balance
01-Jan-05	A/C Opened				$0.00
24-Jan-05	Haverton Retail	REM	$717.10		$717.10
25-Jan-05	Withdrawal	ATM		$325.00	$392.10
01-Feb-05	J Gregor Account 10545463	TFR		$200.00	$192.10
12-Feb-05	Cash Withdrawal	ATM		$150.00	$42.10
24-Feb-05	Haverton Retail	REM	$717.10		$759.20
25-Feb-05	Cash Withdrawal	ATM		$325.00	$434.20
01-Mar-05	J Gregor Account 10545463	TFR		$200.00	$234.20
17-Mar-05	Cash Withdrawal	ATM		$150.00	$84.20
24-Mar-05	Haverton Retail	REM	$717.10		$801.30
25-Mar-05	Cash Withdrawal	ATM		$325.00	$476.30
01-Apr-05	J Gregor Account 10545463	TFR		$200.00	$276.30
15-Apr-05	Cash Withdrawal	ATM		$150.00	$126.30
24-Apr-05	Haverton Retail	REM	$717.10		$843.40
25-Apr-05	Cash Withdrawal	ATM		$325.00	$518.40
16-May-05	Cash Withdrawal	ATM		$150.00	$368.40
24-May-05	Haverton Retail	REM	$717.10		$1,085.50
25-May-05	Cash Withdrawal	ATM		$325.00	$760.50
01-Jun-05	J Gregor Account 10545475	TFR		$275.00	$485.50
15-Jun-05	Cash Withdrawal	ATM		$150.00	$335.50
24-Jun-05	Haverton Retail	REM	$717.10		$1,052.60
25-Jun-05	Cash Withdrawal	ATM		$325.00	$727.60
01-Jul-05	J Gregor Account 10545475	TFR		$275.00	$452.60
17-Jul-05	Cash Withdrawal	ATM		$150.00	$302.60
24-Jul-05	Haverton Retail	REM	$717.10		$1,019.70
......several months later.....					$0.00
01-Nov-05	J Gregor Account 10594832	TFR		$300.00	$346.00
14-Nov-05	Cash Withdrawal	ATM		$175.00	$171.00
24-Nov-05	Haverton Retail	REM	$717.10		$888.10
25-Nov-05	Cash Withdrawal	ATM		$325.00	$563.10
01-Dec-05	J Gregor Account 10594832	TFR		$300.00	$263.10

Loan Accounts					
Date	Description	Details	Receipts	Payments	Balance
01-Jan-05	A/C Opened			$18,000.00	-$18,000.00
31-Jan-05	Interest	DD		$75.00	-$18,075.00
01-Feb-05	J Gregor Account 10545463	TFR	$200.00		-$17,875.00
28-Feb-05	Interest	DD		$75.00	-$17,950.00
01-Mar-05	J Gregor Account 10545463	TFR	$200.00		-$17,750.00
31-Mar-05	Interest	DD		$75.00	-$17,825.00
01-Apr-05	J Gregor Account 10545463	TFR	$200.00		-$17,625.00
02-Apr-05	Loan Repayment	Cash	$17,625.00		$0.00
01-May-05	A/C Opened			$37,500.00	-$37,500.00
31-May-05	Interest	DD		$156.25	-$37,656.25
01-Jun-05	J Gregor Account 10545475	TFR	$275.00		-$37,381.25
30-Jun-05	Interest	DD		$156.25	-$37,537.50
01-Jul-05	J Gregor Account 10545475	TFR	$275.00		-$37,262.50
31-Jul-05	Interest	DD		$156.25	-$37,418.75
01-Aug-05	J Gregor Account 10545475	TFR	$275.00		-$37,143.75
01-Aug-05	Loan Repayment	Cash	$37,143.75		$0.00
01-Sep-05	A/C Opened			$45,000.00	-$45,000.00
30-Sep-05	Interest	DD		$187.50	-$45,187.50
01-Oct-05	J Gregor Account 10594832	TFR	$300.00		-$44,887.50
31-Oct-05	Interest	DD		$187.50	-$45,075.00
01-Nov-05	J Gregor Account 10594832	TFR	$300.00		-$44,775.00
30-Nov-05	Interest	DD		$187.50	-$44,962.50
01-Dec-05	J Gregor Account 10594832	TFR	$300.00		-$44,662.50
03-Dec-05	Loan Repayment	Cash	$44,662.50		$0.00

This example demonstrates the use of loan accounts as a vehicle for laundering money:

- The customer takes out a loan.
- They pay a few instalments on the loan as arranged.
- They suddenly produce the cash funds to clear the loan.
- The loan account is closed.

Unless there is a reasonable explanation for the source of the funds used to pay off the loan, this has to be regarded as suspicious.

In this example, the customer has in fact taken out three separate loans, one after the other. In each case, the loan payments are made as normal for the first three months. At the end of three months, the customer suddenly makes a cash repayment for the outstanding balance of the loan. For the first loan, the cash balance paid was,$17,625.00. For the second loan, the amount paid in cash was $37,143.75. For the third loan, the cash repayment was $44,662.50. The customer receives a regular payment of $717.10 from Haverton Retail and has no other apparent sources of income, which is nowhere near enough money to pay off any of these amounts in one go.

WWW Note: a training film dealing with money laundering through loan accounts can be previewed at http://www.antimoneylaunderingvideos.com/player/red_flags_aml.htm.

Sample Account 10

Account Holder: Curanic Commercial Services (London)					
Current Account					
Date	Description	Details	Receipts	Payments	Balance
01-Jan-04	A/C Opened				€0.00
24-Jan-04	Hipocanthus Financing Prague	REM	€112,500.00		€112,500.00
25-Jan-04	Counter Withdrawal	Cash		€14,500.00	€98,000.00
01-Feb-04	Aramis Consulting	TFR		€23,000.00	€75,000.00
12-Feb-04	Counter Withdrawal	Cash		€13,900.00	€61,100.00
26-Feb-04	Anapolis Professional Services	REM		€25,043.00	€36,057.00
03-Mar-04	Cash Withdrawal	ATM		€14,755.00	€21,302.00

Curanic Commercial Services has taken receipt of a large amount of money from a third party account overseas. There are no further deposits to the account, but a substantial number of withdrawals. Some of these withdrawals are in the form of transfers to third-party businesses with vague and non-specific names, such as 'Aramis Consulting' and 'Anapolis Professional Services'. In short, Curanic does not appear to do a lot other than transfer money around. It receives money from overseas, and it moves money on to other third parties. This behaviour is typical of a shell company, which has no business purpose other than to act as a conduit for the receipt and transfer of funds.

The receipt of large sums from abroad, followed by large numbers of withdrawals is one of the patterns of behaviour identified by the Financial Action Task Force as an indicator of potential suspicion.

'ACCUMULATION OF EVIDENCE' CASES

Suspicion can be something that grows. The exact time at which one moves from an attitude of caution or uncertainty into one of suspicion is a moot point. The following cases address that issue.

Each case study has five stages, so that the relevant information builds to form a complete picture. Read each stage and consider your reactions to it. Is there anything unusual, unexplained or which goes against what you might expect to see in an account of that nature? Do this for each stage, then check your reactions against the comments that appear at the end of each case.

Case 1: Feron Resources

Stage 1

Feron Resources first opened an account with your bank when it was incorporated as a company five years ago. The company provides business administration and accounting services and consultancy. It currently employs 20 people, and has a client base of approximately 50 companies, most of which are small, privately owned businesses.

Stage 2

About six months ago, Feron Resources underwent a change of ownership. The previous owners were well-known to your bank. The new owner is a corporation called 'Commercial Enterprises'. The owner of this corporation is given as a consortium of wealthy entrepreneurs, all well-known public figures but with no previous history or relationship with your bank.

Stage 3

In the past five months Feron has acquired several new and extremely profitable clients. These companies all buy an extensive range of services from Feron. The amounts invoiced to them has increased month by month, until in the last month they accounted for roughly 50 per cent of Feron's total income. None had done business with Feron previously.

Stage 4

Although the invoiced volume of business has increased substantially in the past six months, there has been no real change in staffing levels, and staff themselves do not seem aware of a change in the volume of work. The only new recruit to the company has been Ms Yeretzi who was appointed by the new owners to manage their business on their behalf.

Stage 5

Feron's recent outgoings include several substantial payments to a company called Infotek. These payments are recorded in Feron's accounts as 'consultancy fees', 'business development fees', or simply 'fees'. When the bank enquired, the only person who had any knowledge of Infotek was Ms Yeretz, and she was unavailable.

Observations
Feron Resources

Stage 1

There is nothing particularly suspicious or alarming here. In fact, it seems clear that Feron has been operating as a perfectly legitimate business for a number of years. The business seems quite healthy, there is nothing to suggest any wrongdoing.

Stage 2

The change of ownership is a possible cause for concern, although the owners in question are well-known public figures and the bank presumably knows quite a lot about their reported activities. However, the bank has no previous banking experience of these individuals, and no direct knowledge of these people's banking habits, or of their actual assets. What is the association between them? What is 'Commercial Enterprises', and what does it do? Why is 'Commercial Enterprises' interested enough in Feron Resources to want to own it? These are all important questions.

Stage 3

There is evidence here of a change in Feron's business pattern, and this change coincides with the new ownership. Where do these new clients come from? Why are they suddenly interested in doing business with Feron? Why do they seem to buy substantially more from Feron than any other client (they have 50 per cent of the business, and yet they constitute only a small proportion of the total client base)? Does this change in the pattern of business seem legitimate?

Stage 4

Even though the volumes invoiced would suggest a greatly increased volume of business, this does not appear to be reflected in Feron's staffing patterns. Could it be that Feron is using false invoices as a cover for receiving criminal money? Does Feron *really* do the work for which these companies have been invoiced?

Stage 5

The relationship with Infotek is not clear. What is Feron *really* buying from Infotek? What service is it getting in exchange for the fees apparently paid to Infotek? Or is Feron simply being used as a vehicle through which to channel criminal money back to its criminal owners, hiding behind the name of Infotek? Also, who is the mysterious Ms Yeretz? Is she an innocent employee, or is she knowingly supervising a money laundering operation?

Case 2: Mr Julian Chellis

Stage 1

Mr Chellis is a resident citizen and wishes to open a personal account, with an opening deposit of €5,000. He would like the account to be set up immediately, so he can take receipt of a payment he is expecting. He is unable to visit the bank right now as he is overseas but he will visit the bank to complete the documentation later.

Stage 2

Mr Chellis has now opened his account and completed the documentary requirements, sending his brother initially in order to provide the necessary documents which included a copy of his passport and a mortgage document bearing Mr Chellis' name. The payment that he was expecting (€9,000 from an account overseas) has arrived, but the purpose of the payment and his connection with its originator are not clear. Mr Chellis has been asked to visit the bank to discuss this matter. He seems reluctant to give any additional information about the payment in question, or about his business connections in the overseas country

Stage 3

It is two months later, and apart from the opening deposit of €5,000 and the €9,000 received from the overseas country, there has been very little activity on Mr Chellis' account. In the past three weeks, however, the account has received deposits of more than €53,000 from three other third-party accounts outside the country.

Stage 4

Mr Chellis' account has received a further €15,000 in various instalments this time from an account in his name from outside the country. You have checked Mr Chellis' account application and you see that he has no declared overseas business interests. His account also shows no regular payments from overseas relatives. Yet he has received a total income from overseas of tens of thousands in the past two to three months

Stage 5

Over the past 10 days, Mr Chellis has ordered five wire transfers to different overseas accounts in third-party names. Each wired amount is €9,800. Mr Chellis has just contacted the bank to inform it that he wishes to close his account, and for the bank to prepare a banker's draft for the outstanding deposit in the account, to be collected on his behalf by his brother.

Observations

Mr Julian Chellis

Stage 1

Mr Chellis is putting pressure on the bank to provide him with banking services *before* he has properly identified himself or provided any proof of identity.

Stage 2

Is Mr Chellis really unable to attend the bank, or is it simply that he does not want to be identified? Any apparent reluctance to meet banking staff might be considered suspicious. Also, the use of an intermediary is one of several ploys which might be used by a person to try to keep their true identity hidden (although it is also consistent with a wealthy individual who cannot be bothered with such details). In this case the intermediary has a copy of Mr Chellis's passport rather than the original passport. The copy has not been certified and may not, therefore, be authentic. Copies are easily forged and banks usually protect against this, by requiring to see either the original document itself or at the very least a certified copy. Finally, the mortgage agreement presented as proof of Mr Chellis's residence is useful in proving that he has a house, but does *not* prove that he actually lives in it. He could be living anywhere. Information about a customer's permanent residence is one of the key pieces of identifying information that needs to be obtained by banks, when opening new accounts.

Stage 3

Mr Chellis's account has lain dormant for some time, but has suddenly become very active. The account has received substantial deposits, and it is unclear whether these deposits are consistent with Mr Chellis's legitimate employment or business. Does he really earn or have legitimate access to this amount of money and why is it coming to him? The deposits received by Mr Chellis come from three accounts outside the country but there is no indication as to what Mr Chellis's relationship is with the third parties who remitted the funds.

Stage 4

This information confirms that Mr Chellis is now receiving deposits from overseas accounts in his own name, despite there having been no indication of this when he opened his account. This is therefore unexplained activity, it needs to be investigated and, if credible explanations cannot be established, treated as suspicious.

Stage 5

Mr Chellis has suddenly decided to empty and close the account. Rather than have the money transferred to an account in his name elsewhere, he has asked the bank to produce a banker's draft for the amount. Banker's drafts are drawn on the bank's deposits rather than on a specific customer account, so when this money is next paid into an account it will be difficult to identify Mr Chellis as the source. Also, Mr Chellis still seems very reluctant to come into the bank – he has sent his intermediary along to collect the banker's draft

7

International Cooperation

Background

Modern structures of organised crime and terrorism

Mechanisms and tools of international cooperation

International cooperative bodies

BACKGROUND

International cooperation is the mainstay of international efforts and is referred to time and time again in many of the international conventions and treaties referred to in Chapter 2, which contain many provisions designed to mandate or encourage it. The phrase refers to the capability and willingness of different parts of the world to assist each other in the task of bringing criminals and terrorists to justice, depriving them of the fruits of their crimes and preventing their attacks upon society. This has become even more important with the expansion of so-called 'TransNational Organised Crime' (TNOC) and international terrorism. International cooperation can occur at the state/governmental, agency or institutional/individual level.

Example

State/Governmental level

The governments of two countries agree a bilateral treaty of extradition, meaning that a person who is alleged to have committed a crime in Country A, but who is currently physically present in Country B, can be legally transported or 'extradited' from Country B to Country A in order to stand trial.

Agency

Information on the same trading company is shared between Financial Intelligence Units (FIUs) and police forces from three countries regarding Suspicious Activity Reports (SARs) which all three FIUs have received independently from financial institutions in their countries, regarding large 'in and out' deposits. This information is in turn shared with authorities in a fourth country, where the trading company is incorporated and has staff, leading to a coordinated asset seizure across all countries and the prosecution of two of the company's directors for money laundering.

Institutional/Individual

A Compliance Officer within X Bank receives an internal SAR regarding the deposit of an unusually large sum by B Bank, a small bank based in an offshore jurisdiction, which only recently underwent and passed client acceptance checks. Simultaneously, X Bank receives notification from a third party that the money represents the proceeds of a fraud, and that the deposit is an attempt to launder the proceeds, using X Bank as a conduit for the stolen funds. Together with X Bank's in-house lawyer, X Bank's Compliance Officer speaks to the Compliance Officer of the third party's bank, Y Bank, and obtains important information which enables it to freeze the funds received, and make a full report to the FIU.

The Financial Action Task Force (FATF) has published a number of such examples of international cooperation, demonstrating that when governments, agencies and financial institutions cooperate across borders in the spirit intended by the various treaties and conventions, then it is possible for successes to be achieved, despite the formidable obstacles posed by the existence of multiple jurisdictions.

However, at both the state, agency and institutional levels, experience points to a number of serious barriers to achieving the level of international cooperation which is actually necessary to facilitate the effective combating of transnational organised crime. On the face of it, in theory it should be in all parties' interests to cooperate to the maximum degree possible, yet conversations with law enforcement officials reveal continuing challenges in achieving international cooperation.

The barriers identified include:

- *Corruption* – do you trust the other country's police with the information you are giving them? Can offenders bribe judges to refuse requests for assistance and will this compromise your own investigation?
- *State complicity* – where nations may actually benefit economically from the crimes complained of (e.g. the economic benefit derived by the military junta in Burma from the production of opium, or the way in which the Taliban derived revenue from Al-Qaeda when it was hosting Al-Qaeda in Afghanistan).
- *Politics* – governments can oppose mutual assistance on political grounds (e.g. dislike of another country's foreign policy or when trying to extract concessions during international negotiations).
- *Sovereignty* – closely connected to politics, this is where national pride and historical enmities come into play; effectively, disliking another country and what it stands for, more than you dislike your own criminals.
- *'Turf'* considerations at the agency level – sometimes members of an agency in one country dislike the idea that agencies from another country should be getting involved in their affairs. It is a case of 'this is my area, you can't tell what me to do'.
- *Conflicts of laws* – this is a major problem and very complex to resolve. Conflicts of laws occur where what is legally defined as a crime in one country is not a crime in another, or where a defence applies which would not be available in the other country, or where observing the law in one country would entail breaching it in another (e.g. bank secrecy laws) or where enforcement in one country is viewed as being harsh/immoral/illegal in another country (e.g. the death penalty).

- *Breach of contract and poor customer relations* – at the institutional level, many financial institutions are reluctant to extend cooperation across borders to other financial institutions for fear that their actions may result in legal action by their own customers against them. For example, this may occur when a bank is requested to release information regarding a customer's account by another institution (breach of confidentiality) or when it is requested to freeze an account (breach of mandate).

MODERN STRUCTURES OF ORGANISED CRIME AND TERRORISM

As was seen in Chapter 1, organised crime is growing and exerting an increasing effect on the world and its societies. Between $500 billion and $1 trillion each year is estimated to be laundered through the world's financial system, controlled by organised criminal enterprises, some of which are better known than others. Having this kind of money allows criminal groups not just to enjoy luxurious work-free lifestyles, but to subvert international agendas, bribe corrupt politicians and government officials to pass laws which protect them and allow them to expand their criminal activities unchecked by law enforcement. If left unrestricted, such criminal groups could control entire countries and regions, destabilise world markets and strike lucrative deals with terrorist groups to permit training and organisation on their territory and provide sanctuary.

The battle against money laundering as it is played out within the financial community rests upon the theory of interdiction. Throughout history, and into the future, profit motivates criminal activity. This is represented in Figure 7.1. But the amount of profit produced by criminal activity these days is so large that an additional stage needs to be added for criminal organisations, which is the processing of the profits from crime. Modern international anti-money laundering strategy is predicated upon the assumption that if you can disrupt the processing of criminal proceeds – effectively interdicting them within the global financial system – then you can disrupt this 'magic circle' of causation.

Figure 7.1 **The circle of criminal causation**

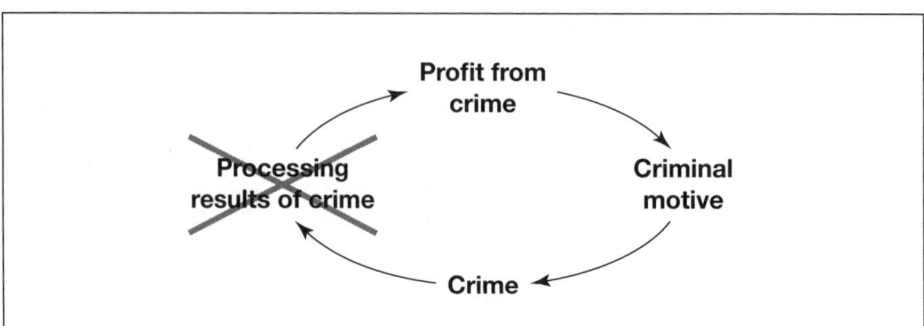

Clearly such a strategy will never result in the elimination of crime. Rather, it is aimed at reducing the flow of criminal funds and trying to ensure that criminal activity should be made as risky as possible for those minded to undertake it, with no degree of profit certainty at the end of it.

Modern TNOC has several features that make it distinctive from more traditional stereotypes. (The following information and commentary is drawn from McFarlane, J. (2005) 'Regional and international co-operation in tackling transnational crime, terrorism and problems of disrupted states', *Journal of Financial Crime*, 12(4)). Modern transnational criminal groups will not organise according to traditional, hierarchical structures (compared with the rigid family hierarchies of the mafia type organisations, for example). This makes them harder to predict and penetrate. They are, rather, network based, using specialists on a 'one job only' basis (much the same as contracting firms may use sub-contractors only for specific, finite work).

For example, a modern TNOC syndicate might use different resources for importation of goods; transportation of those goods in-country; fraudulent documentation to legitimise the presence of goods in a particular country; street enforcement; and money laundering. This lack of formal structure and rapid appearance and disappearance of different combinations makes the organisation more secure. It also makes it more efficient; there is less scope for 'gang politics', with the organisation being purely profit driven and completely ruthless in the pursuit of its objectives.

According to this model of TNOC (see Figure 7.2), the global financial system is especially vulnerable to abuse because of the use of a wide range of professionals and others with traditionally easy access to the financial system, as fronts for introductions and the conduct of financial and business transactions. Examples of these representatives and agents are well known, but include:

Figure 7.2 **Model of transnational organised crime**

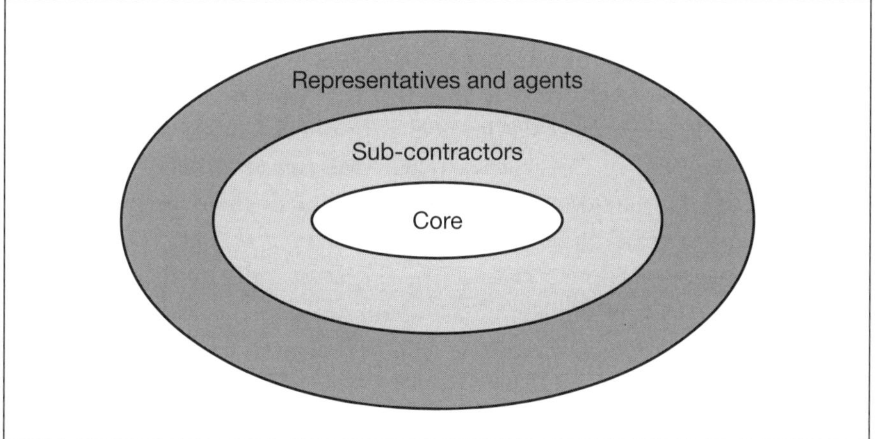

- lawyers
- accountants
- financial advisers
- bankers
- stockbrokers
- IT specialists
- business people
- politicians
- civil servants (judges, magistrates, police officers, customs, military personnel)
- compliant media professionals
- clerics.

In relation to terrorism, after the collapse of the socialist world, the spread of 'new' terrorism, different in form from 'old' traditional terrorism, has taken place. New ideologies, new factors and new sponsors have entered terrorism, and 'new' terrorism is arguably much more difficult to deal with than 'old' terrorism. 'Old' terrorism was 'political': it was all about achieving concrete political aims and tasks. It supported left wing ideologies such as Marxism and Maoism, and also nationalism and separatism. 'Old' terrorists were invariably ready to negotiate: they promised to stop terrorist action in exchange for concrete political compromises and, for the most part, they did not feel any particular affiliation with religion. Indeed religious figures of all denominations often condemned them and their actions.

Old terrorism still exists and its most recent high profile exponents have probably been the LTTE (or Tamil Tigers) in Sri Lanka (who, despite their apparent military defeat in 2010, may yet re-emerge as a coherent force). However, it has been superseded in recent years by the rise of 'new' terrorism, most notably stemming from the Islamic world, but also, it is important to note, from many other areas and from deep within what is generally considered to be the world's most active anti-terrorist state, the US.

A feature of 'new' terrorism is that it often appears to possess no concrete, achievable political goals. Its goal is to destroy modern societies and much of humankind in the process. It uses the concept of the 'asymmetrical threat', at the heart of which lies the doctrine of the superiority of the attackers against their target *at the specific location of the attack*, despite the terrorists' relative weakness against the target overall. Its focus is on the design and execution of indiscriminate attacks to spread panic and make life unlivable, or at least to cause people to question their own lives and views and those of their governments, whether elected or unelected. Eventually, it has to be assumed that Weapons of Mass Destruction (WMD) may be accessed and used thereby allowing a very small terrorist organisation to mount an attack that causes destruction that is totally disproportionate to its numbers.

In the US itself, besides the radicalised Islamist groups known to be operating or attempting to operate, groups and movements such as the Animal Liberation Front, the Earth Liberation Front, the Nation of Islam, the neo-Nazis and skinheads of the 'Aryan Front', the World Church of Creator, the National Alliance and, of course the Ku Klux Klan (KKK) have all engaged in terror attacks.

Many serious terrorist groups are evolving new organisational structures that are harder to detect and infiltrate. These groups are often a collection of factions with common interests which form, change and regroup in response to a specific agenda or planned actions. The groups ally themselves according to religious, ethnic or ideological affinities – often based on major grievances against the US, the world's sole remaining superpower. They are not controlled or directed by any overall 'director of operations'. Instead they tend to be autonomous in their planning and decision-making functions. The large number of these groups, as well as their lack of central direction and changing organisational structures, makes them very difficult to track and interdict.

As they have become more violent, terrorist groups have also expanded the range of targets they consider to be legitimate. As long ago as 1996, Brian Jenkins, senior adviser to the President at the RAND Corporation and an internationally recognised expert on terrorism, noted three potential reasons for this trend:

- First, as generational replacement has occurred within terrorist organisations and their affiliates new leaders have become less concerned with ideological constraints and adverse public opinion.
- Second, in the media age the new leaders desire above all to maintain media attention, and to receive attention they have escalated their levels of violence and used bolder, more shocking tactics.
- Finally, the international dynamics of terrorist groups require that the organisation should demonstrate to its members that it is moving inexorably towards its goals. Increasingly violent tactics generate the impression amongst members and supporters that things are heading in the right direction.

MECHANISMS AND TOOLS OF INTERNATIONAL COOPERATION

The UN Convention Against Trans-National Organised Crime, 2000 (the Palermo Convention)

The Palermo Convention is currently the main international treaty detailing the obligations of signatory countries to combat cross-border organised crime. Articles 5, 6, 8 and 23 of the Convention identify four offences, which states are required to criminalise, these being:

- participation in an organised criminal group
- laundering the proceeds of crime
- corruption, and
- obstruction of justice.

A serious crime is defined in Article 2 of the Convention as, 'an offence punishable by a maximum deprivation of liberty of at least four years or a more serious penalty'.

Article 3 defines the scope of the Convention as addressing such crimes 'where the offence is transnational in nature and involves an organized criminal group', and goes on to explain that an offence is transnational in nature if it is committed:

(a) in more than one state
(b) in one state but a substantial part of its preparation, planning, direction or control takes places in another state
(c) in one state but involves an organised criminal group that engages in criminal activities in more than one state, or
(d) in one state but it has substantial effects in another state.

An organised criminal group is defined in Article 2 as 'a structured group of three or more persons, existing for a period of time and acting in concert with the aim of committing one or more serious crimes or offences … in order to obtain, directly or indirectly, a financial or other material benefit'. Examples of such crimes would include:

- drug trafficking
- money laundering
- trafficking in women and children
- trafficking in illegal fire arms
- smuggling of alcohol, cigarettes and higher-value goods
- illegal immigration
- protection racketeering

- intellectual property piracy
- corruption
- terrorism
- proliferation of WMD.

The Palermo Convention describes certain core areas where international cooperation is required:

- cooperation with international requests for assistance in the confiscation and repatriation of criminal assets
- extradition, and
- mutual legal assistance.

Extradition

Historically, extradition (from *extradere*, meaning the forceful return of a person to their sovereign) was sought for political opponents not common criminals. The earliest recorded extradition treaty dates back to 1280 BC in Ancient Egypt. By the mid-nineteenth century, however, countries were becoming concerned to fight crime and preserve social interests, with the growing acceptance within public international law that countries should either 'extradite or punish'. In other words, if a criminal from another country was on your territory, you should either punish that person yourselves or extradite them back to their own country for them to be punished there.

This general obligation, however, has become considered insufficient and accordingly has been replaced by treaty obligations, either bilateral (between two states and applicable to no other states) or multi-lateral (applying to lots of states by international agreement). Because of the sensitivities of extradition (see above), the principle of a 'speciality' also features. This means that a state must only prosecute a person for the offence in respect of which they were extradited (this, presumably, to prevent 'political prosecutions' becoming embedded within the extradition system).

Mutual legal assistance

This is also required under the Convention (subject to exceptions, see below) and includes providing assistance to other states in the following areas:

- taking evidence or statements
- effecting service of judicial documents
- search, seizure and freezing of assets
- examining objects and sites
- provision of information, evidence and expert evaluations

- asset tracing and 'any other type of assistance not contrary to ... domestic law ...'
- joint investigations and the use of 'special investigative techniques' (e.g. surveillance, electronic listening, phone tapping, controlled delivery, etc.)
- transfer of criminal proceedings from one State Party to another
- transfer of prisoners serving custodial sentences in one country, for the purpose of giving witness evidence in another country
- facilitation and admission of video evidence of witnesses unwilling or unable to travel to the country of the proceedings.

Mutual legal assistance may be refused in the following circumstances:

- if the request does not conform with the provisions of the Palermo Convention
- if the request 'is likely to prejudice the sovereignty, security, public order or other essential interests...' of the requested State Party
- if domestic law would prohibit the action requested
- interestingly, State Parties may *not* refuse requests on the *sole* ground that the offence is also considered to involve fiscal (tax) matters.

INTERNATIONAL COOPERATIVE BODIES

In the Anti-Money Laundering (AML) and Counter Terrorist Financing (CFT) arena, there are a number of important bodies that exist to promote international cooperation, as follows.

The Financial Action Task Force (FATF)

This is the international body set up by the OECD countries in 1989 to promote good anti-money laundering practice around the world, described earlier.

International Cooperation Review Group and its predecessor the Non-Cooperative Countries and Territories (NCCT) List

In 2000, FATF took perhaps its most dramatic new initiative to 'name and shame' what it designated as 'Non-Cooperative Countries and Terroritories' (NCCTs). These were jurisdictions not participating in the general move towards stricter financial regulation and greater international cooperation and which were instead offering financial services under strict banking secrecy and without sufficient control or regulation by the authorities.

The NCCT initiative proved a successful one – at least in getting countries to address the issues through legislation and infrastructure. Of the 47 countries whose systems were initially reviewed by the FATF in 2000 and 2001, a total of 23 countries were listed as NCCTs. By 2000 the number had reduced to 15 and by 2001 the list was down to just eight countries. By the end of 2007 the list was empty, because all of the designated countries took steps deemed sufficient to get themselves removed, and passed AML and CFT laws.

If there was one criticism of the NCCT regime, it was that it was a very blunt instrument; it made no distinction between different severities of deficiency and you were either on the list or you were not. It was therefore replaced in 2007 by the International Cooperation Review Group (ICRG), which aims to be less 'black and white' in how it describes the world, instead attempting to engage in a dialogue with countries to improve their AML and CTF regimes, whilst also publicising those countries where it believes that varying degrees of problems still exist. It currently has three levels of sensitivity, being countries which the FATF has urged should be subject to a call for counter measures, countries subject to a call to consider the risks of transactions involving them, and countries which have made progress, but where strategic deficiencies still remain to be addressed in their AML regimes.

Moneyval

This is the body set up by the council of Europe in 1997 for the mutual evaluation of members states' AML and CFT measures for Council of Europe and Member States which are not members of FATF.

Along with FATF it is influential in applying peer pressure to countries to get their AML and CFT regimes up to International Standards.

Interpol

This is the international criminal police organisation. It has 190 member countries and was created in 1923. It facilitates cross-border police cooperation and supports and assists all organisations, authorities and services whose mission is to prevent or combat international crime.

The Egmont Group

This is the coordinating body for financial intelligence units worldwide. It was formed in 1995 to promote and enhance international cooperation in AML and CFT (see Chapter 2).

8

Modern Money Laundering and Terrorist Financing: Two Case Studies

Where you see the **WWW** *icon in this chapter, this indicates a preview link to the author's website and to a training film which is relevant to the AML CFT issue being discussed.*
Go to ***www.antimoneylaunderingvideos.com***

INTRODUCTION

The two fictional case studies in this chapter provide an in-depth opportunity to consider some of the main issues discussed in this book in a practical, work-based context. Both have been researched and carefully scripted to reflect the day-to-day challenges which arise in trying to make AML policies work amidst the pressures of modern business.

Smoke and Mirrors tells a story of global financial institution AlnaBank's relationship with a Cypriot investment firm, J Dalea Investments and, through Dalea, its unwitting exposure to political corruption, organised crime and terrorist groups in the near Eastern country of Moldachia and beyond.

Too Good to be True, set in another time and drawing heavily upon the private banking scandals of the 1990s and early 2000s, tells the story of Alna's relationship with Halit Kransky and its unwitting laundering of a $83 million fortune built from narcotics and people trafficking.

WWW Soft copies can be requested by emailing info@lessonslearned.co.uk, and both case studies are available to purchase as high-quality film docu-dramas for use in training, which can be previewed on www.antimoneylaunderingvideos.com at the following links.

WWW
- *Smoke and Mirrors*: http://www.antimoneylaunderingvideos.com/player/smoke_mirrors.htm

WWW
- *Too Good to be True* – http://www.antimoneylaunderingvideos.com/player/tgtbt.htm.

SMOKE AND MIRRORS: ALNABANK AND THE MESSENGERS OF GOD

Organisational context and operation of the risk-based approach

After the great financial crisis of 2008/09, in which AlnaBank suffered heavy losses and had to take government bail-out money, it sets its sights firmly on renewal and a revival of profitability and shareholder value. As the crisis recedes and growth returns, Alna's risk focus is very much on those operational risks which were the cause of the crisis, not on money laundering. This 'de-emphasis' of Anti-Money Laundering (AML) and Countering the Financing of Terrorism (CFT) risk in relation to other risks is encouraged in part by the adoption of a new, systematic and very process-driven method for managing AML risk, known as the risk-based approach.

Under the risk-based approach, all a bank like Alna has to do to manage its AML risks effectively is to assess its clients before taking them on as either higher or lower risk according to a number of set criteria (country of residence/

incorporation/regulation, business type, transaction type/volume, etc.), and thereafter adjust the level of due diligence and monitoring according to the perceived level of risk: enhanced due diligence and monitoring for higher-risk accounts and standard or lower due diligence for lower-risk accounts.

Leading AlnaBank's drive for revenue and growth is the Global Relationships Division (GRD), that is aggressively seeking new business opportunities and is therefore very interested when approached by a Cypriot investment firm called J Dalea Investments that is interested in placing initially €1 billion with GRD for management.

Relationship origination, reliance and the AML governance structure

Because of the importance attached by AlnaBank to customer due diligence (CDD), a special unit has been formed in GRD called the Business Unit Support (BUS) group to assist the Relationship Managers (RMs) with obtaining all the documents and verifications required under AlnaBank's group AML policy – particularly for higher-risk accounts where the CDD burden is greatest. What develops under this arrangement, however, is a 'disconnect' between the RMs on the one hand, who see their role very much as revenue earners for the bank and who generally believe that the CDD process has become too complex and time-consuming, and the BUS team members on the other hand, who believe that the RMs don't take CDD seriously enough ...

This division comes to a head over the Dalea Investments account. Under AlnaBank's own policy and also under international standards, where a financial intermediary client is being taken on, that in turn has its own clients on its books, it is acceptable to rely on the CDD conducted against those end clients by the intermediary itself, as long as the intermediary agrees to such reliance and as long as it is incorporated and regulated in an 'equivalent jurisdiction' (which Dalea Investments, incorporated in Cyprus, an EU country, is). The personnel in GRD, right up to its Group Executive Director, Daniel Johnson, believe that this is sufficient and don't wish to undertake further due diligence against Dalea's own clients if it isn't necessary. The BUS personnel, however, consider that further due diligence is not only justified but necessary, given the fact that Dalea Investments is relatively unknown, that the sums involved are so large and given also that the jurisdiction in question (Cyprus) has in the past been associated with inflows of money from high-risk jurisdictions, such as countries of the former Soviet Union.

The issue goes for a decision to the most senior level within the bank and results in a corporate decision, communicated by the Chief Executive, Greg Jonas, that further due diligence will need to be undertaken against Dalea Investments' own clients. The communication from Jonas, however, makes it clear that he expects BUS to be aware of the very demanding revenue targets that the bank is pursuing and to work with the business 'as a team' to help achieve those targets.

Further due diligence and client acceptance

BUS therefore conducts further, deeper due diligence against Dalea Investments' own clients by accessing Dalea's own CDD records, which reveal that the main client is a group of companies based in the former Soviet Republic of Moldachia, with an extremely complex corporate structure consisting of multiple layers of shell and holding companies. Nevertheless, it appears that Dalea Investments has done its due diligence against this structure, as required, and what it reveals is that the ultimate beneficial owner of the Xavier Group is a local lawyer and businessman by the name of Yulian Garbov. One unresolved issue is a rumour (no more than that) in Moldachia that apparently Yulian Garbov is a 'front' for an unnamed Moldachian politician. But Dalea Investments' due diligence reveals nothing on that, and despite the fact that the BUS group want to conduct further, deeper investigations into this allegation, it is also mindful of how much time has already been spent on due diligence and, under strong business pressure, the Head of Compliance, Ottily Marks, agrees to the opening of investment accounts for Dalea Investments. She stipulates that although Garbov himself is not technically a Politically Exposed Person (PEP) under the bank's policy, nevertheless he poses similar risks and should be treated as such, that the account should be the subject of regular, enhanced monitoring and that the Head of GRD, Daniel Johnson, should sign off on the account. In fact, Johnson never does sign off on the account.

When the account is opened, €3 billion is received instead of the €1 billion initially promised. Furthermore, a correspondent bank account relationship is opened in AlnaBank's New York office one year later with KVP Bank, a wholly owned subsidiary of the Xavier Group, based substantially on the existing due diligence against Xavier Group.

The real position: PEP ownership, political corruption, organised crime and terrorism

Following a revolution in Moldachia, details emerge of the extent of corruption in the previous government, particularly by the former Minister of Transport, Vassiliy Chernov, who had been accepting large political donations from a Moldachian businessman named Radovan Kaltan, who was also rumoured to be the ultimate controller of the main Moldachian organised criminal group. Aware, now, of Kaltan's political donations to Chernov, and aware also of the rumour that Yulian Garbov was not, in fact, the ultimate beneficial owner and controller of the Xavier Group, Moldachian journalist Judi Shimanova suspects that Vassiliy Chernov has been the true owner and controller of Xavier Group all along and that he has allowed Kaltan to launder criminal funds through it in return for his donations.

Using information from ex-employees of Xavier Group, Judi Shimanova discovers hundreds of millions of dollars-worth of apparently fake transactions between companies in the Xavier and Kaltan groups, involving large payments against invoices issued for items that are difficult to physically trace and assess, such as consultancy services, intellectual property rights on designs, outsourcing services etc. What nobody has previously been aware of, however, is that Radovan Kaltan has been secretly cooperating with an Islamist terror group known as the Messengers of God that provides security for his illegal gambling, prostitution and alcohol operations in neighbouring Maluchistan in return for the use of some of Kaltan's companies for terrorist financing purposes. As part of these transactions, funds originating in Iran have made their way through Kaltan-controlled shell companies to the Xavier Group pocket bank, KVP Bank, which now of course has correspondent banking relationships with AlnaBank in New York ...

In the US, investigators uncover a plot by the Messengers of God to use some of these funds to explode a dirty bomb in downtown Manhattan.

Questions on due diligence deficiencies and failures

At the time of account opening, what did AlnaBank do, or fail to do, that exposed it to the risk of money laundering and terrorist financing?

The failures were notable and extreme, but perhaps not unpredictable, given the extreme performance pressure which business units of the bank were under and the failure of the governance structure (see below).

Risk assessment

Those involved failed to assess the risks of the relationship with Dalea Investments correctly. Particularly on the business side, the assumption was that as long as Dalea came from within the EU, it could effectively be treated as 'low risk', which isn't necessarily the case. Factors such as the size and reputation of the intermediary in question and the recent financial and economic history of the jurisdiction should all be taken into account.

Depth of due diligence

Even though the above point was eventually accepted, the acceptance seemed to be reluctant and almost certainly influenced the depth of the further due diligence undertaken. AlnaBank seemed to satisfy itself with simply checking the due diligence records which had been obtained by Dalea Investments and failed to conduct its own investigations. The minimum requirements in terms of paper documentation, certificates of incorporation, passport copies, etc. seemed to be there. There was also evidence from corporate reports and local newspapers that Xavier Group was a genuine business. What was missing, however, was any real investigation into Xavier Group's business, its source of wealth (i.e. what produced its revenues) and its business counterparties and trading partners. The journalist Judi Shimanova started asking these questions and quickly got answers. Why didn't AlnaBank? Was it really not possible for it to discover the business connections between Xavier Group and companies controlled by Radovan Kaltan? And was there really no way in which they could have discovered Kaltan's dubious reputation within the country? Likewise, even though Dalea Investments claimed to have reached a dead-end in determining the 'rumour' that Yulian Garbov, the supposed ultimate beneficial owner of Xavier Group, was connected to an unnamed senior political figure, AlnaBank again made no attempt to get to the bottom of the matter. Had it done so, the connections with the Minister of Transport, Vassiliy Chernov, may have been detected.

Failure to conduct proper due diligence against a correspondent bank

After the Dalea Investment accounts were opened, a correspondent banking relationship was set up between AlnaBank's New York office and a wholly-owned banking subsidiary of the Xavier Group called KVP Bank. The due diligence relied upon for that account was the same flawed due diligence in existence for the Xavier Group. In other words, the bank assumed that because the Xavier Group had been deemed acceptable, then any subsidiary – including a banking subsidiary – would also be acceptable. Alna took none of the required CDD steps referred to below against its new respondent, KVP Bank. Had it done so, that would have provided another route for the discovery of Xavier Group's connections with Kaltan-controlled companies.

What do international standards and well drafted procedures and controls require in relation to customer due diligence?

FATF Recommendation 10 sets out that financial institutions must conduct due diligence against entities with which they form business relationships. 'Due diligence' means:

- establishing and verifying the identity of the person or entity concerned
- establishing the beneficial ownership of the asset concerned – meaning the natural person who owns or controls the asset, or on whose behalf transactions are being conducted
- establishing the purpose of the business relationship, and
- conducting ongoing monitoring to ensure that transactions are consistent with what is known about the customer.

It also states that due diligence should be conducted on a risk-sensitive basis and Recommendations 12 and 13 go on to state that in relation to higher-risk relationships involving PEPs and cross-border correspondent banking relationships, additional measures should be taken.

In relation to PEPs, these measures are:

- developing risk management systems to determine whether the customer or the beneficial owner is a PEP
- obtaining senior management approval for the commencement of the relationship.
- taking reasonable measures to establish the PEP's source of wealth (that is, the economic activity that has generated their wealth) and source of funds; and
- subjecting the relationship to enhanced, ongoing monitoring

In relation to cross-border correspondent banking, the additional measures are:

- assessing the correspondent bank's business and customer base
- assessing the strength or otherwise of its AML/CFT controls, the quality of its supervision and whether it has been the subject of investigation or regulatory action
- documenting the responsibilities of each institution
- obtaining senior management approval for the commencement of the correspondent banking relationship, and
- ensuring that where the respondent bank's (i.e. KVP Bank's) own customers will be accessing its accounts with its correspondent bank (i.e. AlnaBank), the respondent bank has identified its own customers and can and will provide CDD records in relation to them upon request.

In practical terms, a bank's policies and procedures would require extensive due diligence against a corporate group such as the Xavier Group and its subsidiary bank, KVP Bank. The complex corporate structure would need to be unwrapped and understood, and also the *reason* for the complexity of that structure. Natural persons owning 25 per cent or more of the shares or voting rights in the corporations in question would need to be identified, and their sources of wealth established. In particular, investigations would need to be undertaken into the business activities of the corporate group, how it made its money, who its trading partners were, the type and amount of transactions which it conducted, and also its status and reputation within the country – not just from local newspapers but also from multiple, independent, unbiased sources. Some banks would employ the services of professional investigations consultancies in these circumstances, with access to a wide range of sources and contacts both public and non-public.

Due diligence investigations in high-risk situations such as this, whether they are in respect of individuals (e.g. Garbov) or corporate groups such as the Xavier Group, need to be thorough and detailed and supporting evidence needs to be obtained and retained on the file.

Questions on beneficial ownership and PEPs

What mechanisms were used by those involved to disguise beneficial ownership and political connections?

Use of fronts

The former Minister of Transport, Vassiliy Chernov, used the lawyer and businessman Yulian Garbov as a 'front' to disguise his own ownership and control of the Xavier Group. The use of fronts in this way is very common and is extremely difficult to detect, because there will usually be no formal record or document confirming the controller's interest (that, after all, is the whole point). When fronts are used, the true controller's name doesn't appear anywhere in the documentation relating to the account, trust or company concerned. When a suspicion exists, therefore, that a front may be being used, one is often left with less than satisfactory indicators. These include:

- the credibility of the suspected front
- the extent and credibility of market rumours and information about whether a relationship between the suspected front and suspected controller does in fact exist, and if so its nature and extent
- careful and detailed searches through public records using not only subscription products such as World-Check but also general search engines such as Google, searches in online international, regional and national newspapers (although these can be suspect – see below) and other information sources such as society magazines and informal conversations with other banks, companies and professional firms such as lawyers and accountants.

In addition, there is personal questioning – often referred to as 'the smell test'. A succession of meetings at which a range of important and detailed questions are asked over a period of time can assist in developing an accurate impression. A person's demeanour, the confidence with which they speak, the extent of their knowledge and mastery of the relevant issues, whether they change their minds on important issues without apparent reason, whether they give different answers to the same questions asked (deliberately) at different times during the process, are all matters which can be taken into account.

Ultimately, it is extremely hard to spot a controller–front relationship if it has been carefully constructed. The important thing is that a bank should be able to show that it has gone through a structured – and not necessarily easy or trouble-free – process to arrive at a decision. Nobody can ask that you get it right all the time, but they can – and do – ask that you make a reasonable and genuine attempt at finding out. Simply saying 'It's a rumour, maybe it's true, maybe it isn't' won't suffice.

Complex structures

Complex structures can develop for legitimate reasons, such as during and after a series of corporate acquisitions when there has been no opportunity to simplify the corporate structure. But they also have a more sinister use in that they are an ideal mechanism for hiding ownership. The more complex a corporate structure is in terms of the number of companies, the ownership layers and the degree of inter-company ownership, the harder it is to determine the natural persons who are actually in control.

A bank should adopt a clear policy that unless the reason for it is clearly understood, any corporate structure at or above a certain number of layers of ownership (e.g. three or four) should automatically be designated as a higher-risk account and therefore subject to enhanced due diligence and enhanced ongoing monitoring. Enhanced due diligence in these circumstances would entail peeling back the corporate structure (something which can take many weeks or even months) so as to fully understand it and determine the identity of the natural persons holding 25 per cent or more of the shares or voting rights or who otherwise appear to be individuals who are exercising significant influence over the affairs of the company/structure concerned.

During this process, the investigations themselves and the conversations that are had with officials and managers of the company can often assist in developing a sense of whether or not it would be appropriate to proceed. Ultimately, if, at the end of the process, one simply isn't satisfied that the true beneficial ownership of a complex structure has been established, then the business should either be refused or requirements expressed as to the level of transparency and restructuring which would be necessary in order for the Bank to proceed.

Public disinformation

People wishing to hide their control over a company or its assets are fully aware that banks these days will look to a wide variety of sources of information in trying to establish true beneficial ownership, and are often prepared to disseminate false or deliberately misleading information in order to improve perceptions about themselves. The purpose of this may be either to help persuade you that a rumour of a connection isn't true, or to enhance the credibility of a front as a genuine owner/controller. Articles in newspapers, journals and websites, internet blogs, even official announcements from government bodies (where these have been corrupted) mingle with other information and are, to all extents and purposes, indistinguishable. In such circumstances, the quality of the information obtained – and in particular an assessment of the quality of the source of that information – becomes paramount and this is an area where many financial institutions again turn to professional investigation firms and the specialist services they offer.

Money laundering and terrorist financing

What mechanisms do criminal and terrorist groups use to move money around and launder it?

Money laundering

Radovan Kaltan was apparently laundering the proceeds of his Moldachian criminal activities out of the country and into Cyprus by getting shell companies which he owned and controlled to engage in apparently legitimate business transactions with Xavier Group companies. These funds would then be transferred to the 'pension fund' and onward to Dalea and AlnaBank.

Whilst some of these trading transactions were no doubt genuine, others will either have been completely fabricated or substantially over- or understated, and will have involved tactics such as false invoicing, over-invoicing and under-invoicing.

For example, a false invoice for a fake transaction from an Xavier company to a Kaltan company would provide an apparently legitimate business purpose for the transmission of funds from the Kaltan company to the Xavier company, then to be fed on out via the pension fund to Dalea Investments in Cyprus and thence on to AlnaBank. Laundered funds coming back the other way could be transferred back to other Kaltan companies under cover of similar invoices issued by those companies to Xavier companies.

The process therefore involves the laundering of criminal funds in a sophisticated scheme involving genuine companies and shell companies, genuine transactions and fake transactions, a corrupt politician, his 'front' and the business structure beneath him, a regulated financial intermediary and an international financial institution. Through this network, the criminal provenance of some of the funds in the AlnaBank accounts is hidden from view. AlnaBank sees initially only Dalea, and subsequently the Xavier

Group and Yulian Garbov. It doesn't see behind them Vassiliy Chernov, Radovan Kaltan or the Messengers of God (see below).

Terrorist financing

The terrorist financing undertaken by the Messengers of God in the film utilises many of the money laundering features outlined above, in particular, the use of shell and front companies as cover for the transfer of funds.

The added element in the case is the use of the Xavier Group pocket bank, KVP Bank. (A 'pocket bank' is a bank owned and controlled by a particular corporate group, or sometimes even a particular individual, and which often has only one customer, or a relatively small number of customers who are associated with the group or the individual). Following the transmission of funds from Iranian shell companies to the accounts of the Kaltan-controlled companies with KVP Bank in Moldachia, the funds are then wired to KVP Bank's dollar clearing account with AlnaBank in New York, for onward transmission, presumably to other companies and individuals inside the US. By this method, the Messengers of God would make funds available to its accomplices inside the US for its purposes there; much the same as happened with the 9/11 attacks, only on a larger scale due to its (expensive) ambition of exploding a dirty bomb in downtown Manhattan.

Criminal groups and terrorist groups will sometimes cooperate when it is expedient to do so. The most high-profile example of this in recent years was the cooperation between the Taliban (pre-2001) and those engaged in drug trafficking from the poppy fields of Afghanistan, which suited the needs of both groups. The Taliban were able to finance their regime and the drug lords were able to continue with their lucrative, illicit trade.

What does the law require you to do if you become suspicious of money laundering or terrorist financing?

You *must report* suspicions of money laundering or terrorist financing *immediately* to your Compliance Officer or Money Laundering Reporting Officer, who will advise you further on what is required.

Failure to report a suspicion and/or warning or 'tipping off' a customer that a report has been filed and that they may become the subject of an investigation are *serious criminal offences* in almost all jurisdictions.

If you are in any doubt at all, speak to your Compliance Officer or Money Laundering Reporting Officer.

Questions on organisational responsibilities for CDD

In what way or ways did AlnaBank's AML/CFT governance structures fail it in this case?

The division between business-getters and business-controllers

Whilst the division of responsibilities in AlnaBank between the RMs and the BUS group made sense in theory – and is indeed a model followed in many financial institutions – in practice it didn't work out. The RMs came to the conclusion that the BUS group was simply there to stop them doing business (as evidenced by the acronym they attached to the 'New Client Acceptance' system or NCA – 'No Clients Any More'). The BUS group clearly came to the conclusion that the RMs wanted any kind of business, regardless of risk. Thus, the two parts of the bank were fighting each other instead of cooperating towards a common goal.

Senior management contribution

The main players involved fell well short of their responsibilities. The business head, Daniel Johnson, was too focused on the GRD's revenue targets and on the contribution which the Dalea business would make to them – preferably at minimal cost – to appreciate the wider risk implications of AlnaBank getting involved in that business. As part of the GRD business structure, the BUS group would have felt completely undermined by what was happening.

For her part, the Head of Compliance, Ottily Marks, and her Compliance team whose role was to support the BUS group from outside of business reporting lines, had clearly failed to make the case for effective CDD to the business team in GRD, which indicates a failure in the training and communication strategy. Whilst a degree of awareness and sensitivity to other people's positions is always required, her most serious mistake was in agreeing to allow the accounts to be opened when both she herself and those on the BUS team who had been working on the case in detail were fundamentally dissatisfied with the extent of the due diligence which they had reviewed from Dalea. Thereafter they failed to follow up on the enhanced monitoring and relationship sign-off that Daniel Johnson should have executed, which she had stipulated was necessary in her account opening approval email. Had monitoring taken place, it is possible that warnings would have been raised and suspicious activity reports filed in relation to the receipt of *three times* the expected funds from Dalea (€3 billion instead of €1 billion).

The Group Chief Executive, Greg Jonas, whilst seemingly supporting the Compliance Department's position that the bank needed to look behind J Dalea Investments, nevertheless appeared to do so reluctantly and his approval words contained a barely-disguised warning that Compliance and the BUS group within GRD would be expected to display a little more understanding in future. This was probably influential in Marks' later decision not to push for further, extensive due diligence on the rumour about Garbov's political connections and on the real nature of Xavier Group's business activities in Moldachia.

What might individual senior managers appearing in the case have done differently?

Daniel Johnson, Head of GRD

He could and should have insisted that CDD be done properly. As a senior business leader, Johnson should have been aware that it was he and his business which was primarily responsible for customer due diligence and that scrimping and saving on it in terms of time and money is a false economy, especially when dealing with relationships which are not 'plain vanilla' low risk, which was definitely the case with the Dalea Investments relationship.

If Johnson had problems with the way in which the BUS group was doing its job, instead of expressing this in the form of tactical fights on specific cases, he could have sought to engage the BUS group and the compliance department in a discussion about how the two could work together for the general benefit of the business.

Ottily Marks, Head of Compliance

Seeing the way things were going, Ottily Marks as the Head of Compliance could and should have sought to address the divisions between the business and the BUS group in GRD through a programme of training and communication. As part of this programme she could have obtained their views on ways in which the CDD process could be streamlined and made to work more efficiently, whilst also stressing of course that the fundamental requirements of knowing the customer and establishing beneficial ownership, political connections, etc. would need to remain.

Marks should also have tried to use her powers of persuasion – with both the Head of GRD, Daniel Johnson, and the Group CEO, Greg Jonas – to convince them that the risks of proceeding with the account without undertaking further and more detailed checks in Moldachia, were too great.

Greg Jonas, Chief Executive of AlnaBank Group

He should have been far less equivocal in his communication about the requirement for effective CDD at all times. Instead of planting the seeds of doubt about his support in Ottily Marks' mind with his email, he could instead have insisted that both Johnson and Marks together lead a joint project between GRD, the BUS group and the Compliance Department to review the Bank's CDD policy and procedures as part of a programme to start reducing the unhealthy tension which was contributing to the creation of unacceptable risks for the bank.

TOO GOOD TO BE TRUE: ALNABANK AND THE LAUNDERING OF THE KRANSKY MILLIONS

Background checks and account opening

Halit Kransky was introduced to AlnaBank by Hegit Milrich, a long-time client of AlnaBank's Private Banking division in London. At an initial meeting Milrich provided a strong personal reference which allowed Kransky to open an account.

Two months later, Alison Carter (a Senior Relationship Manager with AlnaBank) flew to Vresk, the capital of Moldovia and Kransky's given place of residence, to obtain Kransky's signatures on the required account opening documentation. Milrich had introduced Kransky as a brother of the former President of Moldovia. Kransky had, according to Milrich's testimonial, held a succession of posts at state-run agencies within Moldovia. Carter did not check this information. She did not investigate Kransky's employment background, his financial background or his assets. Nor did she seek references other than the one which had been provided by Milrich. Nevertheless, she recommended that Kransky should be accepted as a client of AlnaBank. This recommendation was approved by Carter's Divisional Head, and multiple accounts were opened in London. AlnaSecor, the Private Bank's trust in Switzerland, also discussed with Kransky the setting up of additional accounts in the name of an offshore shell corporation.

An AlnaSecor employee wrote to his senior managers suggesting that a detailed reference should be sought from Carter and signed off by her Divisional Head, before opening these accounts. Although this reference and sign-off were never obtained, AlnaSecor proceeded to set up the shell structure discussed with Kransky.

Secrecy products and services

The structures that AlnaBank had been asked to set up for Kransky and the methods to which the Bank agreed in its handling of his affairs were complicated and shrouded in secrecy.

The shell corporation set up by AlnaSecor was called Fasco, and was registered in the Cayman Islands. AlnaSecor also used three nominee companies to act as Fasco's board of directors, and a further three to serve as its officers and principal shareholders. AlnaSecor controlled all six of these nominee companies, which it used routinely to function as directors and officers of shell companies owned by Private Bank clients. Initially the recorded owner of Fasco was Kransky himself. However AlnaSecor subsequently established a trust, identified only by number, to serve as the owner of Fasco. The result of this elaborate structure was that Kransky's name did not appear anywhere in Fasco's incorporation papers.

Additional accounts were opened for Fasco in Switzerland, together with a special name account for Kransky under the name of 'Caesar'. Kransky had requested the utmost secrecy in relation to the Fasco accounts. As a result, the Private Bank in Switzerland did not disclose the name of the Fasco shell corporation to anyone other than the AlnaSecor personnel who administered the company, and those Swiss Private Bank personnel who were required by law to know the beneficial owner of the Swiss accounts. Not even Alison Carter knew about Kransky's ownership of Fasco.

Meanwhile, Carter had returned to Vresk where Kransky introduced her to his fiancée Svetlana Sevatskaya, a former model and night club owner. Kransky explained that he wanted to move funds out of Moldovia. However, he wanted to do this very discreetly, since if the extent of his personal wealth became known, it could be politically damaging to his brother, the former President. Kransky requested that Sevatskaya be allowed to bring Moldovian rouble cashiers' cheques from various banks in Moldovia into the Vresk branch of AlnaBank, where they would be converted into dollars and wired via New York clearing to a special account in London. This special account was called the 'Accumulation Account'. It was used by AlnaBank in London for administrative purposes, commingling funds from various sources before transferring them on to other accounts. The Accumulation Account was not intended for use by clients. Nor had Carter ever operated for other clients a system such as the one suggested by Kransky. Even so, she acceded to his request.

Carter also agreed that Sevatskaya would use an alias when presenting the cashiers' cheques at AlnaBank's branch in Vresk. As a result of this arrangement Kransky was able to move funds via an indirect route into secret accounts in Switzerland, without leaving any audit trail to connect either himself or his fiancée to the origins of those funds, or their destination.

Account balances and account monitoring

Carter had estimated early on that the relationship with Kransky had potential in the \$15 million to \$20 million range. She did not, however, attempt to conduct independent checks on the sources of this anticipated in-flow of funds. The first deposit was from a \$2 million cheque drawn on an account in Milrich's name. Carter did not query this transaction, nor did she raise any comment when, in a period of less than three weeks shortly after the accounts were opened, the accounts received deposits from cashiers' cheques totalling \$40 million, at least twice what Carter had anticipated for the relationship. She raised no comment either, when deposits totalling \$87 million were made over the next six months – the vast majority of these once again made via cashiers' cheques. In all, the total deposits by far exceeded Carter's estimate of Kransky's net worth, and yet at no stage did she see fit to enquire about or report this anomaly. Nor did she make enquiries to establish the source of the funds used to obtain the cheques, nor even whether Kransky had accounts at the Moldovian banks which had issued them.

Suspicion reporting and other matters

Roughly two years after Kransky had initially approached AlnaBank, he was arrested on murder charges. In the trial that followed evidence emerged of the deep links between Kransky and an East European organised crime syndicate known as 'Kratev'.

At the first sign of trouble, AlnaBank's instincts were tough and self-interested. Alison Carter's Divisional Head recorded in a memo his view that the Private Bank should seriously consider moving funds in London over to Switzerland, where their existence might stand a greater chance of remaining undiscovered. The same memo also recorded his view that the Private Bank should consider exercising set-offs, so as to avoid being out of pocket as a result of their involvement with Kransky. Control of the Kransky accounts was handed over to the Private Bank's legal department, who changed Alison Carter's extremely limited entries in the client profile database so as to emphasise and expand upon her stated beliefs about Kransky's source of wealth. It was not until nine months after Kransky's arrest that AlnaBank finally filed a suspicious activity report with the authorities in London and Geneva.

Questions on anti-money laundering deficiencies and failures

What did AlnaBank's Private Bank staff do and omit to do, that increased the risk of exposure to money laundering?

What procedures and controls are you required to operate within your own private banking business that are designed to minimise your exposure to such a risk?

In most countries there is a legal and regulatory obligation on banks and banking staff to operate certain minimum anti-money laundering measures in their handling of client business. The sequence of events described in this case could, in a large part, be attributed to a number of deficiencies and failures in complying with these measures.

Know Your Client (KYC)

It is incumbent upon private banking staff to take reasonable steps to ensure that clients really are who they claim to be, and that the information they give about themselves and their sources of wealth is accurate. This includes carrying out background checks independently of the client, in order to verify the information given.

Alison Carter accepted as the only means of verification the personal reference of Hegit Milrich. She did not seek other references for Kransky or carry out further background checks into his stated employment and financial interests.

Management supervision

Managers have a supervisory responsibility for private banking staff within their jurisdiction. This includes monitoring for compliance with required anti-money laundering procedures, in particular where approving or signing off on new client business.

Alison Carter's recommendation that Kransky be accepted as a client was approved and signed off by her Divisional Head without question. He failed to note or even to enquire into the absence of the required background checks.

Account monitoring

Private banks should operate procedures for monitoring a client's business activity and flag up any unusual or suspicious activity which does not match the true and likely nature of a client's known business and business needs.

Even if AlnaBank had such procedures, Alison Carter clearly failed to apply them adequately. The in-flow of funds from Kransky by far exceeded her estimation of his known net worth, yet she raised no comment.

Ownership of assets

One of the key principles of anti-money laundering is to ensure that the bank knows the identity of any real persons behind the assets and structures it manages. The nature of private banking is such that quite complex structures may be set up for clients, often with built-in secrecy features such as special named or numbered accounts. Nonetheless, the identity of the real person behind such structures and accounts should always be the subject of a bank record and known to relevant personnel. It is also clear that banks should take particular care with due diligence procedures, in respect of clients who request such products and services.

In setting up Fasco as it did, the bank facilitated a structure in which Kransky's name did not appear in incorporation documents, or ultimately even as the owner of the Fasco accounts. This was compounded by the fact that the Fasco accounts were held in Switzerland and were therefore subject to very strict banking secrecy laws. Whilst the bank did nothing wrong per se in providing this service for Kransky, it is clear that the provision of such complex and secret structures to clients about whom little is actually known constitutes a very high risk of exposure to money laundering. The bank was negligent in its duties in a couple of important respects: firstly, in failing to carry out the required due diligence before accepting Kransky as a client; and secondly, in failing to obtain the detailed reference from Carter and sign-off from her boss (as had been internally recommended) before setting up the Fasco structure and accounts.

Source of funds

From an anti-money laundering perspective it is important to know both the origin and destination of funds. Where the source of funds is unknown, it is incumbent upon private banking staff to take reasonable steps to establish the sources and, where a satisfactory explanation cannot be found, to report the funds as potentially suspicious.

Kransky used a method for the placement of funds that was designed to disguise their origins as far as possible – cashiers' cheques, drawn on a variety of Moldovian banks and presented under an alias, for subsequent transfer to his accounts in Switzerland. Carter made no enquiries as to the sources of the funds to obtain the cheques which, as cashiers' cheques, gave the banks on which they were drawn as the payees. Nor did she enquire as to whether Kransky even held accounts at the banks that had issued the cheques. Even if this method of disguising a source of funds is unusual, there are a number of other more common methods which should be noticed, for example receipt of funds from shell corporations not usually associated with the account, or of fund value in the form of redeemable bearer instruments such as bearer bonds and certificates of deposit.

Record keeping

It is a key responsibility for private banking staff to keep adequate and accurate records for their clients and client business. This includes a record of the client's identification evidence and the means of obtaining this, and records of the client's transactions. It also includes a record of any information gleaned about the client from due diligence and background checks.

Carter's records in respect of the required background checks were paltry to say the least. There was little or no record – she had not done the necessary checks. After the arrest of Kransky and, fearing possible censure of AlnaBank's handling of this client, the bank's legal department responded by 'amending' Carter's records to give the impression that she had indeed researched Kransky's background and sources of wealth far more diligently than had actually been the case. Carter was obviously negligent in her failure to do the background checks. But the legal department should never have taken the action it did in amending records after the event.

Questions on recognising suspicions

What features of Kransky's behaviour and the nature of his business with AlnaBank might have alerted Private Banking staff to the possibility of money laundering?

What does the law require of you if you know or suspect that money laundering may be taking place?

It is impossible to anticipate every possible situation which might duly give rise to a suspicion. There are, therefore, no absolute rules for what constitutes suspicious activity, and what does not. In an anti-money laundering context it is the role of each relationship manager to develop a sufficient knowledge and understanding of their client and their business, and to use this information to identify anomalies or discrepancies which might give due grounds for suspicion.

Whether or not a particular circumstance is suspicious is often a subjective judgement, depending strongly on your knowledge and understanding of the client and whether the activity makes sense, given what you know about them. As a general rule, transactions which are economically meaningless, which seem unusual or unexpected for the client or for which you cannot find any plausible or satisfactory explanation are potentially suspicious. This is particularly true for repeating patterns of unusual or unexplained client behaviour.

In the AlnaBank case study, Alison Carter was the relationship manager for Kransky. It was her responsibility to know her client, and to recognise unusual requests or transactions on the part of her client. The summary below outlines the many circumstances which should have given Carter cause for caution or suspicion in her handling of Kransky.

Client's connections with public office

Particular care and attention may be required when a client is linked to public office or positions of power in countries where public corruption and fraud are known to be widespread. Kransky had powerful political connections and had held public offices in Moldovia, a former Soviet bloc republic with a presumed risk of public corruption and fraud. The fact that Kransky fitted a high-risk profile did not automatically make him a suspected money launderer. But the fact that Carter failed to check out his employment or financial background certainly exposed the bank to greater risk.

Receipt of large, third-party cheques

Payment in of large, third-party cheques endorsed in favour of an account holder might reasonably give rise to queries on the part of private banking staff as to why this particular payee is making this particular large payment to this particular client's account. The first deposit into Kransky's account was a cheque from Milrich, for $2 million. Carter did not make enquiries or seek an explanation for this transaction. The cheque from Milrich may, of course, have had nothing to do with Kransky's money laundering activities. Even so, Carter should at least have been curious as to the rationale for this receipt.

Unusual balances and business volume

Where the balance or volume on an account varies significantly from what one would normally expect for a client then this should generate an exception warning, prompting a closer inspection of the transactions in question. Kransky's accounts very quickly showed balances and volumes of in-flow which far exceeded what Carter would have expected, on the basis of her knowledge about the client. Yet at no time did she take action to enquire about the funds or their sources.

Sources of funds

Any receipt of funds for which the sources cannot be satisfactorily identified is potentially a cause for suspicion. The use of cashiers' cheques drawn on various Moldovian banks would, of course, have made it much harder for Carter to identify the sources of the funds behind the cheques. However, she did not approach the banks on which the cheques had been drawn either to establish whether *they* knew the sources of the funds, or whether Kransky even held accounts with them.

Multi-jurisdictional transfers

Large numbers of unexplained transfers across a large number of jurisdictions are always a potential cause for suspicion. The cross-jurisdictional nature of such transactions in particular makes monitoring difficult. Kransky's funds were paid into AlnaBank in Moldovia, before being wired for clearing to New York, wired back to an account owned by AlnaBank in London and subsequently on to Kransky's Swiss-held accounts. No rationale was sought for the additional London leg of the funds route, nor did Carter see fit to query what was an unnecessarily complicated method of transfer.

Unusual client requests

There should be immediate cause for concern where a private banking client requests a level of secrecy which appears extreme or out of the ordinary, and particularly where the services requested may have the specific effect of impeding bank or regulatory oversight. The methods for receipt and transfer of funds to which Carter agreed were unusual to say the least. In particular her agreement to use the bank's 'Accumulation Account' to commingle Kransky's funds before transferring them to Switzerland would have made the funds even harder to trace, and had never been done before.

Questions on senior management responsibilities

In what ways could AlnaBank's Private Banking senior managers be deemed to have contributed to the risks of exposure to money laundering?

What responsibilities do you as a senior manager have under your bank's rules and applicable regulatory requirements?

How does senior management diligence in relation to these responsibilities help to minimise the risks of exposure to money laundering?

A compliance culture can flourish in a bank only where it has the demonstrable support and commitment of senior managers. Banking staff take their lead from the attitudes and behaviours of their senior bosses. Where the attitudes and behaviours are such that they bring the bank into conflict with its duty of oversight, you have a problem.

The events described in the AlnaBank case study could not have developed to the extent that they did if the bank's culture had fostered greater attention to compliance and due diligence matters. The commentaries below go some way towards explaining the culture and attitudes which were prevalent in AlnaBank's Private Banking division, about the time of the Kransky affair. Reading through these commentaries will help you to think about what it means to have a 'compliance culture', and what it takes to develop one.

Pressure for profit

Commentary

'Much of AlnaBank's success in recent years had been generated through the strength of its Private Bank, which had seen its contribution to group profits rise fourfold, such that by 1998 it accounted for nearly 25 per cent of those profits world-wide. This phenomenal growth had been built on the back of a fierce commitment to client satisfaction, combined with an independence of spirit and a willingness to push banking rules and regulations to their limits, an approach which sometimes found itself at odds with other AlnaBank divisions.'

(Adrian Fenn, MD Hayden Bros, Private Bank)

'You know your position within the Private Bank depends on these relatively few, very wealthy individuals whom you have to try to keep happy. A private banker does tend to become an "advocate" for his client within the organisation where he, the banker, works. His job is to find the best ways of utilising the bank's services in his client's interests. In doing so, they often become the client's "voice" within the company, sometimes arguing against other colleagues who wear other hats – particularly risk function hats – in order to try to get particular deals or transactions done.

Senior management attitudes to risk, control and 'rule bending'

Commentary

'Throughout the late 1990s the Private Bank was subjected to repeated criticisms in internal audits and external regulatory reviews, many relating to money laundering control deficiencies and very low audit ratings. This kind of attention was unwelcome, but not seen as particularly disastrous.'

(Saad al Sayyah, former ARM with AlnaBank)

The Private Bank's senior managers had come to associate the success of the business to a certain degree with the existence of bad reports. The unspoken, but unanimously held view was that if you weren't getting the occasional low score in audits, then your business was too control-oriented and you weren't taking enough risk.'

(Karen Chen, former FX trader with AlnaBank)

'I remember on several occasions coming under pressure from the Private Bank. Can you do this trade or that trade, and can you book it on this date instead of that date? This was stuff that you knew was wrong, but they wanted you to do it anyway, maybe for some tax reason. And it wasn't just the relationship managers who would be pushing you. Sometimes you'd get quite senior people who would ring up your boss to try to get the deal through.'

Effect of leadership example on staff attitudes and behaviours

(Saad al Sayyah)

'You see, this is what I have learned about human nature in organisations. People, they take their cue from the top. Because they want to get on and succeed, they adopt the standards and procedures of those who lead them. So that if you say one thing and mean another, they will pick it up. So if you say that you want people to keep proper records … but in reality you show that you're not too concerned about it … then everyone knows.'

As these excerpts illustrate, the culture within AlnaBank's Private Banking division was such that risk-taking outside the rules (as opposed to risk-taking within the rules) was starting to be treated as acceptable behaviour for any private banker who wished to get on within the organisation. The generally accepted attitude was that you got the client what he or she asked for, almost regardless of the risks.

Senior managers are ultimately responsible (through the example they set) for the culture which exists within their business. The rules should be designed to ensure senior management responsibility for and oversight of risk assessment and risk management within the designated area of the business. Senior managers are required to take 'reasonable care' to ensure that adequate systems and controls are in place, and that these are effectively maintained. 'Reasonable care' means ensuring that:

- the business for which they are responsible has been thoroughly assessed for possible risks
- the systems and controls used are sufficient to manage and minimise those risks
- staff within their jurisdiction are made aware of:
  - the required systems and controls
  - how these are to be used
  - the consequences of non-compliance.

Finally, we should not forget Stanley Milgram's warning about human behaviour, issued all those decades ago. Most people will do as they are told, as long as they perceive that the instruction has come from a legitimate authority. If a senior manager allows a perception to develop that they are more concerned about winning new business and hitting targets than they are about compliance with national laws and company policies, then they should know by now what to expect.

Index

THE MASTERING SERIES

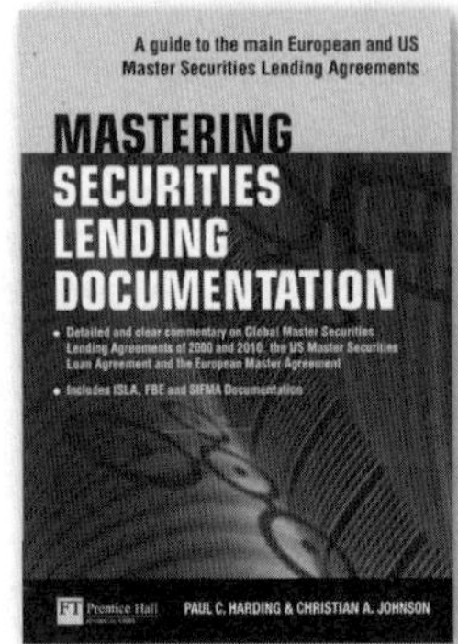

9780273734970

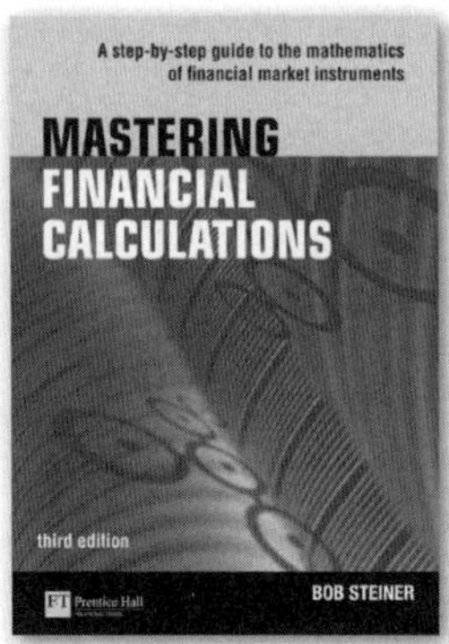

9780273750581

9780273732815

9780273772255

9780273714859

9780273719298

9780273724544

9780273730330

9780273725206

9780273727323

9780273735670

9780273744795

Practical. Comprehensive. Essential

ALWAYS LEARNING PEARSON